**John Obe**

**Applied
Theology for
Youth Ministry**

# Eutychus
# Youth

**Reaching youth on the ledge**

# Table of Contents

# Do I Have Time for This?

**W**hy should I bother to read this book?" I ask myself that question every time I pick up a volume at the local bookstore and start thumbing through it. The question I should ask, however, is, Will I ever read this book? The significance of that question can be found in all the books on my shelves that I've never gotten around to reading.

Why should you bother to read this book? If you are looking for some help in youth ministry in the area of games or ice-breakers, mission trips or finances, planning or liability, then feel free to put this book back down, because you will soon be disappointed. Those are all important topics, but they aren't covered in this book. There are plenty of very helpful resources already available on youth ministry that quite adequately guide even the adult novice who is contemplating to volunteer with the youth at church. Frankly, the world does not need any more books on great games or movie applications for youth devotions. The market is quite saturated at this time.

On the other hand, if you have begun to wonder if theology, and Lutheran theology in particular, has any relevancy for youth ministry, then my advice to you is to read a little farther, because that's what I'm interested in exploring. Is youth ministry such a generic activity that it really makes no difference what my beliefs are about Scripture, justification, or the Sacraments? Is it all pretty much the same?

And if there are a few distinctive qualities brought to youth ministry by Lutheran theology, what are they? How would I notice them? What would they look like in practice? These questions aren't asked because I'm looking to pick a fight with Catholic, Presbyterian, or Baptist youth ministry. This isn't a study in theological polemics applied to adolescent psychology. Rather, I want to examine what Lutheran theology adds to the whole field of youth ministry that isn't found elsewhere.

In my mind, this raises a second question. Have I written this book for you or for somebody else? If you are a volunteer shouldering the responsibilities for youth ministry in a small congregation and your spouse has agreed to go along (though there is some hesitancy) and you really haven't had much theological training beyond confirmation and Bible class, I'm writing for you. Or if you are enrolled in a course of study through which you hope to develop some level of competency in youth ministry as a DCE or lay minister because you really like kids, but you are stressed out because you can't quite make the connection between your theology classes and your youth ministry classes, I'm writing for you. Or if you are a pastor or seminary student who has never quite felt comfortable with the idea of youth ministry, or youth for that matter, but really enjoy theology and are curious how anyone could have a subtitle "Applied Theology for Youth Ministry," I'm writing for you.

Our exploration begins with an introduction to Eutychus, whom you will discover is a paradigm of adolescent development. From there, the chapters are divided into three sections; chapters 2 through 4 provide an overview of youth, youth ministry, and spirituality; chapters five through eight identify Lutheran theology's unique contribution to the youth ministry; and chapters nine through twelve put these theological strengths to work.

What I hope you will discover in these pages is what I have learned: that Lutheran theology's contribution to our understanding of youth ministry, adolescent spirituality, and faith formation is profound but practical, useful without being … utilitarian, and, like the Word upon which it is based, sharper than any two-edged sword.

Dr. John W. Oberdeck

# CHAPTER 1

# The Strange Case of Eutychus of Troas

The accident comes unexpectedly, as accidents always do. Paul's departure is scheduled for the next day. He's spent a week in Troas on the western coast of Asia Minor. Many of his followers, his disciples whom he has accumulated through his mission trips, are with him—Sopater from Berea, Aristarchus and Secundus from Thessalonica, Gaius from Derbe, Tychicus and Trophimus from Asia, along with Timothy and Luke the physician. They, along with many good friends and fellow believers in the risen Lord Jesus Christ, are gathered in an upper room—a third floor meeting hall. Most will never see Paul again. He won't be returning to Troas. So the people listen carefully, never suspecting the spectacle they are about to witness.

The meeting begins with greetings all around, followed by a time of teaching. Paul has an opportunity to talk, something he not only loves but feels compelled to do. He talks about Jesus. He talks about faith. He talks about their bond of love and their calling to be witnesses to the hope that is in them. He keeps talking and talking and talking. Time passes; the evening grows late. Paul keeps talking.

Once darkness settles over the city, the lamps are lit, many lamps casting flickering shadows around the room. There are several windows, but the sea breezes make no impression in a room so crowded. The air is warm and stuffy, tinged with the scent of so many people in so small a space. The evening wears on, but the listeners are attentive—and why not? This is Paul talking to them. Not wanting to miss a word, they fight against fatigue—all of them except one.

A young man, really a teenager, by the name of Eutychus is struggling. He is doing his best to remain alert. Gradually, he moves near one of the windows, hoping fresh air might revive him. He sits in the window frame; now with his attention divided between the street below and the preacher at the opposite side of the room, he hopes to keep alert. Slowly the battle is lost; either bored as Paul drones on or weary at the lateness of the hour, his eyelids flutter and close. For just a moment he's balanced, but only for a moment. He relaxes, he sleeps, and he falls.

While scanning the room to emphasize a point, Paul's eyes have just passed the windows where he's seen the adolescent sitting. Paul is mid-sentence when screams come from the back of the room. He jerks his head to the source of the screams and sees a woman pointing at an empty window. In an instant, all orderliness in the room disappears. Others start shouting. Those near the door are already leaving, rushing down the stairs from the third floor. Like a funnel, the doorway channels the distressed crowd down to the street below.

Paul is the last to descend the stairs. By the time he's at street level, the crowd is circled around the body. People are in shock; some are crying. A few hold torches. They see Paul approaching and open a path for him. He looks through the human corridor and there is Luke kneeling over the boy. Luke glances up, shaking his head. Paul moves closer and the crowd moves back. He lies down next to Eutychus and wraps his arms around him. Paul prays.

Moments pass. Muffled sobs can be heard from the crowd. Then Paul says, "Don't be alarmed, He's alive!" Joy, surprise, disbelief, and relief ripple through the mass of people that's now gathered at the street. Not the least of those surprised is Luke, who knows that the fall was fatal. But Eutychus is alive! The magnitude of the miracle soaks in and the astonishment of all gives way to thanksgiving. Paul suggests that they all go back upstairs, and they do.

With Paul, they break bread together and receive the gifts promised by Jesus when the Christian community remembers Him in this unique, close, and personal fellowship. After worship, everyone is still so excited about what they have witnessed, they can't rest; so seizing another opportunity, Paul begins to talk and talks until dawn. And Eutychus is taken home alive and well to the great relief of his family and friends.

# Youth in the Bible

There are only a limited number of candidates in Scripture if we want to find a model for the adolescent Christian life.

By making this observation, I'm not suggesting that the purpose of Scripture is to provide us with models for living in each of the different seasons of life[1] and that somehow the Holy Spirit has short changed us by providing too few examples of teenagers pleasing God. But I do need to explain why I'm going to spend so much time analyzing Eutychus (Acts 20:7–12), a relatively unknown teenager in the New Testament, while spending little time with the other remaining Bible teens of much greater notoriety, such as Samuel, David, John Mark, or Timothy.

After all, isn't Samuel an excellent role model of the early (very early) adolescent who listens to the Word of God and obeys it (Luke

---

1 We know that the purpose of Scripture is to bring persons into a saving relationship with Jesus Christ that leads them to true life and real living in service to the Creator both now and forevermore (John 10:10; 20:31). At the same time, we recognize that the saved life is a changed life. To put it into a Lutheran theological framework, though justification is never confused with sanctification, justification and sanctification never operate independent of each other. Therefore, we benefit by looking at the examples that are provided to us in the Scriptures. We are careful never to make the examples the Good News, as if following examples in Scripture is the Gospel. To do so is to fall prey to moralism. The Gospel is what God has done for us through Jesus Christ. But there is a ripple effect of the Gospel in our lives, because in faith, we honestly desire to live lives that bring honor to Jesus Christ. How do we do that? We do it naturally according to the new person we are through Baptism and faith in Jesus Christ. We do not do it naturally according to the old person we remain in this fallen world. We are *simul iustus et peccator*, simultaneously sinner and saint. In this condition, we need all the examples we can get to live out the life we have already received in Christ (1 Corinthians 11:1; Philippians 3:17; Hebrews 13:7).

11:28)? Here we have a preadolescent (currently labeled "tweener") whom God Himself calls to be His servant and who humbly accepts the role. He hears the message of God and faithfully transmits the message (1 Samuel 3). Bravo for Samuel. But unless our goal in youth ministry is to instill an expectation within our teens that God will speak to them directly late some night, as he did with Samuel, with a message for their parents, pastor, or youth leader, I think the story of Samuel is saying something much more than "Hey, kids—listen up!" I suspect that the deeper message in the call of Samuel isn't that Samuel heard, but that God called and continues to call servants today—even adolescents—to share His Word.

Or consider how often young people are encouraged to be like young David, particularly young people in certain "evangelical" churches. There is a lot to learn from young David; courage against insurmountable odds, trust in the providence of God, faithfulness to friends, and respect for authority even when the authority doesn't deserve it. All of these are admirable values and characteristics that form a template any youth pastor would love to instill in the more unruly members under his care. But the problem with David is the story doesn't end with his youth. The danger is that the adolescent will read the rest of the story—in detail. It doesn't get pretty.

Moving on to the New Testament—and skipping over a few other notable young persons in Scripture, such as Josiah (2 Kings 22), Jeremiah (Jeremiah 1:6–7), and Daniel (Daniel 1)—perhaps the most helpful we encounter is John Mark. He is helpful in this way. John Mark demonstrates the maturing of a young person in the faith. John Mark's mother owns the house to which Peter flees when he is miraculously freed from prison (Acts 12:12). He's related to Barnabas (Colossians 4:10) and sets out with Paul and Barnabas on their first missionary journey. But he gets cold feet, chickens out, and abandons the mission trip in Pamphylia. Later, after the council in Jerusalem as Paul makes preparations for the next mission trip, Barnabas wants to bring John Mark along. Paul rejects the suggestion, and in the argument that follows, they part; Barnabas and John Mark go to Cyprus, while Paul takes Silas with him and goes to Syria and Cilicia (Acts 15:36–41). I suppose one lesson to be learned from John Mark is that youth ministry, and youth doing ministry, can cause division within the church; a lesson that has not been lost on many directors of Christian education and youth directors over the years. Of course,

I can't close the story on John Mark without mentioning that John Mark matures into a faithful helper of Paul (2 Timothy 4:11) and, according to tradition, the companion and secretary of Peter who is inspired to write the Gospel of Mark.

Timothy is an example of someone described as young (1 Timothy 4:12) in the Scripture but who has obviously gone beyond the stage of adolescence by the time Paul writes to him. We learn of his faithful mother and grandmother, who raise Timothy (2 Timothy 1:5), so we can speculate about his early training. We do catch the drift in Paul's letters to Timothy that he may have had some health problems (1 Timothy 5:23) and that he may have been somewhat timid in his ministry (2 Timothy 1:6–7). Nevertheless, what we know about Timothy supplies us with more information about the life circumstances of a young pastor, or a youth pastor for that matter, than it tells us about youth.

## Looking for Authenticity

Why focus on Eutychus? Eutychus is striking because his story relates so readily, simply, and easily to the situation of so many youth both inside and outside of the Church today. Something about Eutychus is so authentic, so genuine, that he begs comparison to our contemporary situation. Growing up under the direction of the priest of the tabernacle or spending one's early years protecting sheep from predators or maturing in a household committed to supporting Paul's mission journeys or being homeschooled by mom and grandma may resonate with a small sampling of today's teens. But finding oneself young, bored, and at risk with no one taking notice matches a multitude. Let's take a closer look at the story to see how each of these elements is borne out in what must be the most amazing event in this young man's life.

First, we see that Eutychus is a young man. How young? What is meant by young man in this context? Is Eutychus of the age in which an adult might well address him with, "Listen here, *young man*, don't you ever sit in a window again. Do you hear me?" In this case, he's a young man mostly in name only, while the reality is that he is very much a minor under parental authority. Or is Eutychus of that age when physical maturation has reached its zenith; a young man of rippling muscles and head full of flowing hair? In that case, the emphasis falls on *man* and not on *young*.

Fortunately, the Greek gives us some help. The first time Eutychus is mentioned, he's described as a νεανία, a term generally held to mean a young man beyond the age of puberty but not yet married. However, later in the account when he's taken home, he is called a παῖς, "boy." One helpful dictionary explains, "The person concerned could have been of such an age that either 'young man' or 'boy' was a possible denotation. In other words, the age reference of νεανία and παῖς overlaps in Greek."[2] If boy and young man overlap, it can mean only one thing. Eutychus is a teenager.

Second, Eutychus is bored. How bored is he? He's bored enough to fall asleep! Now, granted, there may be other explanations for his untimely nap. We can speculate about the possibilities. One helpful clue we don't have is the reason for his attendance. Why is he there? Does he come on his own or do his parents bring him? Does he have friends along or is he alone? Has he heard Paul before or is this the first time? If he is brought to the all-night preaching festival by his parents, we have a pretty good hunch as to why he is bored.

But taking another approach, perhaps like many teens today, Eutychus has a job. Perhaps he is apprenticed to a tradesman or an artisan. Given this scenario, Eutychus comes to the event after a long day at work. Of course he's tired—who knows what kinds of exertion have occupied him? Yet he's motivated enough to come, and he listens and listens and listens until he just can't listen anymore. The many candles have been consuming oxygen in the room just as fast as the people. Moving to the window, he hopes he'll revive, but it doesn't work.

We have to admit that from Luke's account we really can't tell if Eutychus is present voluntarily or by compulsion. We don't know what prompts his interest, if he is interested at all. Nevertheless, doesn't his situation, ambiguous though it may be, add to the authenticity of the account and to its relevance? I suspect that we aren't dealing with an either/or situation; as if he's either bored or tired. Given my experience in youth ministry, the mix of motivations more than likely is both. Whether he's arrived on his own volition after a hard day at

2 Johannes P. Louw and Eugene A. Nida, eds., *Greek-English Lexicon of the New Testament Based on Semantic Domains*, vol. 1 (New York: United Bible Societies, 1988), 108 (9.32).

work or by compulsion, by the time midnight arrives, he is bored *and* tired.

The third characteristic of Eutychus that magnifies his place as an authentic teen representative is that he's at risk. He's placed himself in an open window on the third floor of a building—not a safe place to be. I would use the manner in which Eutychus positions himself as a metaphor for teens at risk, if it wasn't for my own experiences with windows and teens.

I realized as pastor of a large congregation in southern Illinois in the mid-1980s that I hadn't been spending much time with the youth over the previous two years. I needed to reconnect with the young people I had confirmed not so long ago. So I volunteered to accompany our volunteer youth leader and three other adults as we joined another congregation and took our youth to a youth rally weekend in a Chicago suburb. Reconnect I did.

What I learned was never to underestimate, never overlook, and never under plan when working with youth. Look for the unexpected, I now say, perhaps even the unbelievable. How did I learn this? We were housed on the sixth floor of the hotel. The youth from the congregation that joined us were on the fifth floor. Around 3:00 a.m., a room of girls from our congregation put bed sheets out their window and over a ledge that extended at least two feet out from the hotel. The sheets were grasped by two boys from the other congregation in the room below, who then proceeded to climb out of the room, over the ledge, and into the room above. How this was discovered, what disciplinary actions followed, and what implications this had for our youth group is too long a tale to tell here. Suffice it to say that there was ample opportunity for Confession and Absolution. However, news of the escapade did precede us back home, though not as quickly as it would in today's world of Twitter and cell phones. Upon returning, much of my time was consumed defending the volunteer youth leader from parents who were understandably quite upset.

Good grief! I didn't even suspect windows in the upper floors of hotels could be opened! I now have the strange habit of checking windows every time I check into a motel or hotel with more than two floors. The point, of course, is that angels do exist and were willing to protect these two young men (stuck, no doubt, between νεανία and παῖς) from their own "at risk" behaviors. Our youth groups were spared our own dual-Eutychian moment, a genuine blessing—given that neither I nor the pastor from the other congregation could do an adequate imitation of Paul.

Adolescents do place themselves at risk frequently, sometimes realizing it and sometimes not. And doesn't this make the story of Eutychus that much more relevant, authentic, and correlative to youth ministry today? Consider for a moment that in today's environment, the at-risk component doesn't have to be sought out. Teens don't have to go searching to place themselves at risk. More and more, the risk seeks out the teen. The risk is encountered in the daily environment in which the teen lives.

Take, for example, pornography. In my teen years, obtaining pornography required some initiative, some effort. Somebody had to finagle a way to get the magazine, usually through somebody's older brother. Today, pornography is a predator, only two clicks away on the Internet. It is accessible, addictive, and anonymous.[3] To what degree youth are able to imitate young Joseph—another biblical example of youth who was omitted earlier—and flee from the Potiphar's wife of pornography remains a question for not only teens, but adults as well. Of course, pornography is only one example of the risky behaviors that are ready to tempt, entice, and betray young people today.

We now have three of the components presented to us by Eutychus: a young person who is bored and who is at risk. There is only one more component from the story to examine, and in many ways, it is the most troubling. Nobody notices.

What would it have taken to prevent the whole sordid scene? All it would have taken would have been one person, glancing around the candlelit room, who sees Eutychus and notices first that Eutychus is in the window—not a good place to be, and second that his eyelids are fluttering. It isn't that hard to notice someone falling asleep. I'm a college professor. I know what this looks like. All this person would need to do is notice Eutychus drifting off—starting to relax, loosening his grip on the window sill—and then carefully reach over and give him a little nudge. "Hey, Eutychus, come down and sit here on the floor with me."

---

3 For a helpful resource for congregation use in a Bible study/video format, see *Responding to Sexual Temptation in a High Tech Society* (Billings, MT: Ambassadors of Reconciliation, 2008).

Problems dealing with youth begin right here, because too often our response to the young person at risk is a shout. Imagine someone in that upper room, noticing the young man at risk in the window, who then jumps up screaming, "Get out of that window; YOU ARE GOING TO DIE!" This is counterproductive. Had that happened to Eutychus, the shock of the shout would have sent him tumbling.

Eutychus needs a friend, an adult, who is beside him and who gently nudges him and invites him back into the room and to a safer place. He doesn't need a yell that will be interpreted as rejection or judgment, driving him away.

This is what I believe to be the second great challenge for youth ministry today. In the culture in which we live—a hedonistic, consumer-driven, self-centered, and self-actualizing society—all our young people are at risk. Even those whom we as adults deem the most well adjusted and mature have challenges and difficulties that would disturb us greatly if we were aware of them. Are we? Are we willing to notice? Are we willing to nudge? Are we willing to invite, and keep inviting throughout the adolescent years, to a safer place?

If that is the second great challenge, what is the first? The first great challenge is to take the faith we have been given, the theological heritage that belongs to our Church, and put it into practice in youth ministry. You see, the real goal isn't just safer youth. The real goal is forgiven youth, redeemed youth, youth that live in the grace of our Lord Jesus Christ.

Why is this the primary goal? Because some of our youth are falling out the window, some farther than others, and they need to be raised up through the forgiveness of sins given only through Jesus Christ. Others are sitting in the window dozing. They need the gentle nudge that comes through reminders of our Baptism and the strength that comes through dining at the Lord's Table. They need the gentle guidance from caring adults. And still others are the elder brothers who have been with us all the time, neither bored nor at risk. Our attention is required for them as well for two reasons. First, so that they know that they are also loved and have our full attention even if they aren't at risk. And second, so that they understand the true nature of Law and Gospel and do not become judgmental, but instead see themselves also as forgiven sinners who are living by faith in God's grace through Jesus Christ.

We have a theology for youth ministry that communicates to all three adolescent audiences. I believe … that Lutheran theology can inform, respond, and direct youth ministry today in ways that are truly helpful. I believe that Lutheran theology is uniquely gifted to build genuinely effective youth ministry in deep and lasting ways. I believe that Lutheran theology adds depth and insight that others working with youth will also find helpful. And, at the same time, I also believe that Lutheran theology is open to receive the wisdom others have gleaned in working with youth. The time could not be better for us to explore how this can be done and what will be helpful for us to do it. Let's begin.

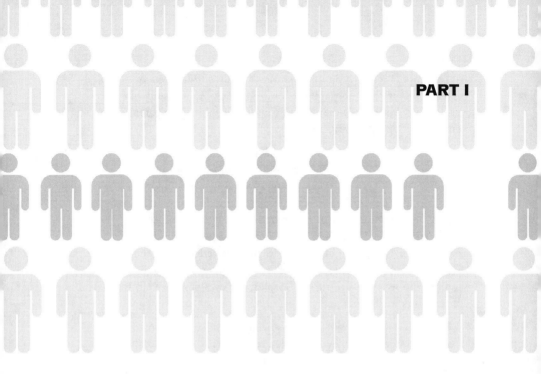

# PART I

# Watch the Window!

How old are you? Are you near enough in age to the youth in your group that you are often mistaken for one yourself? Or does your advanced age betray you, so much that you no longer play in the Frisbee tournament, ride the Screaming Eagle, or make it through the all-night lock in? And if you don't do these things, is it on the recommendation of your chiropractor or your cardiologist?[1]

I'm too old for youth ministry, which on the one hand makes working with youth, studying youth ministry, and writing about youth ministry very difficult. I don't appreciate water parks the way I once did. My own children left adolescence over half a decade ago, and my own adolescence was in a different century; it might as well have been on a different planet. I remember when our party line crank phone number was one long and two shorts. I remember when we got our

---

1 Note to self: Do not play "Dizzy Stick" with college students on a Y-Min Retreat, especially not after lunch, and extra-especially not when one of them is recording it on her phone.

first television. So the baton must be passed to those whose energy levels can sustain them through the long haul servant event and whose constitutions will uphold them at least until 7:00 a.m. when parents come to pick up their offspring.

On the other hand, I believe I'm exactly the right age for youth ministry. I can play the grandparent card! You see—and research tends to confirm this—that ease of communication sometimes skips a generation. The result is that teens can talk to grandma or grandpa a whole lot easier than they can talk with mom and dad. All I have to be is ready with my ears open. Of course, more is involved than just being ready to listen; though we ought not discount the effect on a teen of really being heard. We need to keep our eyes open and watch the windows and see what's going on. Keeping our eyes open is what Part I of this book is all about.

There are three different windows from which we will look, each with its own significant view on adolescence: the front window, the university window, and the window from the Wartburg. Each supplies information that's necessary if we are to watch the windows faithfully.

The front window is the window of our own life and faith. We think often about God. So do teens. We think often about our faith. So do teens. And we think often about how our life matches up with our faith, as do teens. Why don't we think about these things together? The front window acknowledges how much theology plays a role in youth ministry and asks whether or not Lutheran theology has anything to say in the matter.

The university window is the research window through which we discover what experts in sociology and psychology have to say about where teens are in their attitudes and beliefs toward God. Their insights are a corrective if we should fall into the bad habit of assuming teens are empty buckets waiting to be filled with the theology we so eagerly want to pour into them. They are not empty buckets. The subtitle of this book is *Applied Theology for Youth Ministry*, not "A Theology of Youth" or "A Theology by Youth." But such a book could be written because there is a generic set of beliefs held by many teens that constitutes a teen theology. Through this window, we will have a chance to see it—maybe not as clearly as we might want, but it will be there.

The image of the Wartburg window is another way of suggesting that there is a particular way that followers of Luther approach spirituality that has implications for adolescent spirituality. I've heard that from the airy Wartburg castle, Luther had a commanding view of the surrounding countryside. Lutheran Christians not only have a commanding view of spirituality, but we also have a receptive view of spirituality that sets us not only apart from other perspectives but also sets us free in the Gospel of Jesus Christ.

Imagine that your chore is to wash these three windows so that all the smudges are gone, and you can see clearly through each. Once that task is complete, you'll be ready for Part II, where we will, using these three windows as a background, notice Eutychus in our theology. ...

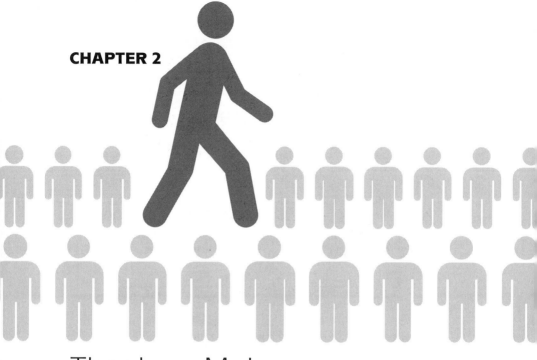

**CHAPTER 2**

# Theology Makes a Difference

H ave you noticed it? Do you feel it? Have you read about it? Perhaps I'm more sensitive to it because every semester I take a group of youth ministry students to conferences of varying lengths with a variety of different presenters; but it seems to me that youth ministry, as conceived by those who do it and those who support those who do it, is going through some kind of major transition.

Those doing youth ministry today seem restless and discontented. There is less certainty, less confidence about objectives, goals, and vision for youth ministry. The more we are encouraged to cast a vision for youth ministry, the thicker the fog of adolescence gets. The more we learn about establishing goals, the less we seem able to put the ball in the net and score those goals. The more competent we are at setting objectives, the more objectionable they get.

# Exploring Our Frustrations

Mark Oestreicher, formerly with Youth Specialties, puts it this way. "The problem is this: The way we're doing things is *already not working*. We're failing at our calling. And deep down, most of us know it. This is why we need an epochal shift in our assumptions, approaches, models, and methods [italics in original]."[1]

Are we failing? Mike King from *Youth Front* points out that if we use retention as a criterion for measuring effectiveness, we don't look all that effective. "According to data from denominations and research organizations, a majority of youth are walking away from the institutional church when they reach late adolescence, and most don't come back."[2]

Strategies and techniques that seemed effective in the '80s and '90s have lost their appeal and some who study the voyage of "youth ministry" within the broad spectrum of American Christendom have identified how we might have gotten off course. Tony Jones, well-known speaker for the "emergent" movement, suggests that relying on an entertainment model involving high-tech bait-and-switch techniques—"getting them in the door with the stuff they like (music, videos, etcetera), and then sneaking in Jesus at the end"[3]—simply reinforces a double-standard view of the Church and Christianity. He describes going to a youth ministry gathering that had all the games, sports, and high-tech music production possible—with five hundred kids in attendance—followed by a devotional message based on Romans 12:2 ("Do not be conformed to this world"). "The whole first hour in the Entertainment Center was rife with cultural influence—and then the students were chided for immersing themselves in secular culture!"[4] The perceptive adolescent realizes more is going on here than just a confused mixed-message from the Church—he or she discerns dishonesty behind the deception.

If there is one thing we can be sure about, it is that young people can sniff out anything that's fake, phony, or disingenuous. Should the

---

1 Mark Oestreicher, *Youth Ministry 3.0: A Manifesto of Where We've Been, Where We Are, and Where We Need to Go* (Grand Rapids, MI: Zondervan, 2008), 20.

2 Mike King, *Presence-Centered Youth Ministry: Guiding Students into Spiritual Formation* (Downers Grove, IL: InterVarsity Press, 2006), 11.

3 Tony Jones, *Postmodern Youth Ministry* (Grand Rapids, MI: Youth Specialties, 2001), 85.

4 Jones, 87.

Church expect them to come back when the Church itself doesn't trust its own message to be the draw, but relies on the very things the world offers, and offers in a more attractive package? Will they come back when what they are looking for is something authentic, genuine, and trustworthy but what they are receiving seems artificial and contrived? Perhaps they do return, but more than likely it's for the entertainment, games, and hanging out with their friends; it's not for a commitment with a community of faith.

So then, is relational youth ministry the answer? By "relational youth ministry," I mean recognizing the overwhelming significance of meaningful relationships in guiding a young person's spiritual journey. Surely, we can avoid the difficulties of too much cultural crossover by focusing on building relationships. Tony Jones says, "At least one thing remains true: most students (and adults) come to church because someone they trust invites them. Relationships with students and volunteer leaders will always be the best investments we'll make."[5]

Nevertheless, relationship building as the center of youth ministry is not above reproach. Youth ministry that uses relationship building as a strategy can easily become manipulative and spiritually smothering. Authenticity and genuineness are quickly lost when the friendship that develops has all the baggage of understated ulterior motives. Andrew Root exposes the problem. "Relationships have been used for cultural leverage (getting adolescents to believe or obey) rather than as the concrete location of God's action in the world."[6] Root calls this a ministry of "influence" and poignantly shares how far short it falls:

> When I tried to influence them, I had neither the patience
> nor the vision to truly share in their suffering, to make it my
> own and to join my own broken humanity with theirs. I was
> so busy making assertions about heaven that I refused to see
> and accompany them in the darkness of their personal hells.[7]

Not only does youth ministry based on relationships of influence distance the youth leader from hearing the real needs of youth, it also has the ability to undermine worship and mission—worship

---

5 Jones, 36–37.

6 Andrew Root, *Revisiting Relational Youth Ministry: From a Strategy of Influence to a Theology of Incarnation* (Downers Grove, IL: InterVarsity Press, 2007), 78.

7 Root, 79.

by making worship about one's own emotions rather than about attending to God's mercy and gifts and mission by making the goal of mission to feel good about one's volunteer service rather than effecting lasting change for those needing help. Root suggests an answer for relationship building in youth ministry. It entails moving from using relationships as a means for influence (manipulation) to recognizing within relationships a shared connection to God through Jesus Christ (incarnation).[8]

What does incarnation in relationships look like? It looks like being truly present with another human being, denying our own agenda—as important as that agenda really is—in order to *be alongside* teenagers in their world of experience. At least this seems to be the understanding of Mark Yaconelli, who eloquently describes how powerful being open and completely attentive to another person can really be. He laments how often youth ministry fails to provide an environment conducive to open, incarnational relationships. "Unfortunately, the last place many teenagers find people open and available is within churches. Instead of a listening ear, they find advice. Instead of a witness to their lives, they're offered programs and activities."[9]

How does one go about creating a truly caring and listening environment? What kind of relationship is genuinely helpful in youth ministry? If all the technology and all of the games are part of the problem, then how do we strategize a solution when the very tools we've been using from our tool box are potentially destructive? No wonder the atmosphere that surrounds youth ministry today is heavy. Not only is there doubt about what we do, but there is also doubt about why we do it. As youth leaders, we have been trained to ask ourselves, "Am I doing all I can to make a difference in the lives of young people?" We have worked hard at training ourselves to be competent by attending conferences, learning strategies, studying adolescent psychology, becoming educated in the fine art of conducting servant events and planning mission trips, making ourselves culturally aware, keeping up with teen technology, and opening our homes and our hearts to those chronologically underprivileged among us. And we know and believe that relationships are extremely

---

8 Root, 79.

9 Mark Yaconelli, *Contemplative Youth Ministry: Practicing the Presence of Jesus* (Grand Rapids, MI: Zondervan, 2006), 23.

important. "Am I doing all that I can to make a difference?" we ask ourselves. We answer ourselves, "All these I have kept for the sake of my youth. What more must I do to be (saved) effective?"

## Looking for the Missing Piece

So, what is missing? Have you ever worked on a jigsaw puzzle—not the little hundred-piece flower pictures, they hardly count—a real jigsaw puzzle of a thousand or more pieces? The secretary with whom I'm privileged to work has a huge framed jigsaw puzzle of Warner Sallman's "Head of Christ" on her wall that must have taken countless hours to complete, given the subtle shades of coffee-colored brown and brunette in the painting.[10]

I was helping my mother-in-law work on a jigsaw puzzle recently when I realized that I have two strategies in play that alternate once the frame pieces are in place. One strategy involves color. Naturally, I first scrutinize the box cover to absorb the overall picture, and then I gather similarly shaded pieces and get to work. But it doesn't take long before frustration sets in and progress stops. Color only gets me so far, and then I must switch my strategy to shape. In fact, shape is the strategy with which the whole process begins, because border-shape pieces provide the boundaries; and without boundaries, I'm hopelessly lost. If I'm going to succeed in completing the puzzle, I've got to establish the boundaries and then work the colors. When I can't place any more pieces using color, I return to shape until it, too, frustrates. And then back to color.

Did you think when I began this jigsaw illustration that I would point out the many pieces that make up youth ministry and then observe that the missing piece is Jesus Christ? That's too obvious; I want more out of this illustration than that. And frankly, I don't believe that we intentionally or unintentionally leave Jesus out of our youth ministry activities. When I'm attending training sessions and youth ministry conferences, no matter how much emphasis is placed on techniques and strategies, "loving Jesus" is never, ever omitted. What is omitted, however, is a careful exposition of what "loving Jesus" means.

---

10 This beautifully framed picture caused one of my colleagues to quip, "Yeah, that Jesus Christ has always been a puzzle to me."

I'm going to draw a different lesson from my analysis of jigsaw-puzzle strategy. The long list of skills, techniques, and strategies is the color of youth ministry. The colors are beautiful and the colors are fun. Together, the colors are what we see of the picture. But beneath the colors is the shape, and shape is the underlying theology that governs the picture. Shape establishes the borders and sets the parameters. The more I study a puzzle, the more I realize there are a limited number of shapes. There may be an unlimited number of different pixilated shades of color, but there are only so many different shapes that I'm working with. Likewise, the theology that describes the infinite God is not in itself infinite, though I may be able to find many ways to illustrate a teaching.

So, what am I saying? Frustration builds in working a puzzle when color is the only strategy. The puzzle must begin with the shape. Likewise, in youth ministry, we can focus on skills, techniques, and strategies only so long before each begins to fail. Times change, technology advances, culture shifts, and what brought youth in by the carloads now gets one big yawn. What doesn't change? What creates the border that gives meaning and coherence to everything else on the table? That is the role of theology in youth ministry.

What I find fascinating is how much the movers and shakers in the field of youth ministry are paying attention to theology these days. In fact, if we are looking for a real movement within youth ministry today, it isn't found in skill building, technology development, or strategic planning. The real movement in youth ministry today is the search for the border pieces of the puzzle, the parameters that will govern the shape of ministry, the theology.

We find it clearly demonstrated in each of the authors I've cited above. Mark Yaconelli comes from a solidly evangelical background—his father founded Youth Specialties—but he writes about contemplative youth ministry and draws deeply from traditional, often Roman Catholic, spiritual practices; as does Mike King, who even brings into his book a discussion of private confession.[11] King is sensitive to abuses of the Law and misstatements of the Gospel[12] and laments the loss of traditions in the Church as losses to youth who, as

---

11 King, 171.

12 King, 28. King addresses how the confusion wrought by moralism harms the proclamation of the Church. "The moralizing message that is communicated by prominent evangelical voices is being viewed as duplicitous and hypocritical" (28).

a result, aren't receiving the "heirlooms" that belong to the family of God.[13]

Andrew Root draws on the writings of Dietrich Bonhoeffer to support his understanding of incarnational ministry—what it means to be truly in a relationship with another person that is neither coercive nor manipulative. To be incarnational is to recognize the presence of God in our relationships and then to allow ourselves to be truly present. In this way, Root expresses how he learns to accept the humanity of adolescents by being truly human himself.[14] Through the application of a theologically-astute anthropology (the doctrine of humankind [Man]), he provides the border pieces of the puzzle that allow the community (the doctrine of the Church [Ecclesiology]) to exist in, with, and under God's grace.

Mark Oestreicher tackles theological epistemology, though he is wise enough not to call it that. How do we come to know and believe? He explains the change that has taken place in the relationship of three important terms—fact, faith, and feelings—by using an analogy of a train with three cars: an engine, a coal car, and a caboose. Growing up, he learned the analogy this way: objective facts (the engine) pull the train down the tracks, while faith (the coal car) gives the engine the fuel it needs. The caboose (feelings) is helpful, but ultimately not necessary.[15] In the postmodern world of today's teenager, the train looks very different. Experience (feelings) is now the engine pulling the train, while faith continues to supply the needed fuel as the coal car. Fact, instead of pulling the train, is now the caboose.[16] The point I'm trying to make by sharing Oestreicher's analogy isn't that Oestreicher has correctly defined how we know or believe or even that he has, in a most helpful manner, described the ascendancy of experience at the expense of objective fact within contemporary culture. The important thing is that he's trying to answer practical youth ministry questions by appealing to a theological framework.

## Theology in Youth Ministry

---

13 King, 100.

14 Root, 120–121.

15 Oestreicher, 100–101.

16 Oestreicher, 102.

But do we really want theology involved with our youth ministries? You might think this is a ridiculous question. Of course we do! But look at the question more deeply for a moment. What are the dynamics that tend to keep theology out of youth ministry? Two elements come immediately to my mind. The first has to do with the underlying, hidden agenda-type goals that exist in youth ministry. The second has to do with theological differences.

The hidden agendas are really not so hidden, and they are no small source of frustration for those in youth ministry. The underlying agenda of the Church is always increased participation: numbers. The underlying agenda of parents is protection: effective youth ministry decreases risky behavior with sex, drugs, and fast cars. When these pragmatic issues govern youth ministry, the line between church youth programs and secular youth programs is nearly invisible. Both are concerned about volunteer background checks, liability issues, and increasing parental involvement; and both claim success when numbers go up and behavior improves.

If there is theology involved in these hidden agendas, it will very often be counterproductive, at least from a Lutheran perspective. Why? Because of the confusion that results with Law and Gospel. If I am led to understand that my relationship with God is established on the basis of the purity of my behavior, if I come to believe that I'm doing God a favor by coming to His events at His church, then I'm missing out on the Gospel. I've learned moralism, but I haven't learned the cross. And if theology isn't involved in the hidden agendas, then why not let secular youth programs do the work? They are probably more generously funded with better facilities anyway.

Avoidance of theology in youth ministry may also come from knowing that theology divides Christians from one another and Christians from non-Christians. When the major concern of youth ministry is providing the best environment and the most nurturing care for the enhancement of adolescent development, the awkwardness of a restricted Communion table or a discussion over the efficacy of Baptism is conveniently avoided. Today's culture prefers not to dwell on differences and discounts them when they are mentioned. They are, after all, divisive.

I have attended several large gatherings of youth leaders from a variety of backgrounds in para-church settings where I've heard speakers tell us that we are from Methodist, Presbyterian, Baptist, Pentecostal, and Catholic backgrounds, but that we can put all that aside because "we are all here to love and praise Jesus." While I will make no judgments about the sincerity of anyone's love or praise for Jesus, the implication is that theological distinctions between confessions make no meaningful differences and get in the way of genuine ministry when, from a confessional perspective, the theological distinctions not only show us the way to genuine ministry, but they also define what genuine ministry means.

I like how Harry Blamires illustrates this point. He asks us to imagine six individuals who disagree very strongly about the place where they all ought to go. So rather than actually work through their disagreement and determine a destination, they all together decide to work building a car "so that, in the long run, they *can* go *somewhere*, easily and comfortably." While this project is in process, any one of the six who dares to ask "But where are we going?" will be considered ill-mannered and rude and likely to be labeled a troublemaker.[17] If the car ever is built, the group still won't know where it is going! But knowing where we are going, and how we really get there, are theological issues. Whether it is rude or not, these questions must be asked. And we aren't so naïve as to think they won't be asked by teenagers.

Earlier, I mentioned how counterproductive theology is for youth ministry when the major concern of youth ministry is providing the best environment and the most nurturing care for the enhancement of adolescent development. Isn't this the crux of the matter? Is enhancement of adolescent development the major concern of youth ministry? Much of my own academic training is in the field of educational psychology. I appreciate, admire, and use the research this, and fields of study like it, provides. But it cannot be the major concern of youth ministry. The major concern of youth ministry is the establishing and/or maintaining of a vibrant relationship with God through saving faith in Jesus Christ accomplished by the Holy Spirit through the Means of Grace.

Well, there now, I've done it. I've thrown Lutheran theology squarely into the center of the youth ministry project. Yet, in so doing,

17 Harry Blamires, *The Christian Mind: How Should a Christian Think?* (Ann Arbor, MI: Regent College Publishing, 1978), 18–19.

I want to be clear that I'm not eliminating the valuable information provided to us through the social sciences or the insights that come from other Christian sources.

Research into youth ministry has, over the decades, worked tirelessly to create environments in which adolescents can "easily and comfortably" reach adulthood as healthy, wholesome people. Helping us in that task has been some of the most informative and insightful research anyone would ever want. No agency has been more helpful in this process than Search Institute and the 40 Developmental Assets the institute promotes. This is wonderful material. One of the programs— with the interesting name of "LOGOS"—is in use across twenty-five different denominations and five thousand congregations.[18] Yet these statistics support the point, don't they? The Developmental Assets are a powerful tool, but only a tool. Search Institute would claim nothing more for them. They are as atheological as the institute can make them, with the result that they are equally suitable for use with community groups, public schools, and churches. Therefore they do not, they cannot, and they are not intended to answer the major concern of youth ministry. The Bible, however, does.

## Theology Applied to Youth

The field of youth ministry is turning toward the study of theology as the source from which to answer the most pressing of practical questions. This is cause for great rejoicing. This isn't to say that youth ministry in years gone by was bereft of theological nuance. It wasn't. But there seems to be a difference. It seems that before, youth ministry literature made the obligatory nod toward denominations and their respective theologies, and then the subject quickly moved to an explanation of the developmental categories (physical, cognitive, moral, psycho-social, emotional) and their significance for a host of activities. Today's popular authors in the field do much, much more than give theology lip service. They see theology as the superstructure within which all the other aspects of the field coalesce. They pay theology close attention.[19]

18 Eugene C. Roehlkepartain, *Building Assets in Congregations: A Practical Guide for Helping Youth Grow Up Healthy* (Minneapolis: Search Institute, 1998), 105.

19 For example, the Association of Youth Ministry Educators had as the theme for its 2009 Conference "Conversations on the Aereopagus: Communicating an Appropriate

So here's the question. If theological differences are attended to with honesty and conviction, won't they inevitably be played out in youth ministry practice itself? Won't there be noticeable differences in how we do things, and what things we do? Here's what I mean. One theological perspective looks at youth ministry as the time for conversion, another as a time for spiritual growth and confession. One theological perspective looks at youth ministry as something filled with purpose that must be driven, another as a time to learn what it means to be forgiven. One theological perspective holds forth the goal of a wholly sanctified life, another as a training ground for daily repentance. One theological perspective seeks the best set of principles by which to be empowered for Christian living, another points to sacraments as the sustaining factor in faith. One theological perspective instills the need of good works for salvation; another catechizes a life of good works in response to salvation.

Now, imagine that a youth group is planning a mission trip, a lock-in, a movie night, a local servant event. How will any of those events be different from each other based on the theological perspectives of the church body? Or won't they be different at all? Or, let's imagine a more difficult scenario, in which a youth leader comes face-to-face with a teen that is cutting, experiencing the break-up of his family, caught using drugs, or pregnant. How different will the youth leader's response be, based on his or her theological perspectives? Or won't the response be different at all?

Do we take the time necessary to review Bible studies and curriculum that we use? Or do we assume that whatever looks good will work out and if there happens to be a theological problem we can manage the discrepancies as we go along? A recent online discussion illustrates the problem of not giving underlying theology due credit. A director of Christian education asks whether or not others have had any experience with a curriculum. The new pastor of the congregation has used it before and wants to introduce it, but the director of Christian education has misgivings. One respondent to the question describes his search of the curriculum's Web site. He quotes from the site's Statement of Faith, in which the organization clearly affirms Baptism by immersion and confesses the Lord's Supper to be a memorial meal—and both without power as a means of salvation. After noting the obvious conflict with Lutheran theology, the

---

Christology in the Midst of a Post-Christian Pluralistic Society."

respondent, Dr. Steve Arnold—the Director of Campus Ministry at
Concordia University, St. Paul, Minnesota—continues,

> Now, one can argue that a curriculum can be adapted. TRUE.
> But, as one who has spent thirty years and many graduate
> hours studying curriculum I can tell you that you cannot
> effectively adapt something that is foundationally different
> because the foundations in a well written curriculum (and [it]
> is a very well written curriculum) are woven throughout and
> become a part of the DNA of every sentence. The statement
> regarding "The Ordinances" is not about grace. Are people
> saved regardless of this belief. I believe so. However, the
> statement as prescribed in the documents leads to anything
> but an abundant life in the grace of God. This view places the
> burden on the believer and, then, even though the believer is
> "saved" is still burdened rather than living in freedom. There
> are strong Law/Gospel issues in their statement of faith.[20]

What we do in youth ministry is informed by our underlying
theology, and if differences based on our theology can't be observed
in our activities, in our curriculum choices, or in our counseling, then
there is cause for concern. Could it be that the underlying theology
itself is weak or nonexistent? Has the need to produce numbers and
safety removed from youth ministry the reason it exists? Texts that I use
for youth ministry courses are excellent resources for learning skills,
techniques, and strategies. They do the social science thing with great
professionalism, and I appreciate how they introduce students to basic
counseling responses and referral skills for traumatic situations. But
they don't teach theology, or, in the limited cases where they do, it's
most often from a perspective other than Lutheran.

Because theology is, if I dare use the term, "emerging" as the
key player in the broad spectrum of youth ministry study, Lutheran
theology needs to be a participant in the discussion. And this needs to
be a discussion. Lutherans have much to learn from other Christians,
but other Christians have much to learn from Lutherans as well. In
order to be part of the discussion, however, Lutherans need to think
more clearly through the implications of Lutheran theology in the
youth ministry context.

---

20 Steve Arnold, e-mail message to author, August 5, 2009.

But have we not done this, over and over? Do we not have nearly five centuries of catechetical resources from which to draw? Yes, we do, and this gives us tremendous depth; our theological well goes very deep. What we need to do is re-examine the bucket and the rope we are using. We have clearly articulated our doctrine, especially in the curriculum we have produced. Have we clearly articulated the connection of that doctrine to teenagers in the twenty-first century? To return to the puzzle illustration—with our border pieces clearly in place, are we managing to account for the different colors within the picture?

I am not suggesting that we develop "a theology of youth ministry." I dislike very much phrases that start with "a theology of" anything. To talk of a theology of youth ministry implies that there are different theologies for different groups. Do we then develop a theology of child-rearing ministry, a theology of mid-life ministry, and a theology of geriatric ministry? There is a better way of saying it: *theology applied to youth*. The theology stays the same; it is the circumstances to which the theology applies that change. God doesn't have something different to tell teens from what He reveals to the rest of us. No, we don't have a theology of youth ministry. What we have is theology applied to youth. Describing it this way keeps us from trying to squeeze our theology into the current culture of adolescence as if this particular age range governs our theological understanding. Instead, theology applied to youth allows us to let the border pieces of the puzzle, the shape of all humanity's relationship to God as revealed in Scripture, guide us as we work with the variety of adolescent colors.

## Preliminaries

Before we begin the task of practical theology—applying Lutheran theology to youth ministry—we need to look at what research tells us about the religious and spiritual condition of youth within our North American culture. How do adolescents view God, faith, and things of … eternal importance? For that discussion, we turn to Chapter 3.

# The World
# of the Adolescent

**W**hat is going on in Eutychus's mind as he sits listening to Paul go on and on? What does he think of God? How does he perceive his relationship with Jesus Christ? Does he sense the presence of the Holy Spirit? Does Eutychus understand what faith is? Must he understand what faith is to be part of the faith community, or is he part of the community before coming to a full understanding of the faith?

If Paul decides to open up the assembly gathered in the third floor meeting room to small-group discussion—a strategy completely foreign to rabbinic teaching methodology—and asks each person to share within the group what he or she believes spirituality to be, what will Eutychus say?

I don't know what Eutychus will say, and to guess how a first-century teenager would respond to the query of no less a luminary than St. Paul is to leap backward over nearly two thousand years of cultural transition as if it didn't exist. First-century adolescent spirituality can only be inferred from what is known of first-century adult spirituality, and scholars don't know as much about that as they would like. Besides, how relevant to youth ministry today is exploring the spirituality of first-century teens?

It may be more relevant than we think, especially when we consider how little we know of the spirituality of twenty-first-century teens. Consider those questions with which this chapter begins. Do we know the answers for the teens with whom we work with any greater accuracy and precision than we know the mind of Eutychus?

I suspect that there is far too much we simply assume. Sure, most of the adolescents in our youth groups have gone through catechesis of varying rigor; many have learned not only Bible passages but can also repeat sizable portions of Luther's Small Catechism and maybe even a hymn or two. They may even be attending church with their parents or with their friends and regularly presenting themselves at the Lord's Table. But what do they think of God? How do they perceive their relationship with Jesus Christ? How do they relate their faith to the lives they are living daily? Often, I fear we have no more insight into the spiritual lives of the teens around us than we have into the mind of Eutychus as he sits in the windowsill three floors above the street.

It is not as if our ignorance in these matters is willful. Adolescents are a tight-lipped group, by and large. Only when strong, authentic, and trusting relationships have grown over time do they cautiously share their inner thoughts and feelings. Parents struggle to maintain clear and deep communication with their teens, so it is no surprise that great effort is required for youth leaders to get a peek into their world.

# Looking Through Trifocal Lenses

Literally, peeking into the teen world for me means looking through trifocal lenses, evidence enough that the world has turned over several times, or so it seems, since I was a teenager. Therefore, I must trust that a cross-generational perspective can be helpful, especially when the source of my glance into the teen world is coming through research that in itself requires careful interpretation.

The purpose, as you well know, of trifocal lenses is to assist eyes that are no longer nimble enough to adjust rapidly to changing distances. The lower lens is for close work—about the distance from my eyes to the keyboard of my laptop. The middle lens handles medium distances—about the length that would be between us if we were standing together in conversation. The upper lens covers far distances—helping me read road signs while driving.

With the same sensitivity to distance, those who study adolescents and adolescent spirituality provide us with important observations and insights. Let me arrange these observations as if we are looking through my trifocal lenses: moving from studies that focus on individuals and small groups of teens who open themselves through close face-to-face interaction to research conducted over a large number of adolescents through surveys and interviews in North America to global investigations into adolescent and college-age spiritual development conducted by sophisticated research institutions.

## The Close-Up View: First Glance

Chap Clark uses the lower, up-close lens as he describes adolescents. He points out that up until a decade ago, we could divide adolescence into "early" and "late" adolescence. Now, with the continually expanding number of years that count as adolescence, a third category is needed that he calls "middle adolescence." To peek into the mid-adolescent world, he doesn't take surveys; instead he spends a year teaching in a public high school where he is a "participant-observer" with mid-adolescents.[1] In that environment, he discovers it takes months of daily contact with students before students feel comfortable enough to share with him what is really going on in their lives. When they do begin to open up, he finds the world they inhabit is much different from the positive predictions made about the millennial generation.

When I first learned of Clark's findings, I was skeptical. I have read the works of Howe and Strauss on generational identities and had found their arguments compelling, so much so that I included their

---

1 Chap Clark, *Hurt: Inside the World of Today's Teenagers* (Grand Rapids, MI: Baker, 2004), 10.

analysis in many of my lectures.[2] Howe and Strauss are the authors who compare the GI Generation with the Silent Generation, the Silent Generation with the Baby Boomers, the Baby Boomers with the Gen-Xers, and the Gen-Xers with the Millennials—those born between the mid-1980s and 2001—today's adolescents.

Howe and Strauss predict very positive futures for the Millennials because, according to their historical analysis, characteristics of generations repeat every fourth generation. Like the members of the GI Generation that won World War II, built the interstate highway system, made family central to their lives, and arranged themselves in community service organizations like Rotary and Lions Club, Millennials will win, build, and organize. Unlike Generation X, the Millennials will be more upbeat, more career oriented, and ready to organize. Though they will display some postmodern tendencies, such as thinking in non-linear ways, they will nevertheless value education, seek altruistic ends, and be more community based. They will value relationships and be more connected.[3] The GI Generation became what it was through overcoming adversity. Writing in 2000, Howe and Strauss expect some adversity for the Millennials too. "No one can foresee exactly what surprises, perils, delights, disappointments, and triumphs lie in store for Millennials. Yet Boomers and Gen-Xers can take some satisfaction in how they are raising a generation fully prepared to accept challenges, live up to their elders' trust, and triumph over whatever history has in store for them."[4] What history has in store for them is the world after 9/11.

Upbeat, committed, positive about themselves and their future— this is my view of adolescents—it is what I see in the church-work students that sit in my classroom. But then I read Clark. There is a different view. Clark suggests that there is more, much more, than what meets the eye when observing the world of adolescents. There is a world beneath.

---

2 Bill Strauss and Neil Howe, *Generations: The History of America's Future 1584 to 2069* (New York: William Morrow, 1991). Neil Howe and Bill Strauss, *13th Generation: Abort, Retry, Ignore, Fail?* (New York: Random House, 1993). William Strauss and Neil Howe, *The Fourth Turning: What the Cycles of History Tell Us about America's Next Rendezvous with Destiny* (New York: Broadway Books, 1997). Neil Howe and William Strauss, *Millennials Rising: The Next Great Generation* (New York: Random House, 2000).

3 Of any prediction concerning today's youth, this has been the most prescient, all with the aid of cell phone technology and development of text messaging.

4 Howe and Strauss, *Millennials Rising*, 362.

The world beneath is the world in which adolescents live. It is the world largely of their own making, and according to Clark, they create it because they are abandoned. In fact, abandonment is the emotional cloud that hovers over adolescent life. The adolescents feel as if they are in a deep ditch and no one notices or offers any help. In response to this rejection, the adolescent culture has pulled a roof over the ditch and have committed to raising themselves. The adult world is not welcome in this world beneath.

Abandonment manifests itself in multiple ways, each communicating to adolescents that if they are going to reach adulthood, they will have to make it on their own. Clark finds evidence of abandonment in the school system, in sports, in the family, and even in the Church. School systems have become institutions for the benefit of the adults in the institution. Controversies in school districts often revolve around contract disputes, administrative needs, and benefits packages rather than over student learning needs. Adolescents notice and feel abandoned.

Competitive sports are touted for building character and promoting physical health and well-being. But even Little League has become a big business for adult entertainment.

Sports (including dance) are no longer about fun, exercise, experience, and play. They are about competition, winning, and defeating an opponent. Sports are no longer child's play; they are a grown-up dog-eat-dog reality.[5] Adolescents notice and feel abandoned.

Who could argue with Clark's observation that the very structure designed to support the child's journey to adulthood no longer sees that function as primary? The frequent lack of a father figure in the home; the sense of loss at divorce; the busy, preoccupied lives of two parent two parent families all communicate quite clearly to the adolescent that his or her needs are never going to rise to the top of the priority list. An intact traditional family in a large suburban home is no guarantee against a sense of family abandonment. The home probably has a large master bedroom on one side of the house, and on the other side, beyond the living room, family, room, dining room, and kitchen, are the other bedrooms. Days could go by without family members ever having to interact with each other. Adolescents notice and feel abandoned.

---

5 Clark, 114.

Even the Church comes in for criticism and in a most surprising way. The well-staffed church with ample facilities has a youth pastor, a youth building, and youth services—all geared to attend to the spiritual needs of the youth. Surely such a program has not abandoned the congregation's young people! Yet, if the youth pastor ministers so that parents are relieved of their role of guiding their children into spiritual maturity, if the youth building exists so that the women's guild doesn't have to share kitchen facilities with messy teenagers, if the youth service is held so the adults can avoid contact with those unruly, rambunctious teenagers, then it is pretty obvious to the teens why they have all the goodies. Adolescents notice and feel abandoned.

A sixteen-year-old girl expressed her abandonment when she told Clark,

> I'll tell you why I don't trust anybody at this school or my parents. Everybody is out for themselves. Teachers, coaches, parents, even my church group leaders—they are all out for themselves. *Nobody* gives a (expletive) about me! *Nobody!*[6]

The result of abandonment is the adolescent "world beneath." In order to survive in the world beneath, adolescents form clusters: groups of students who hang together. Clusters can have as few as four and as many as ten members. They are usually gender specific, but a male cluster might affiliate with a female cluster. Clusters usually form in the latter months of the freshman year of high school. Cluster members commit to one another, not so much because of common behaviors and activities, but as a place in which to be safe. Each cluster develops its own set of mores, and clusters within a school filter themselves into a pecking order. Members may associate with teens one or two clusters above and below their own rank, but rarely beyond those boundaries.[7] Clusters aren't cliques or gangs. Their goal isn't supremacy

---

6 Clark, 167.

7 Clark comments on the implication of this for church youth groups that are drawing students from different schools and different clusters. "The church tries to bring young people from a wide variety of schools and clusters into what they call fellowship. These and countless other programmatic assumptions may have a noble intent, and in some cases may even appear to the adults in charge to be somewhat workable, but they do not take the changing youth culture and relational shift seriously. As a result, young people are once again offered up on the altar of an adult agenda at the cost of their personal sense of safety" (85–86).

or dominance—their goal is survival, together, through the treacherous high school years.

The fragmentation of society creates fragmented selves. Clark calls the adolescent ability to live life in layers "multiple identity candles." The adolescent compartmentalizes life—placing a different candle in each window (context) of life.[8] It means being a different self in each setting, yet each self is real. From the adult perspective, this is being untruthful, false, and disingenuous. But the adolescents are seeing themselves as they are supposed to be in the given setting—whether at church, at school, in the world beneath, or at the beer party.

Clark says we can't go down into the world beneath. We can only sit at the steps and be ready with a secure, loving presence and the offer of authentic, genuine, and trusting relationships with truly caring adults.[9]

So which is the accurate portrayal of the Millennial Generation—Howe and Strauss or Clark? This question nags at me. I follow the arguments of Clark, and they make sense in our culture, yet my students in class and the youth at my church don't seem to reflect the anger and frustration that abandonment brings. On the other hand, what if my positive perception of youth is simply evidence of how incredibly effective the world beneath has become in shielding the true teen experience? What if my students are simply the survivors who made it through high school or the brilliant couriers, double agents, who bridge the gap between the adult world and the world beneath?

I decided to put the question to the test. I described the Millennial Generation and the world beneath to my youth ministry class and asked for their opinion: which seems real to them? An articulate young lady responded, "You just teach church work students, don't you?" Other students in class were smiling. She answered my question with a question that answered my question.

What is she saying? She was telling me that I really am teaching some very special young people when I have a class of church work students. I'm not hallucinating when I see before me upbeat young people of strong yet maturing faith ready to learn what they can do to bring Jesus Christ to the world. She was also telling me that the world

8 Chap Clark, "Youth Ministry 2007" (lecture, Houston, TX. January 6, 2007).

9 Clark, *Hurt*, 171.

beneath exists. Both are real.[10] If I fail to notice the world beneath, I reinforce once more the abandonment by the adult world felt by many adolescents.

# Close-up View: Taking a Second Look

Carol Lytch also uses the lower, up-close lens, but rather than looking at adolescents in their school environment as does Clark, she explores their church youth group setting. For over a year, Lytch attached herself to three different youth groups in Louisville, Kentucky, one Roman Catholic, one United Methodist, and one Evangelical nondenominational, that share a rather unique characteristic—each retains a large number of adolescents through their senior year of high school. She wanted to know how these churches manage to avoid the drop off in participation experienced by so many congregations during the junior and senior years of high school. She interviewed students, leaders, clergy, and parents. She attended worship services, teen nights, Bible classes, and mission opportunities. She looked for the glue that keeps the teens attached. The answer she found is different for each of the three youth groups, but common threads among the three provides insight into the spiritual lives of teens.[11]

She calls these threads "a sense of belonging, a sense of meaning, and opportunities to develop competence."[12] This sounds vaguely familiar. This sounds very similar to the three formative needs in adolescent development that Robert Kolb connects to catechesis. He puts them in a different order, "identity, security, and meaning," but the concepts are comparable.[13] If I have a sense of belonging, then I have security. If I have a sense of my own competence, I'm better equipped to understand who I am, my identity. If I have meaning, then—it's a match! I have meaning!

---

10 Since that conversation, I've had the opportunity to teach a required religion course for nonchurch-work students. While some well-catechized students going into other fields aced the course, other students struggled. For some, the course was their first exposure to the Christian faith. They were filled with questions. Others couldn't hide their boredom. A few never came up from the world beneath.

11 Carol E. Lytch, *Choosing Church: What Makes a Difference for Teens* (Louisville: Westminster John Knox, 2004).

12 Lytch, 25.

13 Robert Kolb. *Teaching God's Children His Teaching* (Hutchinson, MN: Crown Publishing, 1992), 2–1.

Notice that Lytch worked with a different population than Clark, so there is no surprise that her findings do not reflect the darker aspects of the world beneath. In contrast, Lytch seems to have uncovered practices that assist in creating the kind of young people who later on decide to become professional church workers. Now, how are they doing it?

Lytch examined a number of variables: age-graded divisions in the Christian education program, number of young people in the congregation, number of activities offered, amount of space assigned to the youth program, amount of human resources dedicated to the youth program, and the kinds of relationships fostered with leaders and clergy. She found one variable often considered of prime importance to be quite negligible—the age and gender of the youth minister.[14]

The Roman Catholic youth came to their youth group, but were sporadic in attendance at mass, except for special events and holy days. What held them together are the experiences that they share under the guidance of a caring adult who gets deeply into their lives. Their leader knows them, and they know they will be missed if they don't show. Her example of faith was a model for their own growing religious and spiritual understanding, particularly when the group experiences tragedy.

> Faith transmission was "working" at Transfiguration as teens had powerful experiences that they interpreted as experiences of God. It is no coincidence that these experiences often happened in experiences of death, on retreats . . . , and during the senior year.[15]

Symbols and rituals that were learned and practiced years earlier now come into play and allow the young people to interpret life experiences within a God-filled framework. No wonder even college students on break returned—they are drawn by comforting rituals and supportive relationships.

The United Methodist youth also had strong relationships with their leaders, but these relationships stem from another source. The worship experience of the congregation was musically rich, and the

---

14 Lytch, 32.

15 Lytch, 67.

youth from early on had not only been invited to participate, they had been heavily relied upon. They were key participants who have gained skill and competence within the worshiping community. Their absence would be a denial of their gifts and a betrayal of the community. But they wouldn't think of missing—they are needed. The relationship with the leader (director) was warm and genuine, and the director was not without opportunity to model forgiveness when members of the group messed up. They also returned on break from college and slid right into the choir or music ensemble. There were youth, however, who don't fit into the music program. If they stayed involved, it was because of friends and family. Some found deeper spiritual experiences on retreats with parachurch groups.[16]

The energy level of the nondenomination youth group was high. They were the largest of the three groups, and as with the other two, relationships with the youth leaders provided much of the sticking power. They attended the youth services at their church because Jesus Christ is exciting, and they were learning how to share Him with others. Their leaders showed up at their high schools for lunch and watched their extracurricular activities. They saw themselves as missionaries to their peers. "Teens reared at Riverland Heights professed high levels of loyalty to their religious tradition. Only at Riverland Heights did any of the teens say they intended to pursue a professional church vocation."[17]

Lytch's findings from the programs of the three congregations provides the backdrop for what I consider the most cogent analysis in her work, that regarding family influence. She draws three conclusions regarding the family:

- First, teens are influenced in the most lasting way by how their parents connected them (or not) to the church from a young age.

- Second, parents influence teens in what they believe and how they practice their faith by maintaining a church attendance rule even into the teen years.

- Third, parents influence teen religious loyalty by

16 Lytch, 71.

17 Lytch, 71.

choosing carefully a church to which they link the teen.[18]

Am I surprised by these findings? Not at all. She confirms what I have seen throughout my ministry. Of particular interest is the second bullet. According to Lytch, parents that permit their teen to decide whether or not to attend church are abdicating a lynch pin position in their influence of their teen. (I'm assuming that the parents themselves are weekly attendees.) Parents, perhaps recalling their own adolescent years, fear their teens will accuse them of "shoving religion down my throat." Many times, I've heard the same from a fallen away adult trying to excuse his own rejection of God by blaming his parents. Nevertheless, what Lytch heard from the teens in these three congregations should dispel that worry. She writes:

> The teens who were most heavily socialized in their tradition and grew up with the understanding "in our family we attend church" are also the ones who say emphatically that their *church participation is something they would choose* even if it were not a family requirement [italics added].[19]

What do I learn from Lytch? The Christian faith provides meaning. The Christian community provides belonging. And the youth group is a place to practice competencies for adulthood. Kolb is correct. It's about identity, security, and meaning.

## A Middle View through the Middle Lens

Christian Smith and Melinda Lundquist Denton are a little more removed from adolescents in their research, taking the middle-lens perspective—still close, but not developing the kind of long-term relationships that Clark and Lytch establish. They report the findings of the National Study of Youth and Religion (NSYR). To accomplish their research, they conducted a phone survey with over thirty-two hundred teens between the ages of thirteen and seventeen. Then, in order to validate the survey results, they conducted 267 in-depth personal interviews that covered similar issues of the teen's religious,

---

18 Lytch, 187–188.
19 Lytch, 192.

spiritual, family, and social lives.[20] What they learned from their research is assuring on one level, but on another, it paints a very disturbing picture of spirituality among youth in North America.

What is reassuring? Well, a large number of adolescents in the United States consider religion and spirituality important if not defining features in their lives.[21] On the other hand, an equally large number of youth feel other influences in their lives compete with their spiritual lives.[22]

The researchers summarized the difficulty more conservative churches face. For most conservative Protestant churches there is a large gap between the church's confessional stance and what students actually say they believe.[23] For example, the researchers report that 33 percent of conservative Protestant youth "maybe or definitely" believe in reincarnation. The same percentage believes in astrology, while a slightly smaller percentage believes in communicating with the dead.[24] Of all United States teens, less than a third say there is only one true religion, a little over half believe one can practice more than one faith, and two-thirds do not believe it's necessary to be part of a congregation in the exercise of their religion or spirituality.[25]

Rather than continuing to share specific statistics from the study, let me summarize the broader findings, at least those things that struck me as most relevant to youth ministry in a Lutheran context. First, the researchers found that teens are, by overwhelming majorities, not able to use the language of faith when asked to describe their beliefs about God. In more than two hundred interviews with teens, the resurrection of Jesus Christ was mentioned only seven times, God as the Trinity only four times, salvation six times, but sin or being a sinner forty-seven times. Teens were more likely to talk about grace in reference to the title of a now cancelled television show than in the actual concept of grace.[26]

20 Christian Smith and Melinda Lundquist Denton, *Soul Searching: The Religious and Spiritual Lives of American Teenagers* (New York: Oxford, 2005), 292, 302.

21 Smith and Denton, 27.

22 Smith and Denton, 28.

23 Smith and Denton, 77.

24 Smith and Denton, 44.

25 Smith and Denton, 74–76.

26 Smith and Denton, 166–167. As a point of information, in the study, LCMS

Second, just as the language of faith seems foreign to the teens, so do the doctrines of the faith.[27] In fact, what the researchers gleaned from the survey and interviews concerning the belief systems of most teens, they summarize in what they call "Moralistic Therapeutic Deism." Moralistic Therapeutic Deism (MTD) is summarized in five statements.

> 1. A God exists who created and orders the world and watches over human life on earth.
>
> 2. God wants people to be good, nice, and fair to each other, as taught in the Bible and by most world religions.
>
> 3. The central goal of life is to be happy and to feel good about oneself.
>
> 4. God does not need to be particularly involved in one's life except when God is needed to resolve a problem.
>
> 5. Good people go to heaven when they die.[28]

MTD bears little resemblance to the historic Christian faith, but it does bear an uncanny similarity to what might be called American civic religion. In a consumer-oriented society, it should come as no surprise that religion and spirituality are transmogrified into commodities designed to please the individual. The researchers wonder, and so do I, if MTD is simply the teen reflection of the overarching common adult perspective on God, faith, and religion.[29]

How much a problem is this, and is it a problem for Lutheran teens? The study actually does break down the responses by denomination. Smith and Lundquist discovered that no one religious group was more likely to retain their faith or lose their faith through the high school years. Those youth who were disaffiliated from their denomination of origin were found to be in the same percentage as

---

respondents were placed in the Conservative Protestant Category along with WELS respondents. ELCA respondents were considered Mainline Protestant.

27 Smith and Denton, 136.

28 Smith and Denton, 162–163.

29 Smith and Denton, 165.

the rest of the population. Lutherans are 3.4 percent of the total study population, and they are 4 percent of the disaffiliated, and it is much the same with other groups.[30]

The actual breakdown for Protestant youth is found in a second report with over fifty questions analyzed by denomination.[31] While most responses by the LCMS youth in the survey are average and do not stand out in a significant way, there are several that do stand out, and I can't help but share them. In response to "Shared Faith with Person not of their Faith" in the last year, 77 percent of the LCMS respondents answered yes—ten percentage points ahead of the next closest denomination.[32] While 87 percent of all surveyed youth would attend the same church if the choice was left up to them, 95 percent of LCMS youth, the highest percentage, would attend the same church.[33] In a question dealing with sometimes feeling confusion over right and wrong, the researchers had this to say, "Only 6 percent of Episcopalian teens and 9 percent of Missouri Synod Lutheran teens say they sometimes feel confused about what is right and wrong,"[34] percentages lower than many other denominations.

Before celebrating over the evangelism, loyalty, and moral clarity of our teens, however, we should also take note that the Missouri Synod teen respondents also scored second highest (80 percent) on cheating in school during the last year[35] and lying to parents often (11 percent) over the last year.[36] I'm hesitant to ask the Lutheran question, "What does this mean?" because the answer seems to be that LCMS youth are not confused at all; they know exactly when they are doing wrong. And yet, like most other youth, there is uncertainty about what is ultimately right and wrong. One question reads, "Some people say that morals are relative, that there are no definite rights and wrongs for everybody. Do you agree or disagree?" LCMS teens were right in

30 Smith and Denton, 88.

31 Phil Schwadel and Christian Smith, *Portraits of Protestant Teens: A Report on Teenagers in Major U.S. Denominations* (Chapel Hill: National Study of Youth and Religion, University of North Carolina, 2005).

32 Schwadel and Smith, 40.

33 Schwadel and Smith, 49.

34 Schwadel and Smith, 53.

35 Schwadel and Smith, 56.

36 Schwadel and Smith, 57.

the middle with most other groups, with 50 percent agreeing to moral relativism.[37]

Many other questions could be analyzed from the study, but these are sufficient to inform us that our youth are under the same pressures and living in the same culture as adults. I think the researchers feel their work is a wake-up call for the Church today that we not underestimate the power of culture and media to shape attitudes and beliefs. They see Moralistic Therapeutic Deism as a threat to the historic Christian faith, and yet it is a view that can't sustain itself. They call it parasitic faith. Unable to sustain itself, parasitic faith attaches itself to existing religious traditions.[38]

Smith and Denton conclude their study by offering some serious advice to faith communities that can be summarized as follows:

- If you want teens involved, get their parents involved.

- Teens are teachable and need to be taught the faith intentionally.

- Religious teachers need to clearly articulate the faith.

- Appeal to teens' individualism can be used against culture's negative effects.

- Both teens and adults need work on articulating firmly-held beliefs in nonoffensive speech.[39]

That's enough to look at for a while through the middle lens of our trifocal lenses. Let's try looking into the distance.

## Looking into the Distance through the Top Lens

The fourth source of information we look at uses the upper lens, gaining perspective from a distance. The Center for Spiritual Development in Childhood and Adolescence, an initiative of Search Institute, wants to learn as much as possible about what adolescents

---

37 Schwadel and Smith, 52.

38 Smith and Denton, 166.

39 Smith and Denton, 267–269.

think of spirituality, religion, faith, and God. Rather than just studying North American teens, however, this research takes a global perspective. Spiritual experiences of 6,500 young people between the ages of twelve and twenty-five from eight different countries are reported, along with the findings of focus groups involving 175 young people in thirteen different countries and thirty-two personal interviews conducted in India, Jordan, Kenya, Peru, the United Kingdom, and the United States. Guidance in constructing the survey instruments is provided by "a network of almost 120 distinguished leaders, social scientists, theologians/philosophers, and practitioners from around the world"[40] representing all major religions. Broad and inclusive, these researchers want to know what is held in common and what is different about adolescent development and things spiritual. They want answers to questions about adolescent spirituality like "*How do they think about this aspect of life? Is it important to them? What helps them on this journey? What gets in the way? How does it influence who they are and who they are becoming?*" (emphasis in original).[41]

The researchers analyze spirituality, so naturally they explore the relationship between religion and spirituality among youth. They find that 34 percent feel themselves to be spiritual and religious, while 24 percent consider themselves spiritual but not religious. Most think religion and spirituality are both good elements to have in one's life, but "a third view religion as 'usually bad.'"[42]

The study makes several assumptions about spiritual development:

- Spiritual development is an intrinsic part of being human. It includes processes that are manifested in many diverse ways among individuals, cultures, traditions, and historical periods.

- Spiritual development involves both an inward journey (inner experiences and/or connections to the infinite or unseen) and an outward journey (being expressed in daily activities, relationships, and actions).

- Spiritual development is a dynamic, nonlinear process

---

40 Eugene C. Roehlkepartain et al., *With Their Own Voices* (Minneapolis: Search Institute, 2008), 8.

41 Roehlkepartain et al., 5.

42 Roehlkepartain et al., 7.

that varies by individual and cultural differences.

• Spiritual development, though a unique stream of human development, cannot be separated from other aspects of one's being.

• Spiritual development can be conceptually distinguished from religious development or formation, though the two are integrally linked in the lived experiences of some people, traditions, and cultures.[43]

These assumptions raise some interesting and potentially troubling questions about what is spiritual and what is not. We will look at these questions from a Lutheran theology perspective in our next chapter. But in the meantime, given these assumptions, what do we learn about teens through this research?

Well, we learn that teens around the world vary in their relationship to spirituality. Most, the study reveals, believe a spiritual dimension exists in their lives, and some interpret their life experiences as meaningful through their spiritual understanding; although, others don't. These researchers find that adolescents like to talk about spiritual things, and most don't see themselves as having any problems in their spiritual lives. They do tend to look at their spirituality as a choice they make, yet at the same time it is "part of who you are." When asked "What does it mean to be spiritual?" about 36 percent answered "believing in God," 32 percent answered "believing there is a purpose to life," 23 percent answered "having a deep sense of inner peace or happiness," and 7 percent answered "I don't know" or "I don't think there is a spiritual dimension to life."[44]

When youth are asked what helps them in their spiritual development, youth mention everyday experiences, relationships with family and friends, time alone, helping others, and having religious or spiritual activities modeled for them by their parents. While most mention how others are helping them, 20 percent say they aren't helped by anybody.[45]

43 Roehlkepartain et al., 4.

44 Roehlkepartain et al., 13.

45 Roehlkepartain et al., 29.

In reporting their research, the authors share in-depth descriptions of some of the young people who are interviewed. The young people come from a variety of world religions, and each exudes hopefulness and an upbeat attitude toward life. They are talented, articulate, and honest in either their adherence or rejection of the spirituality they learn at home. You just know that if these young people were in your youth group, they would be the leaders; you'd love them—and you would have to scramble to keep up with them.

The findings of the study conclude by saying that spirituality for young people around the world has to do with "being connected" and that the "awareness or awakening" that comes with their spirituality provides them with hope and purpose.[46] Because the researchers want to learn more, the insights gathered from this study are forming the theoretical framework for further study and research. Nine different areas have been identified that can be explored regarding adolescent spirituality. The core of research in spirituality explores the inner, personal life of young people, as exemplified in (a) awareness or awakening that takes place as adolescents gain the capacity for deeper understanding and meaning; (b) the sense of interconnection and belonging that spirituality provides; (c) the way of living that flows from the beliefs that are held; all influenced by (d) other dimensions of development (physical, emotional, cognitive, moral, etc.). Around the core are the external, environmental influences that to one degree or another affect the personal inner dynamic. These include (e) the social context of family, peers, school, congregation, neighborhood, and so forth; (f) the culture that surrounds the social context, including media and ethnicity; and (g) the metanarratives that provide the interpretive keys to understanding and meaning—the sacred scriptures and stories that surround the young people. All these are influenced by (h) the passage of time and the significant life experiences of the teens, both personal and collective. From this rich mixture, the researchers look for (i) the outcomes—healthy spiritual development or harmful spiritual development.[47]

---

46 Roehlkepartain et al., 39.

47 Roehlkepartain et al., 41.

# A Lens for Looking Beyond High School

What happens to the spirituality of young people when they leave the nurturing environment of their congregations? If we are serious about our service of the Gospel to young people, it certainly means that we will want to know if our efforts done in one stage of life find fulfillment in the next. Interestingly enough, there are researchers in secular universities who are interested in the same question.

One final glance into the distance through the upper lens comes from the Higher Education Research Institute (HERI) of the University of California—Los Angeles. Beginning with the presupposition that higher education has overemphasized the mind at the expense of the spirit, and therefore the spiritual life needs more attention, the researchers at UCLA surveyed over 100,000 incoming freshman college students on several measures of spirituality and then followed up their findings with another survey of the same students when they were juniors.[48] At the same time, the researchers noted the importance of measuring the religious and spiritual understandings of faculty, so they conducted a survey with 421 colleges and universities involving over 40,000 faculty members.[49]

What can we discover from these two research projects? We learn some things that are common to everyone and other things quite specific for Lutherans. First, let's look at the general findings. Most incoming freshmen expect their college experience will help them in their "personal expression of spirituality." They are looking for input from knowledgeable persons with multiple letters behind their names. For most, however, this hope is not fulfilled.

> More than half (56%) of the students who completed the pilot survey say that their professors never provide opportunities to discuss the meaning and purpose of life. Similarly, nearly two-thirds (62%) say professors never encourage discussion of spiritual or religious matters.

48 Alexander W. Astin et al., *The Spiritual Life of College Students: A National Study of College Students' Search for Meaning and Purpose* (Los Angeles: Higher Education Research Institute, University of California, Los Angeles, 2004), http://spirituality.ucla.edu/results/index.html/ (accessed March 18, 2009).

49 Alexander W. Astin et al., *Spirituality and the Professoriate: A National Study of Faculty Beliefs, Attitudes, and Behaviors* (Los Angeles: Higher Education Research Institute University of California, Los Angeles, 2004), http://spirituality.ucla.edu/results/index.htm/ (accessed March 18, 2009).

> ... Nearly half (45%) report dissatisfaction with how their college experience has provided "opportunities for religious/spiritual reflection."[50]

This disappointment needs to be understood against the precarious position of faculty in a pluralistic culture. Faculty members are divided on the question of whether or not spiritual development ought to be a consideration in undergraduate education. We can certainly understand the hesitancy faculty may have with bringing their own spirituality into the classroom where they may find themselves censured or accused of proselytizing. Yet it seems as if segregating spirituality out of higher education fails to account for the full range of human experience and produces an unsatisfactory educational result.

This tension is felt in different ways in different institutions. I teach at an institution that not only encourages faculty to integrate faith and learning in higher education, but it also evaluates faculty teaching through student evaluations regarding faith and learning. This is one way in which the university sustains its commitment to the mission statement "Concordia University is a Lutheran higher education community committed to helping students develop in mind, body and spirit for service to Christ in the Church and the world." While not intending to be self-serving, I can't help but suggest that teens heading off to college would do well for their own spiritual well being to consider the overall goals and intentions of faculties when making their choice.

Back to the college students—in general, they have a full range of attitudes and perceptions about religious and spiritual matters. This doesn't surprise us in the least; and what we find encouraging is that spirituality is on their minds and in their experience. Only 15 percent of the student respondents say they aren't interested in spiritual/religious matters. Another 15 percent are conflicted; 23 percent are seeking; 10 percent doubt; and 42 percent report themselves secure in their spirituality/religion. Changes take place during the college years. For example, in terms of religious behaviors, the HERI study finds that over half of freshmen (52 percent) attend religious services frequently, but attendance drops by the junior year to less than one-third (20 percent). At the same time, interest in things spiritual rises.[51]

---

50 Astin et al., *Spirituality and the Professoriate*, 1.

51 Alexander W. Astin et al., *Spiritual Life of College Students*, 6.

Through statistical analysis of survey responses, researchers identified twelve different measures of spirituality and religiousness. Described briefly, they are

- *Spirituality*—believing in the sacredness of life and spirituality of all

- *Spiritual Quest*—interest in finding answers to meaningful questions of life

- *Equanimity*—feeling at peace even in times of hardship

- *Religious Commitment*—following religious teachings for personal strength

- *Religious Engagement*—attending religious services, praying, reading sacred texts

- *Religious/Social Conservatism*—opposition to casual sex, abortion; belief in punishment for unbelief

- *Religious Skepticism*—universe arose by chance, no life after death, science will explain all

- *Religious Struggle*—unsettled about religion, feeling distant from God, questioning

- *Charitable Involvement*—community service, donating money, helping friends

- *Compassionate Self-Concept*—self-ratings on kindness, generosity, and forgiveness

- *Ethic of Caring*—commitment to helping others, reducing pain, making the world a better place

- *Ecumenical Worldview*—interest in world religions and different cultures, believing love is the root of all great religions

For each of the measures, percentages of high scorers and low scorers out of all the respondents are provided. For example, in the measure of Spirituality, 17 percent scored high, while 25 percent scored low. Everyone else was somewhere in between. The measure that has the largest percentage scoring high (37 percent) is Religious

Commitment, followed by Compassionate Self-Concept (30 percent), Spiritual Quest (25 percent), and Religious/Social Conservatism (23 percent). On the other side, the measure with the largest percentage scoring low is Religious Struggle (36 percent), followed by both Charitable Involvement and Ethic of Caring (tied with 26 percent), Spirituality and Compassionate Self-Concept (tied with 25 percent), and Religious Engagement and Religious Skepticism (tied with 24 percent).[52]

What does this mean? It means that fewer college students overall are involved in a religious struggle or are captivated by skepticism as we might think. It means that commitment to religious teachings and a belief in a higher power is more prevalent than we might have thought overall. It means that involvement in charity and in caring for others isn't very high on the priority list for college students overall, and that some measures are comfortably in the middle.

This data takes on more meaning when we observe how different groups of students, like Lutheran college students, respond. Lutheran students fell into average ranges in most of the measures, but were below average on four measures: Religious Skepticism, Religious Struggle, Spiritual Quest, and Ethic of Caring. The study adds, "Their average scores on these last two measures are the lowest of all groups."[53]

What are we to make of this? Well, if we are to make use of it in determining if there are any distinctives to having been raised as a Lutheran Christian, I think we have an answer. Yes, while there are ways in which Lutherans are very much like others, there are some ways in which Lutherans are different. Scoring low on Religious Skepticism means Lutheran college students are less likely to think the universe arose by chance or to deny life after death. Scoring low on Religious Struggle means they are less likely to feel unsettled about religion or feel distant from God. Having the lowest score of any group on Spiritual Quest means they are less likely than others to be searching for the meaning and purpose of life or striving to find a meaningful philosophy.

Some might be tempted to take these three measures and interpret them negatively, as if Lutheran college students aren't thinking hard, aren't interested in struggling with religious or spiritual questions, and

---

52 Alexander W. Astin et al., *Spiritual Life of College Students*, 8.

53 Alexander W. Astin et al., *Spiritual Life of College Students*, 22.

aren't predisposed to want to find meaning in life. I suggest that here is a place where putting the best construction on everything will get us closer to the truth. I interpret these findings to mean that Lutheran college students are well grounded in their beliefs and tend to doubt them less. They aren't, by and large, questioning their beliefs, nor do they tend as a group to feel distant from God. Moreover, rather than being disinterested in finding a meaningful worldview and philosophy of life, their low score may reflect instead the responses of a group that feels comfortable with the worldview and philosophy of life it already has.

I'm not sure that I can find a way to put the best construction on the last area in which Lutheran students score lower than other groups, the Ethic of Caring. This measure includes such things as community leadership, working to change things that are unfair, reducing pain and suffering, and getting involved politically. Historically, Lutherans have been under-represented in public office, and this data would indicate that trend will continue. On the other hand, Lutherans have been in the forefront of social services, refugee resettlement, and World Relief. Perhaps more needs to be done to model Christian servanthood for our young people.

If my analysis of this data has any validity, it means that what we do as parents, pastors, teachers, and youth leaders does have an influence and needs to be taken very seriously.

## Summary

Does it strike you as problematic that my review of research on adolescent spirituality appears contradictory? For example, Smith and Denton found no real awareness of the religion/spirituality divide, while the Center for Spiritual Development in Childhood & Adolescence found it to be a very live variable in their worldwide survey. Likewise, Clark paints a very dark picture of a world beneath in adolescence, one not recognized by the adult world, while Lytch sees churches successfully involving youth and keeping youth involved long beyond what might be expected. One thing does seem consistent: what happens during the formative years of childhood and the exploratory years of adolescence does have an effect, however subtle, when and if the child leaves the nest and takes flight.

I'm not ready to accept that these research projects, with their
... different portraits of adolescence, are in contradiction. Instead, I
believe each provides an accurate view, given the angle from which
the snapshot is taken. Each provides us with a picture, sometimes from
below, more often from above, but each time a picture that lets us see
something that we otherwise hadn't observed and that we need to
notice if we are going to serve our Eutychus-like youth wisely and
well.

Of all the concepts discussed in this chapter, the construct of
spirituality ought to create the greatest level of discomfort for us as
Lutheran Christians. We may have a clear understanding of what the
researchers mean by the term, or we may not; but we surely ought to
have a clear understanding of what we mean by it. Defining spirituality
is the task we will tackle next.

# CHAPTER 4

# Lutheran Spirituality

E ach view of adolescence that we gain by looking through
the trifocal lenses of the previous chapter provides us
with helpful information for youth ministry. We learn
that teens are deeply spiritual and are often passionate
about what they believe. Nevertheless, in looking at
the research, we discover that words like "spiritual" and "spirituality"
are used in ways unfamiliar to us—or if not unfamiliar, then at least
in ways of questionable theological value. How do people today
understand these terms? And more important, how do adolescents
understand them? Before moving forward in our application of
theology to youth ministry, we will be well served by looking at
the variety of ways in which people use the words "spiritual" and
"spirituality."

For example, there is the distinction drawn by many today between
being religious and being spiritual. At one time, spirituality was
considered to be nothing more than a subset of religion.

Spirituality and spiritual practices were simply the means by which one practiced one's religion. Today, however, if I am religious, it means I am restrictive, dogmatic, judgmental, and denominational; but if I am spiritual, then I am open, experiential, nonjudgmental and free to express belief in God whatever way I choose.[1] In social science research, the separation of the religious from the spiritual is often even more pronounced. "Spirituality" may not even have anything to do with religion or a deity. As Laura Lippman and Julie Dombrowski define it,

> Spirituality is generally considered to be beliefs, experiences, or practices, such as prayer or meditation, that foster a connection to a higher power that transcends daily physical existence, and *which may be unrelated to the practices of any religion per se* [emphasis added].[2]

Mark McMinn and Todd Hall contrast what we might call secular spirituality with a definition more in line with historic Christianity.

> The contemporary postmodern views of spirituality that surround us are often based on amorphous notions of self-discovery, actualization, and moral relativism. Christian spirituality, in contrast, is deeply rooted in a particular historical tradition and set of epistemological assumptions that defy moral relativism. Christian spirituality, as revealed in scripture and affirmed throughout history, is about knowing God and knowing ourselves.[3]

## Exploring the River Delta of Spirituality

Michael Anthony explains the various perspectives on spirituality by diagramming the different definitional branches. To help understand his categories, imagine for a moment that spirituality is the very

---

1 Mark R. McMinn and Todd W. Hall, "Christian Spirituality in a Postmodern Era," *Journal of Psychology and Theology* 28, no. 4 (2000): 251.

2 Laura H. Lippman and Julie Dombrowski, "The Demographics of Spirituality Among Youth: International Perspectives," in *The Handbook of Spiritual Development in Childhood and Adolescence*, ed. Eugene C. Roehlkepartain et al. (Thousand Oaks, CA: Sage, 2006), 110.

3 Mark R. McMinn and Todd W. Hall, "Christian Spirituality: Introduction to Special Issue—Part 2," *Journal of Psychology and Theology* 29, no. 1 (2000): 3.

beginning of a river delta. If you have seen some of the strikingly beautiful pictures of millions of birds crossing enormous river deltas now available through programs like "Planet Earth," you know the image I'm looking for.

The first divide in the river of spirituality splits *Natural Spirituality* from *Religious Spirituality*. Natural Spirituality involves the study of all things humans consider to be spiritual, but viewed from a perspective that includes only naturalistic phenomenon and excludes anything supernatural. This is the stream of "objective" research. It sees itself as scientific and, while the Natural Spirituality stream will accurately record what it observes, no explanation for phenomenon that includes a real "God" is allowed. Further downstream this part of the delta divides into five more streams: spirituality as studied by the social sciences, as propounded by *humanism*, as dissected by *psychology*, as delved into by *human development*, and as experienced by *existentialism*. As in any river delta, there is crossover among these streams, yet each has some unique component that distinguishes it from the others.

Let's return to the first fork as we entered the delta and follow the other stream toward the gulf. This is the stream of Religious Spirituality, and as Anthony explains, it divides into four different streams, each open to the supernatural where gods or God are welcome: the *New Age* stream with its crystals and other paraphernalia; the *World Religion* stream that recognizes spirituality as varied as the Jewish Sabbath, Islamic five pillars, and Hindu karma; the *Contemporary Religions* stream that opens the door to Gaia, Wicca, and other earth centered, green spiritualities; and finally the *Christian Spirituality* stream. The *Christian Spirituality* stream is by no means a uniform watercourse. It subdivides into *Catholic Spirituality* involving saints and rosaries and *Protestant Spirituality* with its heavy emphasis on cognitive capacities. Oddly, Anthony makes no mention of the icons of *Orthodox Spirituality* or the emotional characteristics of *Pentecostal Spirituality*, but he does split the *Protestant Spirituality* stream into *Mainline* and *Evangelical*.[4]

Now, why have I taken you down the river of spirituality? The first reason is because every river that slows down long enough to form a delta also creates a murky swamp in the process, and that is what we have when we try to find a simple definition of spirituality.

---

4 Michael J. Anthony, "Putting Children's Spirituality in Perspective." In *Perspectives on Children's Spiritual Formation*, ed. Michael J. Anthony (Nashville, TN: Broadman & Holman, 2006), 16.

As Alexander and Carr point out, "Recent philosophical writers on spirituality and spiritual education have invariably begun by observing the difficulty, if not impossibility, of defining the notion of spirituality."[5] In youth ministry, I dare you to find a more difficult concept than spirituality. I don't think you can do it. Spirituality can mean just about anything.

The second reason for sharing this taxonomy of spirituality is to provide sufficient background so that when you are reading something about "spirituality," you can ask the question, "In what stream is this material floating?" Once the appropriate stream is identified, you can separate the data from its presuppositions with the hope of distilling from it something useful, all the while taking depth soundings to be sure that the stream hasn't become too shallow for safe theological navigation.

The third reason for creating a landscape of spirituality, and most important, is that there is such a thing as Lutheran Spirituality. I'm not exactly sure where to place it in the delta. It shares some aspects with Catholic Spirituality and not a few elements from Mainline and Evangelical Spiritualities.[6] Nevertheless, I suspect that Lutheran Spirituality is its own stream flowing from the Reformation, and if that is the case, it deserves its own explanation before we muddy the water with research, whether from the religious or naturalistic flow.

## Roots of Lutheran Spirituality

First of all, we need to acknowledge that Lutherans are suspicious of "spirituality." Why? Not because Lutherans devalue the work of the Holy Spirit or because we want to demean others who call upon the name of Jesus Christ and consider themselves to be "spiritual."

---

5 Hannan A Alexander and David Carr, "Philosophical Issues in Spiritual Education and Development," in *The Handbook of Spiritual Development in Childhood and Adolescence*, ed. Eugene C. Roehlkepartain et al. (Thousand Oaks, CA: Sage, 2006), 74. These authors are working with the concept of "spiritual education" and describe six different continua that will be present in any discussion of spirituality: "(1) confessional or nonconfessional; (2) religiously tethered or untethered; (3) theologically objectivist, collectivist, or subjectivist; (4) independent of or reducible to morality; (5) culturally thick or thin; and (6) pedagogically cognitive or affective. . . . Most leading accounts of spiritual agenda are 'situated' somewhere along each of these six axes," 75.

6 To draw too heavily from those waters in understanding Lutheran Spirituality would be to do the very thing Egon warned against in *Ghostbusters*: "Don't ever cross the streams!"

Lutherans are suspicious because spirituality has been so thoroughly misunderstood so frequently, often with tragic results.

For example, most people think if something is spiritual or has to do with spirituality, it must be good. Lutheran theology does not draw that conclusion. The Bible presents a very different perspective. Spirituality can be very, very good; but it can also be a gateway to unfathomable evil. There is a spiritual world that has been at war since Adam and Eve were in the garden. Christ has won the final victory over sin, death, and the devil by His resurrection from the dead. Nevertheless, the devil, the world, and our own sinful flesh continue to seek our destruction.[7] The mature Christian recognizes the danger and follows the advice John gives. "Do not believe every spirit, but test the spirits to see whether they are from God" (1 John 4:1). The context of 1 John indicates that the spirits about which John is warning are false teachers, false prophets; yet the power behind the falsehood and deception comes from spiritual darkness that seeks our ultimate destruction.

Even being spirit filled is no guarantee that the spiritual is good. The most "spirit-filled" man in the New Testament was the Gerasene Demoniac. Remember the account? Jesus confronts a demon possessed man and asks the demon its name. "My name is Legion," he replies, "for we are many" (Mark 5:9). Jesus drives out the demons, and they go into a herd of pigs—two thousand pigs run down an embankment into the lake and drown. Now that was a man who was truly spirit filled, but it did him no good. You get the point. As Lutheran Christians, we don't approach the spiritual, or spirituality, with open arms; no, we have our deflector shields up—just in case—and this is the biblical posture to take regarding things spiritual.

Lutherans are also cautious when talking about spirituality because of the ease with which emotions and spirituality are confused. Scripture speaks about true spirituality coming from outside of us, not from inside of us—not from our own thoughts or feelings. At the time of the Reformation, the "enthusiasts" claimed direct revelation from God apart from the Spirit working through the Word. Luther responds to this claim. "All this is the old devil and old serpent, who also turned Adam and Eve into enthusiasts. He led them away from God's outward

---

7 See 1 Peter 5:8–9 for the reference to the "roaring lion" and Ephesians 6:12 to be reminded that the battle is against the "*spiritual* forces of evil in the heavenly places" (emphasis added).

Word into spiritualizing and self-pride" (SA III VIII 5). Without some type of action on the part of the Holy Spirit working through the Means of Grace, we remain unspiritual—at least in the biblical way of speaking.

However, on the positive side, there is much to say from Scripture about being spiritual in the God-pleasing sense of the term. The Greek word πνευματικος, can be understood as a spiritual person—"one who has received God's Spirit and presumably lives in accordance with this relationship."[8] Such spirituality is "pertaining to a pattern of life controlled or directed by God's Spirit—'spiritual, of spiritual conduct, guided by the Spirit.'"[9]

When Paul describes what it means to be spiritual, this is what he says:

> And we impart this in words not taught by human wisdom
> but taught by the Spirit, interpreting spiritual truths to those
> who are spiritual. The natural person does not accept the
> things of the Spirit of God, for they are folly to him, and he
> is not able to understand them because they are spiritually
> discerned. The spiritual person judges all things, but is himself
> to be judged by no one. "For who has understood the mind
> of the Lord so as to instruct Him?" But we have the mind of
> Christ. (1 Corinthians 2:13–16)

Spiritual wisdom, spiritual truth comes from the Spirit—as a gift to us and not by human wisdom derived from within ourselves.

What do we learn from this passage? There is a difference between the spiritual and the unspiritual. The spiritual person has a spiritual life unavailable to the unspiritual person. The Spirit of God teaches spiritual truths using spiritual words, and the end result is that the spiritual person has the mind of Christ. The spiritual person accepts the words taught by the Spirit and understands through spiritual discernment. But to those on the outside, it all appears to be foolishness. The unspiritual person does not accept the Spirit's words and therefore does not understand the things of the Spirit. Once again, from a biblical perspective, spirituality doesn't begin inside us through personal experience or action and then move out toward the world.

---

8 Louw and Nida, 143 (12:20).

9 Louw and Nida, 509 (41:40).

Instead, spirituality comes to us from the outside and works its way in. Therefore, John the disciple encourages us to "test the spirits to see if they are from God" (1 John 4:1) because he knows there are false spirits, false prophets multiplying in the world.

In the Bible, the word *spiritual* also refers to more than just spiritual persons. There are several lists of spiritual gifts in the New Testament that are given to believers (Romans 12:6–8; 1 Corinthians 12:7–11; Ephesians 4:11–13). There are also spiritual benefits received by the believer, not the least of which is being raised on the Last Day with a spiritual body (1 Corinthians 15) and a glorified, resurrection body distinguished from but yet the same as our natural bodies. In addition, we have the spiritual teaching of the Holy Spirit already referred to in 1 Corinthians 2, and there are references to spiritual blessings and even spiritual songs found in the New Testament (Colossians 3:16).

The Lutheran Confessions also recognize both the positive and the negative sides of spirituality. The word *spirituality* often describes a man-made attempt at something spiritual and something that should be avoided. In the Augsburg Confession, Melanchthon calls monastic rules and vows "manmade services."[10] In the Epitome of the Formula of Concord, in a section dealing with "Errors that Cannot Be Tolerated in the Church," the confessors refute attempts at meriting righteousness before God through pious behavior, calling it "one's own self-chosen spirituality" (FC Ep XII 5). The same description occurs later in the Solid Declaration of the Formula in a section titled "Erroneous Articles of the Anabaptists" (FC SD XII 10).

What is the point? From the perspective of the Lutheran Confessions, there's something not quite right about spirituality that is self-chosen. Those who are involved in this "self-chosen spirituality" are the monks and nuns doing what they consider to be good works, but works that are not commanded by God nor are part of a God-pleasing vocation. Self-chosen spirituality leads to looking at one's own obedience, piety, and feelings of closeness to God as a true measure of spirituality. The implication for Lutheran spirituality is clear. We have a built-in bias against any spirituality that is dependent upon our works, our piety, or our feelings. As you may already have noticed, this

---

10 Paul T. McCain, et al., eds., *Concordia: The Lutheran Confessions*, 2nd edition (St. Louis: Concordia Publishing House, 2005), 54.

contrasts sharply with spirituality as it is defined by many and has huge ramifications for our understanding of adolescent spiritual growth.

# Spirituality in Lutheran Practice

In an essay on Lutheran spirituality, Frank Senn provides this definition. "Spirituality, therefore, has to do with one's relationship with God, with the way in which that relationship is conceived and expressed."[11] What do we think about our relationship to God? How did it begin? How do we make this relationship known in our lives? What do we do? The answers to these basic questions— what establishes our relationship to God and what do we do in this relationship—are the two poles around which Lutheran Spirituality revolves.

Lutherans believe that the relationship with God is one that is initiated and established by the Holy Spirit working through the Means of Grace: the Word of God and the Sacraments. Therefore, though much of popular spirituality begins with our search for God, that's not where Lutheran spirituality finds its roots. This means once again that Lutheranism is at odds with much of what's considered spirituality.

Note how Lutheran spirituality contrasts with the three most common approaches to spirituality. Each begins with humankind's attempt to establish a relationship with God through human effort. What exactly are these popular approaches? Gene Veith, in *The Spirituality of the Cross*, organizes them under the headings of moralism, speculation, and mysticism.[12]

*Moralism*, as the name implies, is any attempt to establish my relationship with God based on my own efforts. If I am going to relate to God based upon the good I've done, then I'm choosing moralism as my spirituality link to the almighty.

*Speculation* takes a different route. Here my relationship with God is determined by my knowledge and under-standing of God. If I learn the secret ways, words, and signs; I can work my will through the

---

11 Frank C. Senn, "Lutheran Spirituality." In *Protestant Spiritual Traditions*, ed. Frank C. Senn (New York: Paulist Press, 1986), 2.

12 Gene Edward Veith Jr., *The Spirituality of the Cross*, 2nd ed. (St. Louis: Concordia, 2010), 25.

divine power. This type of spirituality takes many forms, but in the Early Church the popular manifestation was called Gnosticism.

*Mysticism* is the third spiritual avenue. In mysticism I seek to become one with the divine; and so I practice rituals, speak mantras, and meditate in a prescribed manner, thereby establishing my link to the center of all things. Through the mystical path I am one with the divine and the divine is one with me.

Veith points out from Scripture the inadequacies of these three approaches.

> In the New Testament, a single verse demolishes each brand
> of human spirituality: "There is no one righteous, not even
> one [so much for *moralism*!]; there is no one who understands
> [so much for *speculation*!]; no one who seeks God [so much
> for *mysticism*!]" (Romans 3:10–11, NIV)[13]

Given the popularity of conceiving the relationship with God through behavior, through knowledge and understanding, and through union with God, we aren't surprised if research into adolescent spirituality at some point reflects each of these approaches to some degree. Our lack of amazement is also attributed to our own self examination. If we have looked into our own spirituality closely, we recognize vestiges of these approaches within ourselves.

Why are we, as human beings, like this? Why do we look to ourselves? There is a theological term that describes this phenomenon. The term is *opinio legis*, the opinion of the law. It is our default mode ever since the fall. It is the persistent belief in the human heart that if we are to be set right with God, the restoration of the relationship must come through our effort. Therefore spirituality begins with us; spirituality is our search for God.

Reality, however, is just the reverse—a complete turnaround—and in some ways a big obstacle for many who don't want to relinquish control. Lutheran spirituality doesn't begin with our search for God, but with God's search for us. Spirituality begins with the shepherd searching for the lost sheep, the woman searching for the lost coin, the father looking down the road waiting for the son to return so he can

---

13 Veith, 34.

run to meet him (Luke 15). It begins with something being lost—us! Veith describes it well:

> Instead of insisting that human beings attain perfection, Lutheran spirituality begins by facing up to imperfection. We *cannot* perfect our conduct, try as we might. We *cannot* understand God through our own intellects. We *cannot* become one with God. Instead of human beings having to do these things, Lutheran spirituality teaches that God does them for us—He becomes one with us in Jesus Christ; He reveals Himself to our feeble understandings by His Word; He forgives our conduct and, in Christ, lives the perfect life for us. (emphasis added)[14]

Now, I realize that this doesn't sound very spiritual, at least not in the way our culture expects spirituality to be. But think about it. What could be more spiritual than God sending His Spirit through His chosen means to enable us to believe? What could be more spiritual than the Spirit dwelling within us and bringing about change in us over the long haul of life? What could be more spiritual than a holy washing for forgiveness and a holy meal for strengthening faith?

The first step, then, in spirituality within Lutheran theology is not the development of spiritual practices, the gaining of religious knowledge, or the elevating of one's spirit to celestial realms. "Admitting one's failure—and agreeing with one's condemnation—is the first step in Lutheran spirituality."[15] Why must confession be the first step? Confession must be the first step because it leads to the cross of Jesus Christ. At the center of Lutheran spirituality is the belief that the cross of Jesus Christ restores the severed relationship between God and humankind. Through the cross, the obstacle of human sin is removed—not by our action, but by God's ultimate act of grace.

Many Christians today shy away from using religious language or theological terms. They feel such technical language erects a barrier for people who aren't willing to tackle the theological terms. But Lutheran spirituality rejoices in the theological terms that describe the centrality of the cross of Jesus Christ. The primary term is "justification." Again, many wouldn't think of the doctrine of

---

14 Veith, 17–18.

15 Veith, 25.

justification as being very spiritual. It sounds too cerebral. Nevertheless, it is where Lutheran spirituality finds the headwaters of every spiritual blessing flowing from our generous and loving God. At the cross, Jesus secured our justification. By His righteous act of self-sacrifice, we sinners are declared righteous before God. Satan can no longer accuse us before God's throne with our sin, nor can our conscience do the same. The debt of sin is paid; there is no more punishment, no more condemnation for us because we are in Jesus Christ (Romans 8:1). Can there be anything more spiritual than this?

John Kleinig calls Lutheran spirituality "receptive spirituality" because "its chief characteristic is reception from Christ, the exercise of faith in Him and reliance on Him for everything."[16] What does this look like? If I want to find a truly spiritual person who can guide me in the spiritual life, what—in Lutheran spirituality—would I look for? If I'm going to guide the spiritually impressionable youth, what ought I look like? Is there something special I should be doing? According to Kleinig:

> When I speak about spirituality, I do not envisage something extraordinary—a superior way of being a Christian that is open only to a religious elite or a more advanced stage in the spiritual life. I have in mind what is given to every faithful person. Christian spirituality is, quite simply, following Jesus. It is the ordinary life of faith in which we receive Baptism, attend the Divine Service, participate in the Holy Supper, read the Scriptures, pray for ourselves and others, resist temptation, and work with Jesus in our given location here on earth. By our practice of spirituality we are not raised to a higher plane above the normal, everyday, bodily life, but we receive the Holy Spirit from Christ so that we can live in God's presence each day of our lives as we deal with people and work, sin and abuse, inconvenience and heartbreak, trouble and tragedy. We are not called to become more spiritual by disengaging from our earthly life, but simply to rely on Jesus as we do what is given for us to do, experience what is given for us to experience, and enjoy what is given for us to enjoy.[17]

---

16 John W. Kleinig, *Grace Upon Grace: Spirituality for Today* (St. Louis: Concordia, 2008), 9.
17 Kleinig, 23.

Spirituality is not other-worldly. Spirituality is part of our ordinary Christian life. As we do the practices of an ordinary Christian life, we are in fact being quite spiritual—with a spirituality that pleases God. How so? This spirituality pleases God by receiving His gifts and responding to His love.

Spiritual practices are useful as a way of responding to the spirituality we have received. Kleinig suggests several such practices. We can meditate on God's Word in a number of different ways. Depending on one's dominant perceptual mode (auditory, visual, or kinesthetic) we can meditate by listening, imagining, or doing. We can use whatever we might find helpful to focus our meditation. Prayer is also an important practice in Lutheran spirituality. Because Kleinig sees our vocations, our Christian callings, as part of our spirituality, he uses the image of Christians as secret agents. We are "citizens of this world, with earthly homes and earthly jobs and earthly identities," and yet we are "citizens of heaven, extraordinary people, aliens, working to promote God's gracious rule here on earth."[18]

If, as Senn suggests, spirituality demonstrates how our relationship with God is conceived and expressed, then we can summarize Lutheran spirituality in this way. Lutheran spirituality is *conceived* as God's intervention into human lives with the Gospel by the work of the Holy Spirit, using the Means of Grace. Lutheran spirituality is *expressed* by receiving God's gifts and responding with faith-filled lives in God-pleasing vocations. The expression of Lutheran spirituality can take many forms, from classic and formal spiritual disciplines to personal and private prayer practices. But it is framed in a posture of receiving God's love through Jesus Christ.

# Building a Bridge

In the previous chapter, we learned a great deal about the lives and the thoughts of adolescents; at least, we learned what can be known through various research methods. In brief, we discovered that

- teens in our culture today feel abandoned and have been left to raise themselves and create their own teen culture;

---

18 Kleinig, 63–64.

- teens that remain active in their churches do so because they sense they are genuine contributors to the life and worship of the community;

- the faith expressed by teens, when expressed at all, isn't the historic Christian faith, but is something called "moralistic therapeutic deism";

- teens nevertheless feel themselves to be very spiritual and look for environments that let them experience the transcendent and the numinous; and that

- as they move out of the teen years, young adults continue to express a need for the spiritual but not the religious.

To think that all of the young people in our churches think and feel as the research reports would be a gross overgeneralization. On the other hand, to think that the young people in our churches are not affected, influenced, or guided by the culture that surrounds them would be naïve.

In this chapter, we have contrasted what society in general tends to think of as spirituality with spirituality as it is defined by Lutheran theology. In brief, we have emphasized that

- spirituality begins with God's search for us, not our search for God.

- spirituality is grounded in God's Word, not in our feelings or emotions.

- spirituality is expressed through faithful reception of God's gifts as we faithfully fulfill God-pleasing vocations.

- spirituality is practiced through a variety of disciplines that focus our attention on the work of Christ for us.

Now comes the hard part, and in fact, the place where youth ministry finds itself today. How can we bring these two chapters together? We need to use the empirical research that is available because it provides the landscape for the environment in which we serve. By means of the research, we get a glimpse of the adolescent environment: the air that teens breathe, the water in which they swim.

If we do not include knowledge gained through the social sciences, we run the risk of thinking that teens today are no different than our own remembrances of our teen years.

This would be a great mistake indeed. It reminds me of something said to a group of parents of teens by youth leader Rich Melheim over a decade ago. He said, "Don't ever say to your teenager, 'When I was your age!' You never were their age, not in 1995." The same can certainly be said whatever year this happens to be. We cannot draw on our own experience of adolescence to inform us about the pressures on teenagers today. My teenage years didn't include computers, cell phones, or the Internet. The environment changes rapidly. Even if you happen to be in your early twenties, enough has changed. There was no threat of "sexting" when you were a teen. Yet the genuine spiritual needs of teens today really aren't any different, and never will be any different, from your teenage years or the teenage years of Eutychus. Every teen bears the burden of sin, every teen needs a Savior in Jesus Christ, every teen needs the release from bondage that comes with forgiveness. These truths remain constant no matter how significant the changes in the culture.

This tension between the constant and the changing finds its way into our thinking about youth ministry. We can be leery, hesitant, and suspicious about using information from current research and from developmental studies because we don't want that information to drive our ministry to youth—and rightly so. A culturally-driven youth ministry disconnects from the heritage and tradition of the Church, selling a priceless inheritance for a bowl of pottage (Genesis 25:29–34). A culturally-driven youth ministry doesn't solve spiritual problems; it assists in their creation.

*Nevertheless*, a culturally-uninformed youth ministry creates its own set of obstacles to rightly dividing Law and Gospel within the teen environment. After all, teens do need to be present if the congregational youth ministry is to have any possibility of having an influence. We need a framework, theologically sound, that encourages us, with good conscience, to make use of all the information we can glean about adolescent culture and use it in the service of a genuine Lutheran spirituality in the day-to-day … experience of ministering to adolescents. I believe that such a framework is readily available to us in Lutheran theology. Let me explain this framework in Part II of *Eutychus Youth*.

# Noticing Eutychus
# in Our Theology

A year ago, I changed cable providers and suddenly found myself with nine different religious channels to choose from. In one of my bouts of habitual channel surfing, I happened upon the area in which these channels are sequestered and began to observe. It didn't take long for me to conclude I wouldn't be coming back to these stations very soon. At least when I'm watching the History Channel's Sunday evening offerings on the Book of Revelation or the Jesus in the New Testament, I know I'm listening to skeptics who bring on screen scholars who left their Christian faith behind years ago. The religious channels, on the other hand, claim a theological high ground that none of them can adequately ascend with any credibility.

Okay, let me scale back that last criticism, inasmuch as the Eternal Word Network is Roman Catholic, and I know where they are coming from theologically. That knowledge provides a level of discernment that lets me commend them for believing that God is actually doing something in the Sacraments. In addition, their programs on G. K. Chesterton are quite helpful. Other than that high point, the only other safe place to be is on the Mormon channel when they are showing reruns of Brigham Young football. Most of the other programming starts out poorly and goes downhill from there. Have these people no shame in what they are promoting? Is there a sucker born every minute?

Okay, let me scale back that last criticism. I must learn to be more sorrowful and less judgmental when assessing the relative theological competence of the general public. The religious channels have been helpful in this regard. It has affirmed for me my hypothesis that theology today is not only all over the map; it is all over the whole atlas.

But to scale back yet again, I ought to remember that Paul wasn't the only religious show in the town of Troas either. What were the choices available to Eutychus? Before how many different deities could he have pledged his undying commitment? The pantheon of Greek and Roman gods was quite crowded, to say nothing of the imports from Egypt or Persia. Yet somehow, Eutychus connected with Paul. He found the right channel, a channel that was broadcasting the truth.

The truth is what we are working with in Part II of this book. We want to locate not merely within theology, but within Lutheran theology, those specific *loci* that most cogently intersect with the development and growth of faith and spirituality in teens. What follows is my attempt to do just that. I make no claim to have done it well or comprehensively. Some doctrines, perhaps your favorites, aren't even mentioned. I fail to refer to the Six Chief Parts of Christian doctrine. The doctrine of justification by grace through faith receives no special treatment—not because I value it less, but because it forms the foundation for everything else; and as in any construction framework from garage to skyscraper, the foundation is pretty much out of sight.

In spite of these weaknesses, I encourage you to dialogue with the framework that I share. See if it isn't helpful to think that all teens are and can be understood as gifts from God. Perhaps these gifts function like a sound two kingdom theology that recognizes God's action in both kingdoms. Then examine how the Law might feel to a teenager or how refreshing the Gospel must be when encountering certain sins for the first time. Rejoice in the spiritual health that is ours as Lutherans because we have the Means of Grace to guide, cleanse, and feed us. And then get ready to see how three doctrines in particular find utility without being utilitarian in the lives of teens: the two natures of Christ, the theology of the cross, and the doctrine of vocation.

There is surely more to be said, and maybe you will be the one to say it. If so, don't hold back; it may be your vocation to exercise God's careful guidance for me. But if not, and you find this framework helpful in and of itself, then by all means find a way to apply it with the youth you serve. Once we've initiated the discussion on finding the place for youth within Lutheran theology, we'll be ready for Part III, where we will look for the place for youth within Lutheran practice.

**CHAPTER 5**

# Trinitarian Youth

How does our theology as Lutheran Christians inform our practice of youth ministry? This question requires close examination of our theological commitments as well as a critical look at longstanding practices in youth ministry. It means reviewing assumptions that we have accumulated along the way and testing them against our core beliefs. Another way of describing this process is to call it "practical theology."

Practical theology, in the minds of most people who even have this phrase in their vocabulary, consists of all the things professional church workers learn in their education that do not neatly fall into the three other categories of exegetical (Bible), systematic (doctrine), and historical (God at work through the centuries) theology. Thus it involves preaching, teaching, leading worship, counseling, and evangelizing. In this sense, practical theology is all the things we do with the information gleaned from the other theologies.

An odd thing has happened in recent years, however, regarding the field of practical theology as it is conducted across denominations. It has moved from simply being the acquisition of technical skills required to function as a pastor, teacher, DCE, DCO, DFL, deaconess, or lay minister[1] to becoming a full-fledged investigation into the way in which all that's been gleaned from the other academic theologies are brought to bear in very specific ministerial contexts. Like youth ministry? No, more specific than that—like how our theology relates to what we do when Jimmy and Jamal have it out in the back of the van on our way to the servant event on the Gulf Coast or like how our theology confronts the fact that nobody notices when Eutychus nods off and reaches street level.

Let's begin by asking a not-so-simple question.

## A Practical Question

What are we trying to accomplish by having "youth ministry" in our congregations? Every youth leader, youth board member, or caring congregation member should carefully consider this question. On the surface, the answer to that question appears blatantly obvious. We have youth ministry in our congregations in order to ... to ... to ... Well, maybe the answer isn't so obvious. In fact, raising this question might bring about hours of interesting and fruitful discussion, while on the other hand it could raise dissension to a fever pitch.

Let's take a few examples of how others have answered this most purposeful question. In 1893, the Walther League was formed as a synodwide youth organization associated within The Lutheran Church—Missouri Synod. To this day, older members of the Synod fondly recall their experiences as Walther Leaguers. If it were in existence today, the Walther League would be a "Recognized Service Organization" of the LCMS, much like the Lutheran Women's Missionary League or Lutheran Hour Ministries. When formed, it declared the following to be its objectives:

"The purpose of this association shall be to help young people grow as Christians through

---

1 DCE—director of Christian education, DCO—director of Christian outreach, DFL—director of family life.

- WORSHIP—building a stronger faith in the Triune God;

- EDUCATION—discovering the will of God for their daily life;

- SERVICE—responding to the needs of all men;

- RECREATION—keeping the joy of Christ in all activities;

- FELLOWSHIP—finding the power of belonging to others in Christ."[2]

Ninety-five years later, Doug Fields wrote what has become a classic in the field of youth ministry, *Purpose-Driven Youth Ministry*. Naturally, with a title like that, he lists what he understands the purpose of youth ministry to be.

A purpose-driven church is built around the five purposes found in the Great Commandment and the Great Commission.

- EVANGELISM Sharing the Good News of Jesus Christ with those who don't yet have a personal relationship with Him

- WORSHIP Celebrating God's presence and honoring Him with our lifestyle

- FELLOWSHIP True fellowship happens when students are known, cared for, held accountable, and encouraged in their spiritual journey

- DISCIPLESHIP Building up or strengthening of believers in their quest to be like Christ

- MINISTRY Meeting needs with love[3]

A brief comparison of the two lists reveals some fascinating consistencies as well as a curious discontinuity. Notice that Worship and Fellowship are listed in both; as well as the similarities of Education (Walther League) with Discipleship (Doug Fields) and

---

2 Erwin L. Lueker, ed., *Lutheran Cyclopedia* (St. Louis: Concordia, 1975), 836.

3 Doug Fields, *Purpose-Driven Youth Ministry: 9 Essential Foundations for Healthy Growth* (Grand Rapids: Zondervan, 1998).

Service (WL) with Ministry (DF). Fields includes Evangelism as a central purpose, while the Walther League doesn't forget the importance of Recreation.

A more significant difference is to be found in the introduction to each list. The purpose for the Walther League is to grow young people as Christians. To be purpose-driven, by contrast, is to act on the Great Commandment and the Great Commission, which is all well and good, except that a ministry built only on commands is seriously flawed. How? It is seriously flawed because the Gospel gets lost in the Law.

Lutheran theology takes very seriously the distinction between Law and Gospel. God's purpose in giving us the Law first and foremost is to point out our sin, accuse us of unrighteousness, cause us to despair of our own righteousness, and thereby drive us into the arms of Jesus—who is our only hope and Savior from sin. The Law has other uses too. It restrains sin and evil in the civil realm, and it provides guidance for us as we seek to please God in our lives. Nevertheless, the Law never loses its bite. It always accuses us.

The Gospel, on the other hand, is the wonderful message that God has done everything in order to bring us fallen creatures back into a loving relationship by means of the righteous life of Jesus lived for us, the sacrificial death of Jesus as the ransom for us, and the resurrection of Jesus from the dead as our justification.

Of the two, it is the Gospel that changes us, saves us, and motivates us for lives of service. This is the flaw in Fields's otherwise masterful description of youth ministry. He builds the theological structure for youth ministry on the commandment to love as Christ loves us (John 13:34) and the commandment to go into all the world and make disciples (Matthew 28:19–20) without laying the foundation on the cross of Jesus Christ. There is a third "great" that we would add to the Great Commandment and the Great Commission, and that is the "Great Promise." Actually, I think I would have to put promise in the plural, because I'm not sure which Bible passage I would choose as the source. First on the list no doubt would be John 3:16, "For God so loved the world," but a close second is John 11:25–26, "I am the resurrection and the life. He who believes in Me will live, even though he dies, and whoever lives and believes in Me will never die" (NIV). And there are more we easily could add to the list.

Now, to be fair, Fields doesn't ignore the message of Jesus' life, death, and resurrection. It's there in the background throughout the book; it's just not in the central position the Gospel deserves as the true motivation for the Christian life of Spirit-empowered sanctification. Before we can respond to the Great Commandment and the Great Commission in youth ministry, we must be grounded in the Great Promise.

# A Practical Answer

But then, let's look once more with a critical eye toward the Walther League's first sentence. The purpose is *to help young people grow as Christians.* This in itself is a laudable goal, but is there a way that we might deepen and enrich this concept of *growth*?

I believe there is, and we can find it in Ephesians 4, a chapter in which we are encouraged to leave behind childishness and *grow up* into Christian maturity.

> And He gave the apostles, the prophets, the evangelists, the pastors and teachers, to equip the saints for the work of ministry, for building up the body of Christ, until we all attain to the unity of the faith and of the knowledge of the Son of God, to mature manhood, to the measure of the stature of the fullness of Christ, so that we may no longer be children, tossed to and fro by the waves and carried about by every wind of doctrine, by human cunning, by craftiness in deceitful schemes. Rather, speaking the truth in love, we are to grow up in every way into Him who is the head, into Christ, from whom the whole body, joined and held together by every joint with which it is equipped, when each part is working properly, makes the body grow so that it builds itself up in love. (Ephesians 4:11–16)

Notice what Paul is teaching us here about the purpose of ministry in general and also about ministry as it is applied to youth.

Growth takes place as it is guided and directed by those entrusted with the task of equipping and building up—those in the office of public ministry. Youth are not to be left to work out their spiritual growth and development on their own. Just as the adults in the Christian community are in need of pastoral care for their faith journeys, so are the youth of the Christian community. Those called to be equippers for the building up of the Body of Christ dare not follow the example of our culture and abandon youth to their own devices.

According to verse 13, the goal of equipping and building up is threefold: unity of faith and knowledge of the Son of God, mature manhood (adulthood), and to the measure of the fullness of Christ. Each of these goals deserves its own comment as we apply them to youth ministry.

*Unity of faith and knowledge of the Son of God*—Diversity is a marvelous gift of God to be embraced and enjoyed to its fullest extent, when the diversity is in regard to personal gifts and talents, cultural artifacts and practices, and manners of creativity and self-expression. But if the subject is faith, then unity not diversity is the goal. We embrace the diversity of subcultures into which youth subdivide themselves. But we do not foster diversity of teaching, doctrine, or confession of faith. We can, without difficulty, acknowledge and even explore the multiple answers to many given questions that youth will raise, but for many if not most of these questions, our youth ministry will uphold the concept, quite unpopular in our culture, that there are right answers and wrong answers.[4] In matters of faith, we believe, teach, and confess that unity is not restrictive, coercive, or punitive. Rather, it is the objective we are trying to achieve. Nowhere more significant is this unity than in matters of who Jesus Christ is (Christology) and what He came to do (soteriology). Nevertheless, we also recognize that true unity is governed by love. Without the love of Christ as the moderating influence, the desire for unity within a fallen world rapidly devolves into cultlike behavior and oppression.[5]

*To mature manhood*—The footnote "Greek: to a full-grown man" alerts us to Paul's intention, which is by no means sexist. He's describing what it means to become an adult. Those called to public ministry and those serving with them will be fully aware of the

---

4 This epistemological position means that there are some limits on the pedagogical approaches suitable for teaching confirmation and youth. For example, discussion groups that conclude with each participant leaving the class fully satisfied with his or her opinion though it diverges from each of the other participants is counterproductive. Where the Scriptures speak with clarity, our goal is a unity of understanding and belief and a humble reception of God's truth.

5 Examples from history teach us that the goal of unity has frequently been twisted into the evil of persecution. While we are called to seek unity in the confession of the faith, we are also called to practice love in the profession of the faith (1 Peter 3:15).

multiple developmental tracks we as human beings follow as we grow. God has created us to grow and change not only with respect to our physical bodies, but also regarding our emotions, our social capacities, our cognitive reasoning abilities, our moral decision making, and our intellectual commitments. As we have already observed, many researchers are also viewing spiritual development as a variable ready for investigation. Viewing spirituality or faith as just another developmental issue has serious consequences that will be addressed later. At this point, we simply recognize that the process of moving from child to adult in all its complexity is a ministry issue for which there is solid biblical guidance.[6]

*To the measure of the stature of the fullness of Christ*—There is no fixed point in this life at which our growing in faith and faithfulness ends. This is simply to say that in this life, we never arrive. Our true destination, the place wherein we hold true citizenship (Philippians 3:20), is always beyond us. Paul's inclusion of this truth as he describes Christian maturity is of great significance for two reasons. First, it offers a link, a connection between the growing, developing youth and the adult world. It reminds the adult world that it, too, hasn't finished the growth process; for *the fullness of Christ* is what we shall receive on the Last Day. Taken in its proper frame, we approach mentoring and catechizing the young with a grain of humility, recognizing that we are still growing toward that fullness of Christ ourselves. Second—and no less significant—is that we see the ultimate, final goal for the ministry of equipping and building up rests in the fulfillment of God's Great Promise by raising us from the dead and giving us life everlasting. That is when we will no longer "see in a mirror dimly, but then face to face. Now [we] know in part, then [we] shall know fully" (1 Corinthians 13:12). The fullness of Christ, of which we get a taste at His altar with our youth kneeling beside us, we then shall have in all its fullness.

The result of equipping and building up is the capacity to discriminate in the best sense of that term. The author of Hebrews describes the mature as "those who have their powers of discernment

---

6 While there is good reason to place value judgments on much of the progress made as children pass through developmental stages (e.g., there really are advantages to thinking in abstractions rather than being limited to concrete operational thinking), there are also good reasons for avoiding value judgments if we are thinking about faith or spirituality as a developmental process. Paul points out his own cognitive development as he moved from childhood to adulthood (1 Corinthians 13:11) as a good thing, yet Jesus extols a childlikeness as a prerequisite for the kingdom of heaven (Matthew 18:3–4).

trained by constant practice to distinguish good from evil" (5:14). We are able to distinguish between what is God-pleasing and God-displeasing, between good and evil in our behavior, and between Law and Gospel in our application of the Christian life. This isn't as simple as it sounds, however. The culture of Paul's day is anything but supportive of a discipleship lifestyle. Questions surround the early Christians concerning pagan rites and sacrifices, appropriate ways of relating to the surrounding culture, and how to conduct themselves as sexual beings. The winds of false doctrine and human cunning and deceitfulness swirl around them. They need to rely on God's Word to provide them with practical theological wisdom. And they also need to study the signs of the times, to understand the ways of the culture not only in order to bring Jesus to the culture, but also to protect themselves from the onslaught of faith's enemies.

The final insight from Paul concerns what happens to the body when all the parts are involved. Individual growth results in corporate growth; or put another way, when all within the Body of Christ are maturing according to their particular station in life (their vocation, or calling), the entire body grows, "builds itself up in love." At that point, the whole is surely greater than the sum of its parts. Within that whole, we, as those entrusted with the instructing, mentoring and catechizing of the young, discover the marvelous two-way quality of the relationship. We learn from the young; just as the young are learning from us.

What have we learned about the purpose of youth ministry? Let's work our way backwards through the text of Ephesians 4. The purpose of youth ministry is mutual growth by young and old, who are learning and practicing practical wisdom, as they express unity in faith and exercise maturity in gifts while anticipating the promised fullness of Christ, accomplished within the community of believers who are sustained by God's gift of Means-of-Grace ministry.

Yes, that is a mouthful. Each phrase is packed with meaning, and it expresses youth ministry that transcends the superficial without succumbing to a Law-oriented drivenness. Youth ministry is more than keeping teenagers away from sex, drugs, and fast cars; even though that sentiment may well be the genuine concern of parents and others. The purpose is more than prevention, more than just a reaction against the devil, the world, and our own sinful flesh. The purpose is reception, a proactive expectation and recognition of God's participation by the teen in her or his life. As we learned earlier, this is what Lutheran spirituality is all about.

# Practical Theology

In articulating a purpose for youth ministry, we are already engaging in practical theology. We are looking for direction from the Scriptures (exegetical theology) as correctly understood (systematic theology) and taking into account what has gone before (historical theology). The next step is to apply the insights gained to a concrete circumstance. Of course, in real life, this works backwards. The concrete circumstance suddenly erupts, and in a flash we find ourselves responding as best we can. The manner of that response, however, will differ between the youth leader who reacts from the gut and the youth leader who reacts from the heart—informed by practical theology.

What will go into that ministry moment? Let me plan ahead a little bit. Of what do I want to be aware when the opportunity for Christian caregiving arises for the young person under my supervision?

I suggest that a healthy practical theology for youth ministry starts with "receptive spirituality" as Kleinig describes it, and particularly in its relationship to the Trinity. "By this reception of life from Christ we are drawn into the life of the Holy Trinity. Receptive spirituality embeds the life of the believer in the family of God and the Church."[7] Spirituality is not something done alone in isolation, but something done within a community. This Body of Christ that is the Church recognizes that it is constantly receiving all that sustains it as gifts from God. Remember Paul's question from 1 Corinthians 4:7, "What do you have that you did not receive?" We have received everything.

# Gifts of the Trinity

What kinds of gifts have we received? What kinds of gifts have our young people received? God's gifts to His people fall into two categories, according to the two ways in which human beings relate to God—God as our Creator and God as our Savior. In the first category are all those things received by all human beings because God is the Creator of all. These are what we call "First Article" gifts, referring to

---

7 Kleinig, 9.

the division of the Apostles' Creed into three articles. Luther's words from the Small Catechism describe well the First Article gifts. Our heavenly Father has

> Given me my body and soul, eyes, ears and all my members; my reason and all my senses, and still takes care of them. He also gives me clothing and shoes, food and drink, house and home . . . land, animals, and all I have. He richly and daily provides me with all that I need to support this body and life. (SC First Article)

For reasons that will become apparent in a moment, I like to call First Article gifts "gifts from below." Everyone receives these gifts, whether they acknowledge God as their Creator and Father or not; these gifts are given in various measures to all.

The second kind of gifts is Third Article gifts. Third Article gifts are the result of the work of the Holy Spirit. The Holy Spirit has "called me by the Gospel, enlightened me with His gifts, sanctified and kept me in the one true faith. In the same way He calls, gathers, enlightens and sanctifies the whole Christian church on earth" (SC Third Article). These gifts I like to call "gifts from above." They belong to those who have saving faith in Jesus Christ.

Now what must be kept in mind within this distinction between gifts from below and gifts from above is that both sets of gifts are from God. Just because I'm calling the First Article gifts "gifts from below" doesn't mean that we have any input into what they are. They all come from God.

"Well, this is all fine and good, and it certainly meshes well with Luther's catechism (though there does seem to be an article absent from the discussion so far). But how is this helpful in understanding a practical theology for youth ministry? This all still seems way too 'theoretical'." If this is the question on your mind right now, I'm pleased; because it means you are following along. So we have First Article gifts from below because God is the Creator and Third Article gifts from above because the Holy Spirit is the Sanctifier. Why is this significant? You should be asking the "so what?" question!

Let me share four ways in which this distinction will be helpful in developing a practical theology for youth ministry.

- By recognizing the First Article gifts, we create a bridge of common experience for ministry not only to our own youth, but also to their friends outside the Church.

- By recognizing the First Article gifts, we open the door for fruitful use of empirical data and research on adolescents as a theologically legitimate source of information.

- By recognizing the Third Article gifts, we acknowledge the Holy Spirit as the power at work through the Word and the Sacraments, establishing restored relationships with God.

- By recognizing the Third Article gifts, we understand our own role as tools in the hands of the Holy Spirit, bringing the message of God's presence into moments of ministry.

Remember that lengthy run-on sentence that defined a purpose for youth ministry?[8] The practical application between First Article and Third Article gifts comes in handy when we observe how the purpose for youth ministry is accomplished. Third Article gifts use First Article gifts for the purpose of Second Article faith. (Ah, there's the missing article!) Let me put it another way. In youth ministry, we recognize that the gifts from above (Third Article—Means of Grace) are received within the context of the gifts from below (First Article—Created Order) as the environment in which maturity in faith in Jesus Christ (Second Article—Faith in Jesus Christ) takes place.

No design of practical theology for youth ministry is truly practical if it fails to lead to Jesus Christ. A Trinitarian paradigm for youth ministry leads us to the cross and empty art notes tomb, to forgiveness earned for sinners by a sinless Savior, to Second Article faith, by affirming the work of the Holy Spirit through Word and Sacrament within the ordinary daily lives of growing and changing adolescents caught in a confused and contrary culture.

---

8 The purpose of youth ministry is mutual growth by young and old, who are learning and practicing practical wisdom, as they express unity in faith and exercise maturity in gifts while anticipating the promised fullness of Christ, accomplished within the community of believers who are sustained by God's gift of Means-of-Grace ministry.

# Gifts from Below

What belongs to the adolescent because he or she is a created being? Have you given that much thought recently? Let's examine this question, but let's do so by concrete life experience rather than by abstract conceptualization—your concrete life experience.

## First Article Gifts

Adam was created in the *Imago Dei*, the image of God. Adam possessed a perfect knowledge of God and a perfectly holy life. Both were lost through the fall. Nevertheless, the characteristics given to Adam that made him different from all the other creatures God made—a soul and a rational intellect—were not lost. Every human being has a soul, and every human being has, to one degree or another, intellect.

But wait, there's more! Because God sees fit to continue giving the gift of physical life generation after generation, we have, through that gift of intellect, come to understand how we change as we go through the stages of life. We change

- Physically: from infancy through early, middle, and late childhood and adolescence, and then into physical maturity (from which everything goes downhill)

- Cognitively: from limited concrete thought processes to deep abstract concepts

- Morally: from decision making based on punishment or approval to decisions based on universal principles

- Emotionally: from being controlled by our emotions to having some management of our own emotions

- Socially: from being the center of our own little universes to being integrated members of functioning communities[9]

Do you recall your own experience of physical development? What is your earliest memory? How old were you when you reached puberty? Can you remember any transitions for yourself as your capacity to think expanded? Were you an awkward adolescent? Or were you socially competent at an early age? Ever run into any moral dilemmas—like determining how much your parents ought to know about your activities as an adolescent?

These aren't insignificant questions to ask oneself when in ministry to youth. My purpose in identifying these categories of development is to tie each one to our condition as created beings. God created us in such a way that we grow, develop, and change. Not only, therefore, is it legitimate in doing practical theology in youth ministry to study the issues surrounding ourselves as created beings, but it is absolutely necessary.

For example, I can't adequately meet the spiritual needs of a mid-adolescent struggling with sexual identity issues if I don't have a grasp of adolescent development and how that development is taking place in the life of the adolescent in front of me. Studying these developmental issues doesn't mean that I've wandered from my theological roots or that somehow I have supplanted the authority of Scripture with the social sciences. Rather, it means that I'm adequately accounting for God's work as Creator and incorporating what I know of human beings as creations of God into art notes my ministry.

## Life Experience

The next layer of gifts from below is the life experience of the teenager. Life experience is the context by which we find ourselves

---

9 The scope of this book precludes any in-depth description of these categories, helpful as they are to understanding adolescents. Here are some helpful resources. Becky Schuricht Peters, *Building Faith One Child at a Time* (St. Louis: Concordia, 1997); William R. Yount, *Created to Learn: A Christian Teacher's Introduction to Educational Psychology* (Nashville: Broadman Holman, 1996); William Crain, *Theories of Development: Concept and Applications*, 5th ed. (New Jersey: Prentice Hall, 2005).

guided, shaped, and formed. From early on, we experience life through several concentric circles of influence. Some speculate that infants perceive themselves as the center of the universe, and indeed from their perspective and experience, they are—everything revolves around them. In actual fact, of course, the infant, though endowed with multiple First Article gifts, is relatively helpless. Those First Article gifts won't begin to manifest themselves for some time. Meanwhile—eat, sleep, cry, and get changed, not necessarily in that order, constitutes the routine for the infant while the parents supply nurturing love and everything else.

As the child grows, it learns about the world and himself through multiple filters, the concentric circles of influence. These also are gifts from below that the child receives, and each one is significant for youth ministry. The first and most powerful filter through which experience is mediated is the family. Recall your own family of origin. Wasn't that the context in which you learned how to read the world around you? Didn't you, in those early years, value what your parents or guardians valued? Comments at the breakfast table, overheard conversations while in the backseat of the car, and daily schedules taught you what was important and what was not. You responded in concert with your environment, or you suffered the consequences.

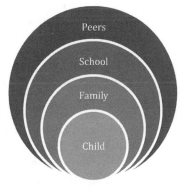

For what seems like ages, developmental psychologists have debated the relative merits of nature (First Article created gifts) and nurture (life experience) as to their influence. A clear divide existed between the extreme views of the "you either got it or you don't" and the "we can make a Mozart out of anybody" schools of thought. Today, as you might expect, most agree the reality is somewhere in the middle. Nature provides the range of possibilities, while nurture determines where along that range a given individual might fall.

Now, rather than work with these concepts in a psychological framework, let's put them in a theological worldview. What do we see? We see the First Article gifts placed within the family circumstances where those gifts will either be enhanced through nurture or atrophy through inattention. But the family circumstance itself is a gift; that is to say, it is received by child, and the child out of necessity adapts.

The next filters through which the child views reality are school and peers. The order of effects will vary depending on the individual child; for some, the teacher's influence is immediate and only later do peers enter the picture, while for others it is reversed. But each in its own way colors how the young person sees the world, relates to the world, and engages the world.

At this point, we might wonder about the wisdom of calling the child's social context a gift. As we look around, we find way too many examples of family and community circumstances that could hardly be called a gift for the child—one deficit after another, creating intolerable obstacles for the child to overcome. Much of the heartbreak in ministry for youth directors and youth leaders comes from watching families and communities fail to function as Christ-centered places of nurture and instead are places of hurt and pain.

Now there are two ways, paradoxically, to comprehend the social context. We first need to acknowledge that we are fallen beings in a fallen world. What did we expect? Don't we know that sin and death has infected this world (Genesis 2:17), that the first death ever recorded was fratricide (Genesis 4:8), and that creation itself cries out in eager longing for the restoration that is to come (Romans 8:22)? Recognizing the effects of sin (original, actual, committed, omitted, involuntary, etc.), we are the best equipped, theologically, to engage a sinful social context because we are fully aware that we are not fighting against flesh and blood, but against principalities and powers (Ephesians 6:12). We aren't at all surprised when the social context— the families—with which we minister (and our own families, for that matter) show signs of extreme dysfunction. The patriarchal domiciles were not always happy places either—just ask Joseph (Genesis 37:28). This isn't to deny that there are many wonderful homes. Many if not most in our congregations are affirming, God-fearing incubators of faith and Christian virtue. But we won't find any perfect ones, no matter how hard we search or how long we wait. And we aren't devastated when the household we thought most sound cracks and falls. That's what happens in a fallen world.

Moreover, the social contexts from which our teens come are not a surprise to God. This is the paradox. Families made up of sinful people nevertheless are gifts of God. How? We could say that it is in the same way that God "sends rain on the just and the unjust" (Matthew 5:45). God as the Creator of all and Father of all provides family for all. While it is true that social contexts vary in quality, every child receives his family and social context as a gift. Our role in service to the Lord Jesus Christ may very well be to take up the slack when the family life is unable to provide a nurturing environment where faith can grow.[10]

Life experience includes more than just social context, especially by the time the child has entered adolescence. Along with the influences of family, peers, and school we find the imprint of the surrounding culture. In fact, we can embed the social context within the cultural setting and present a new set of filters mediating the world to the teenager.

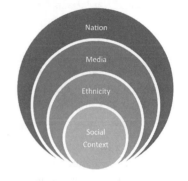

Take the first circle above the social context. How does your ethnicity influence and color your view of the world and your place in it? In the United States today, ethnicity may play a huge role if you are a first generation immigrant child who, because you can master the language more easily than your parents, have become the family link to the outside world; while on the other hand, third generation and beyond may have little or no influence. We are moving rapidly to the day when we will be part of a plurality culture—when no ethnic or racial group will have a majority. A possible result might be a shift in our understanding of what divides groups from one another, with less emphasis on race and more recognition of social/economic status. Whatever the outcome of these population shifts, we can't ignore ethnicity when talking about the gifts from below received by the adolescent.

---

10 Take for example the Old Testament description of how God wants the widows and fatherless (single parent households) to be cared for. They will have justice (Deuteronomy 10:18) and will not be excluded (Deuteronomy 16:14). They have the right to glean the harvest fields (Deuteronomy 24:20; 26:12-23), and they aren't to be mistreated (Exodus 22:22; Jeremiah 22:3). To mistreat the fatherless and the widow is to demonstrate the worst forms of evil (Psalm 94:6; Malachi 3:5), but to care for the fatherless and the widow is a sign of righteousness (Job 29:12). Showing mercy to the family that is struggling is family ministry.

Nor can we, or will we, fail to notice the powerful influence of media and how it is constantly changing the playing field of human relationships, communication, and what is meant by entertainment. Gone are the days of passively sitting in front of the television screen and choosing from among the three rival networks and public television. Today, television is interactive, entertainment is self-created, and communication is ubiquitous.[11]

According to Leonard Sweet, noted cultural commentator, the media-driven culture has made the younger generation, and a sizeable portion of the older generation, EPIC. This means that we have become *Experiential, Participatory, Image Driven* and *Connected*.[12] I was about to summarize these words in a sentence or two when I realized how futile that attempt would be. Nevertheless, something must be said. EPIC means that people expect to be involved in passionate, memorable events geared toward the five senses that make a difference within a community of like-minded persons. I'm sure I've left a whole lot out, but this is enough to let us know that the implications of EPIC for youth ministry are huge.

Finally, the large canopy filter that sets the context on a global scale is the nation. What people are we a part of? What beliefs about ourselves are communicated over and over again to young and old alike that define who we are as a people and what we stand for? There are thoughts, attitudes, and biases that come built in for us based upon our country. Americans see themselves as guardians and helpers within the world. Americans have a "can do" spirit. Americans live in the land of the free and the home of the brave. How these predispositions play out in the life of the adolescent will range from wholesale acceptance to rejection.

## Needs

The capstone on the gifts from below is constructed out of the creative mixture of First Article gifts and life experiences, what the

---

11 When I'm preaching and I begin by saying, "Our text for today is . . ." I can't help but wonder what teens in the congregation think I'm talking about. Obviously that standard opening line has got to go.

12 Leonard Sweet, *The Gospel According to Starbucks: Living with a Grande Passion* (Colorado Springs: Waterbrook Press, 2007). This is the most recent explanation of EPIC.

teen has received as a created being and what the teen has experienced by way of close social contexts and more distant cultural influences. What does the teen do with all this? Doesn't it just look like a soup, with every ingredient available in the kitchen thrown in? Who is going to risk tasting this?

But that is what the teen must do. Teens now take what has been filtered to them and, in their own individual and unique ways, construe it into a picture of the world. From that picture, they establish what they need. This is their opportunity to respond, and within the youth ministry context along with their own First Article gifts and life experience, they bring the gift of their needs. Everything else from below has been from the outside coming in; self expression is the inside coming out.

But clarity is in order here. I'm not including wants among the gifts from below; I'm only talking about needs, and I'm limiting this aspect of the gifts from below for one simple reason. Wants can have no limits, whereas needs can to some degree be met. Wants can soar off into fantasy, whereas needs are found in requirements that ought to be fulfilled. Wants satisfy the human heart's desire to curve in on itself, whereas needs can be understood and rewarded within well-meaning and God-centered relationships.

So what kind of needs am I talking about? Needs fall into four categories that can be expressed as follows:

- *Felt Needs:* This is the unsettled feeling that things are not right, that life is confused; felt needs drive behaviors that mystify adults and are unexplainable by teens. "Why did you do that?" is answered honestly by "I don't know!"

- *Expressed Needs:* These subsurface felt needs rise to full awareness and find expression with peers and parents. These aren't simply the "I wants" of a consumer society, but also the awareness of why the object is wanted— what it means to have the desired object.

- *Comparative Needs:* These needs are discovered by comparison. More often than not, comparative wants ("I want what he's got!") are mistaken for comparative needs ("Why am I not like others?"). Comparative needs focus less on objects and more on characteristics and are often the source of teens' low self-esteem and depression.[13]

• *Normative Needs:* These are knowledge and behaviors not necessarily desired by teens but required in order to fit into the social and global contexts. While the other kinds of needs come from within, normative needs are imposed from the outside. Much of what passes for curriculum throughout one's schooling is normative rather than desired. Confirmation instruction is a normative need.

Could there be more included among the First Article gifts received by teens? I'm sure there would be if we think more deeply of the life circumstances of the teens in our youth ministries, but this discussion is sufficient for us to understand the enormous range of helpful information that is available to us through sacred and secular sources for our youth ministries. We can better understand the youth and their friends as we serve them, and we can serve with full comprehension that no aspect of youth ministry is atheological.

# Gifts from Above

In the receptive spirituality of Lutheran theology, what constitutes gifts from above? Three areas immediately come to mind. The work of the Holy Spirit through the Means of Grace, the work of the Holy

---

13 Once the adolescent achieves "interpersonal perspective taking," self-consciousness creates hyper self-criticism. Appearance, intelligence, and resources ("I'm not pretty enough, I'm not smart enough, I don't have enough money, and people don't like me") become the criterion for self-evaluation and determining self-worth.

Spirit through the creation and preservation of the Church, and the work of the Holy Spirit in forwarding the Gospel into the world through the Office of the Holy Ministry. In the gifts from above, we see the Spirit at work as the Spirit "calls, gathers, enlightens, and sanctifies the whole Christian church on earth" (SC Third Article).

## Third Article Gifts

Unlike the First Article gifts from below that are received in varying degrees by every human being, the Third Article gifts from above belong to believers in Jesus Christ alone. You know these gifts very well, because each one involves the work of the Holy Spirit, the same Spirit that was received by you as a gift in your Baptism. When I describe Third Article gifts, I'm reminded that all we have received as brothers and sisters in Christ we have because of God's mercy and grace through Jesus Christ. Every Third Article gift is predicated on the work that Jesus Christ has completed on our behalf through His life, death, and resurrection. Faith in Jesus Christ is a Third Article gift received through the applied Word of God in the water of Baptism (Acts 2:38–39). Faith is a Third Article gift received by hearing the Word as it is preached, taught, and read (Romans 10:14–17). Faith is a Third Article gift strengthened through the forgiveness of sins received in the Sacrament of the Altar, that special meal prepared for believers wherein the true body and blood, in with and under the bread and wine, are distributed for us to eat and drink (Matthew 26:26–28). These are the gifts that bring saving faith in Jesus to us and strengthen and nurture that faith for us. The same is true for teens, who need to be reminded (probably a normative need) of their Baptism and be prepared to receive the Supper through a catechetical curriculum that recognizes and accounts for First Article gifts while it gives all glory to God for the Third Article gifts.

## Christian Community

Third Article gifts are received within the Christian community. The congregation is a gift for teenagers, and I like to think of it as a gift from above. Others may find fault with our congregations for the many ways in which they fall short of fulfilling all they could be. Perturbed parishioners and frustrated church workers may, more often than they wish, begin to disparage the congregation and point out its flaws. In our most honest moments, we know this is true.

Therefore, first, for the sake of the young among us, especially teenagers, we ought to be very, very careful what we say about the Christian community of which we are a part. We may have the strength of conviction and the wisdom as adults to recognize that the Church is made up of sinful human beings and that in this life it can be no other way. The teens do not have the perspective and experience that will maintain them in spite of the congregation's flaws. If you complain about the youth board, the elders, the Ladies Aid, the pastor, or whomever—remember that impressionable minds are hearing your words, and teens react. If there is one thing teens despise, it is institutional hypocrisy. Your verbalized frustrations could easily add to the list of reasons why a teen doesn't like church, doesn't want church, and walks away from Jesus Christ. Second, however, remember that the Church is the Bride of Christ, the new Jerusalem (Revelation 21:2), and we must be very careful how we talk about the Bride of Christ. This is the Bride that Christ loved all the way to the cross, and Jesus Christ did that knowing full well every blemish, pimple, scar, and sore on His Bride. There were many times when I held my tongue because I remembered that if Jesus could love this Church, who was I to mock or belittle it? There is no compliment for the groom by insulting the bride.

Besides all that, the congregation is a gift for the teen through the many ways the congregation nurtures faith received in Baptism and gives the teen opportunities to exercise faith and grow in sanctification. The congregation is the Church in the eyes of the teen. The home congregation defines for the teen what church is all about and what it is supposed to do. This is why the congregation needs to be very much aware of its place in the teen's life. Whereas the gift from below of family nurtures faith in the private life, the gift from above of congregation nurtures faith in the public life by providing nonparental examples of Christian adulthood. Teens learn that their own parents aren't so weird; other adults do the same things!

So the ministry to youth by the congregation is extremely important, yet it is often overlooked and underestimated. The congregation is where the Christian life is observed, absorbed, and absolved by teens. The life is observed as teens see adults living out their Christian commitments. The life is absorbed as teens participate in the worship life of the congregation gathered around Word and Sacrament. The life is absolved as teens are drawn into the ebb and flow of a life lived in Confession and Absolution.

This is what congregations, as gifts from above, provide as an essential component of adolescent spiritual growth. At Trinity or St. Paul's or Zion or Mt. Calvary or Crave, they receive a community dedicated to worship, nurture, fellowship, outreach, and service.

## Servant Skill

The third and final gift from above consists of you, the servant leader who has taken upon yourself the challenging task of guiding, molding and shaping youth. You might be a Masters-Degree-holding pastor, the young associate who naturally must have youth ministry skill because you are younger, or the teacher in the parish school who has youth ministry attached to your portfolio though youth ministry was not in your undergraduate curriculum. Maybe you are the director of Christian education who has had more youth ministry courses and youth ministry experience than all who precede you on this list or the young lay couple who so enjoyed your own youth ministry experiences that you've volunteered to replicate the experience for the youth of your congregation. Or you could be the parent who passionately wants your children to grow up in the faith and since no one else was willing to work with the youth you volunteered, much to the chagrin of your own teens.

Regardless of the category under which you serve youth, God is using you as a gift for the youth you serve. You are a gift *from above* because you demonstrate faith-filled lives of service, and in that service you use God's Word—the Gospel—the power of God for salvation (Romans 1:16). In my diagram, servant skill forms the touch point of the gifts from above because in your role, you are the point of contact where personal ministry touches teens. For pastors and commissioned ministers of religion, this is their responsibility by virtue of the Office of the Public Ministry. Pastors in particular have a pastoral responsibility to train, support, and monitor the work done by the priesthood of all believers.

When I think of being a gift for others, I find myself humbled. But I can't stay immobilized in humility, because there is so much to do—and do well. My servant skill is everything God has made me to be in service to those entrusted to my care. This involves my training, my faith, my public witness in word and deed for Jesus Christ, and my theological wisdom. Theological wisdom is another way of saying "able to rightly divide Law and Gospel," and let me assure you that theological wisdom is necessary for faithful youth ministry.

What, then, is required of you in youth ministry servant skill? We might begin with a heart for teens as a prerequisite. If you find it difficult to love them, then perhaps your servant skill points to a different group of God's people. But what is also required is a desire to improve your ministry skills. Effective and efficient youth ministry includes organizational skills, planning skills, and a repertoire of icebreaker games and activities. Though important, those skills are not the focus of this book.

What I'm more concerned about is our skill at theological wisdom. Can we use the Law without falling into the ditch of moralism? Can we apply the Gospel without falling into the ditch of antinomianism on the other side of the road? Do we even know what these terms mean? By the way, we don't have to know the terms to be able to practice theological wisdom, but it does help in recognizing our strengths and our areas of greatest potential growth!

We began this chapter recognizing a gap in youth ministry. We need a theological framework for noticing Eutychus, one that accounts for both his spiritual and his physical development. By observing how God the Father, Son, and Holy Spirit impact our lives, we have found just such a framework. Eutychus has gifts from below and gifts from above.

By sharpening our awareness of these gifts, we multiply our own ability to take notice. Third Article gifts use First Article gifts for the purpose of Second Article faith. The gifts from above (Third Article: Means of Grace) are received within the context of the gifts from below (First Article: Created Order) as the environment in which maturity in faith in Jesus Christ (Second Article: Faith in Jesus Christ) takes place. The place where gifts from above and gifts from below meet is the ministry moment. It is for that moment that we are preparing.

# Forgiven Youth

The expression of relief on his face is so honest, so genuine, and so real that tears well up in my eyes too. My right hand has just left his head and completes the sign of the cross between us. I have said the words and the words are believed. "As a called and ordained servant of the Word, I announce the grace of God to you, and in the stead and by the command of my Lord Jesus Christ, I forgive you all your sins; in the name of the Father and of the Son and of the Holy Spirit." He looks at me, waiting for me to say more. But I don't. There isn't anything to add to what has already been said. The work of Jesus Christ is complete. We look at each other for a few moments, deeply, both feeling the fullness of God's love, God's presence. He gives a little smile and stands; I motion him toward the door. As he leaves, he turns. "Thank you," he whispers. "Not me," I whisper back, with an upward nod of my head.

A conscience at peace is a wonderful thing to behold. Beholding many such consciences is what draws me into youth ministry, and the serious study of youth ministry, more than anything else. In 1996, my son tried to get me to attend a Lutheran TEC (Teens Encounter Christ). He'd been trying ever since he attended one the year before. Naturally, I supplied one valid excuse after another; at least they seemed valid to me. But then he conspired with one of his religion teachers at his Lutheran high school to provide me with a title and a role at a TEC weekend to be held in June; I was to be the Assistant Spiritual Director. Well, now I didn't have any excuses left, so I went.[1]

Because the TEC experience is meant to be one of many blessed surprises, I was not given an agenda in advance. I was simply told, "Participate; don't anticipate." Participate I do, and what I learn altered my view not only of adolescence, but of the Office of the Public Ministry as well. Without giving away too much, I can tell you this: LCMS TEC weekends teach private Confession and Absolution in memorable, meaningful, and profound ways.

In my first TEC, I learned that teen consciences are no less burdened by the weight of sin and guilt than adult consciences. This prompted me to study adolescence in greater depth and to appreciate the pressures under which teens live today. Lutheran spirituality, as we learned in a previous chapter, begins with the admission of one's limitations, weaknesses, helplessness, and sins. Lutheran spirituality begins with confession. Teens need Lutheran spirituality.

I also learned the spiritual strength of a properly constituted authoritative voice speaking to the heart that's burdened by sin. Dietrich Bonhoeffer, in his exposition of private Confession and Absolution, points out that when one has confessed sin openly before another who is acting as God's ears, the power of sin to torment within one's own mind is drained away.[2] Why? Because what seems unreal but haunting in the mind is now—in fact—real. The sin is spoken, out in the open, heard by another, and can't be taken back again. In the utter shame of that moment, the sin that cannot be forgotten because it is locked deep inside is finally released outside where it is revealed and then forgiven. In Confession, there is no more running, no more hiding. We are exposed, vulnerable, and helpless.[3]

---

1 "Show-Me Lutheran TEC" is the name of the LCMS Teens Encounter Christ program in St. Louis. See http://www.showmetec.org/index.html.

2 Dietrich Bonhoeffer, *Life Together* (New York: Harper & Row, 1954), 112–113.

3 A theological term for this is *Coram Deo*, "before God." It is a frightening thing to be before God without a defender or advocate. We have an advocate in Jesus Christ.

In this condition, the word of a friend is somewhat helpful, but it may be uncertain. The word of a parent or teacher is comforting to a degree, but it may carry the uncomfortable certainty of consequences. Only the word of someone who actually receives authority to put an end to guilt and forgive sin provides relief that the accuser cannot contradict. We know what that word sounds like because we hear it often from Scripture. "Man, your sins are forgiven you," Jesus says to a paralytic (Luke 5:20). "Your sins are forgiven," Jesus says to a woman torn by guilt (Luke 7:48). "Neither do I condemn you," Jesus says to a woman whom others are going to stone (John 8:10). Jesus is the authoritative voice that must be heard. But how will His voice be heard today?

Wouldn't you know it! Jesus provides a way for His voice to be heard; the one true voice speaking through cross and empty tomb against the sin that binds. He gives authority to His disciples, to His Church, to speak on His behalf. "If you forgive the sins of any, they are forgiven them; if you withhold forgiveness from any, it is withheld" (John 20:23).

I did not know the young man whose confession I heard. He told me his name, but I have since forgotten it. This is as it should be, for there is nothing special about me in the memory I share. But there is everything special about Jesus Christ, and there is something special about the Office that speaks on behalf of Jesus Christ to announce forgiveness. This statement doesn't deny that one Christian may absolve another, something that we are all given to do. Rather, the point is that when people are uncertain about their forgiveness and uncertain whether or not their friends' words are trustworthy, there is a God-ordained office that is specifically empowered to absolve the sins of the penitent sinner. Part of the TEC weekend helps to establish the teen's relationship to that Office. For that reason, only pastors serve as confessors at TEC weekends. It isn't just anybody who speaks the Absolution above his head in the candlelit room, it is a pastor. This isn't lost on the boy. He understands.

Now, why is Confession and Absolution so important in youth ministry? As we examine this question, keep in mind two things. First, Confession and Absolution is the doctrine of justification by grace through faith—the doctrine by which the Church stands or falls—put into practice; it is applied forgiveness for the penitent sinner. Second, Confession and Absolution describe the end result of the foremost interpretive tool in Lutheran theology—Law and Gospel. When the Law fulfills its most important function, we are driven to confession. When the Gospel attends to our greatest need, we are absolved.

# The Misplaced Center of Youth Ministry

At the heart of Confession and Absolution is the cross of Jesus Christ. So also at the center of youth ministry is the proclamation of forgiveness in Jesus' name. Yet so often this center gets misplaced and frequently overlooked. Why might this be the case?

A probable answer is found by looking at the congregation and parental goals for confirmation instruction and youth ministry; and here I'm not talking about the well-written and highly commended curriculum goals that we all promote; nor am I talking about the interlocking relationship of the Great Commission and the Great Commandment with the Great Promise. I'm speaking about the hidden curriculum, the underlying motives that are never quite absent and that sometimes rest just below the consciousness.

For a congregation, the underlying motives may include sustaining the institution, maintaining membership, and raising up the Church for tomorrow.[4] For parents, the underlying motives for involvement in the congregation through confirmation and youth group may be clustered around one word: safety. An overwhelming consideration for a loving parent is the safety of his or her child. Some rather unrealistic expectations—again more than likely at a subconscious level—easily come into play. If the pastor does his job correctly and the congregation does its job correctly and the youth director performs as the congregation prescribes, then my child will not ingest controlled and illegal substances, will not become promiscuous, and will always wear a seat belt—especially when another teen is driving! Oh, that we actually could put teens in hermetically sealed bubbles far out of the reach of the devil, the world, and their own sinful flesh. (That last one is the really hard part!)

---

4 This begs the question about teen membership today. Teens are the Church of tomorrow in the sense that, barring the Lord's return, the youth will be the Church when the current crop of older adults is in the Church Triumphant. However, if the phrase "Church of tomorrow" is taken to mean the teens aren't part of the Church today, then there is a problem regarding the understanding of "Church." Teens are the Church of today too.

Mark Yaconelli suspects that adult anxiety about youth is really the driving force behind most youth ministry in North America.

> Look behind most youth ministry programs and you'll
> find pastors and church boards nervous about declining
> memberships, parents afraid their kids lack morals,
> congregations worried the Christian faith has become
> irrelevant to younger generations, and the persistent
> frustration among adults that something ("anything!") needs
> to be done with "those kids!"[5]

He describes serving as a consultant to a congregation that had a youth program called "Youth Power," which wasn't drawing the young people. After studying the program in detail, Yaconelli suggested they change the name to "Nice and Safe." The response of the parents to the suggestion was laughter—they knew that wouldn't work. But one parent caught what Yaconelli was really saying and responded. "You know, I bet the reason our kids don't like coming to church is because they know it's all about us. . . . They know that despite all the outings and activities the program is really about our desire to teach them to stay out of trouble."[6]

Staying out of trouble is not a bad goal. If confirmation and youth group experiences result in safer, more moral (read "sanctified") teen lives, I certainly won't object. But that is not the central focus for youth ministry. Youth ministry is in danger when themes, curriculum, and activities become prevention-oriented. The reason for this is clear if we look at the track record of prevention education through the framework of Law and Gospel.

In the mid-1980s, I became involved in our small town with a drug prevention program called "Chemical People." The national figurehead for the program was Nancy Reagan, and the program was geared toward training and awareness through a community-based outreach. We were supplied with booklets for distribution, one of which still stands out in my memory. Each page had about twenty pictures of different pills, and below each picture were the scientific names, the more common names, the street names, and a listing of the anticipated effects of each. Now the intention, I'm sure, was to teach young people

---

5 Yaconelli, 36.

6 Yaconelli, 64.

what to avoid. Unfortunately, the same booklet functioned just as well as a catalog indexing the very items for which to look! The only thing missing was the price. The presupposition of the program was simple. If young people have sufficient information, they will choose wisely. You see the problem? Information, no matter how accurate or extensive, doesn't guarantee wise choices.

A second approach to prevention looks to self-esteem as the answer. If the young person has enough self-esteem, he or she will choose wisely. Is low self-esteem a problem among young people? Yes, and this has been known for some time. But will high self-esteem engender moral behavior? Unfortunately, it seems that self-esteem is not at all correlated with positive achievement outcomes. What does that mean? It means that I can think very highly of myself even when I am (or because I am?) doing things harmful to my neighbor.[7] From a Lutheran perspective, a fallen human nature is a very poor source of accurate information about oneself or about what one ought to do. And here again is the problem. Thinking well of myself won't lead me to choose wisely; it may just as often lead me to trust my own inadequate judgment.

There are two other approaches often used in prevention; one focuses on social competence and the other on activities. Like the two previously mentioned, each fails to provide an adequate grounding for choosing wisely. Social competence may help, as the less awkward I feel among my peers the less likely I'll be to find myself goaded into some risky behavior in order to prove myself to the group; yet this isn't sufficient to help me in choosing the peers with whom I associate. Likewise, the strategy to keep teens busy enough so they won't have time to get themselves into trouble is highly dubious. In this model, extracurricular activities such as sports or time-consuming activities like part-time jobs will prevent teens from inappropriate behavior. Once again, while the intentions are admirable, the effect is weak. Sports teams get into trouble with hazing practices, and the teen that's busy with a part-time job is also the teen who can afford the drugs.

---

7 Research has found that "favorable self-regard is linked to violence. . . . When large groups of people differ in self-esteem, the group with the higher self-esteem is generally the more violent one." However, the authors also note that high self-esteem is also a characteristic of exceptionally nonaggressive individuals. Roy F. Baumeister, Brad J. Bushman, and W. Keith Campbell, "Self-Esteem, Narcissism, and Aggression: Does Violence Result From Low Self-Esteem or From Threatened Egotism?" *Current Directions in Psychological Science* 9 (February 2000), 26, http://www.sju.edu/academics/centers/ ivrp/pdf/Baumeister.pdf (accessed May 23, 2009).

The issue we are really dealing with is much deeper than how much we know, what we think of ourselves, whether or not we have social skills, and how busy we are. The issue is the same one that Paul struggles with, "I do not understand my own actions. For I do not do what I want, but I do the very thing I hate" (Romans 7:15). Paul continues by describing the sin that is in him, that is part of who he is as a fallen, sinful human being. Recognizing his inability to keep himself pure and his propensity for sin, he cries out, "Wretched man that I am! Who will deliver me from this body of death?" (v. 24). He answers his own question with the only answer possible: "Thanks be to God through Jesus Christ our Lord!" (v. 25).

It is not only unrealistic, but it is impossible for any youth ministry program to insulate and isolate youth from the effects of temptation or the results of their own sinfulness. To read some youth ministry curricula, we might think holiness of thought, word, and deed is within our grasp if only we put forth enough effort. The reality of a fallen human nature and the persistent effects of original sin is that we are not capable of choosing wisely, not all the time. When we do choose the God-pleasing course of action, it is to God's credit, not our own.

The belief that we can, through our behavior, offer God a better reason for granting us forgiveness than He has given us in His undeserved grace, mercy, and love has a name in Lutheran theology. It is called a "Theology of Glory," and we will look at that in greater detail in Chapter 8. In the meantime, let me be very careful to correct any misunderstanding this discussion might give. I'm not saying that Lutheran youth ministry cares nothing for the training of young people in a God-pleasing, moral way of life. Luther does, after all, include the Ten Commandments in the Small Catechism. We will do all we can to promote purity of mind, body, and spirit for youth, but we won't be caught off-guard or surprised when our teens mess up. Nor will we hold youth to a higher standard than we do the adult world around us, which offers daily examples of adults messing up in ways teens haven't thought of.

If not prevention or perfection, then what are we trying to do? We are trying with the Word of God to build a foundation on the rock of Jesus Christ so that when the storms of sin and stupidity strike, teens aren't blown away. Can they trust that whatever it is they have done—and some teens do truly emotionally and physically devastating things—they have an advocate with the Father in Jesus Christ (1 John 2:1)? Do they, when gut-wrenching awareness of guilt flattens them, believe in the forgiveness of sins for Jesus' sake? The teen that is pregnant or the teen that just wrecked dad's new car or the teen that didn't pick up on the friend's suicidal tendencies in time may believe that their guilt—whether genuine or not—is unforgivable. Our calling is to assure them that there is only one unforgivable sin the Bible mentions, and their failing isn't it. Our desire is that teens believe, as the Apostles Creed says, "in the forgiveness of sins."

What this provides teens is a growing realization, through the working of the Holy Spirit through the Word, of their true condition before God as saints and sinners, *simul justus et peccator*. Of course, this is a lifelong process in which all the adults in the congregation, including the professional church workers, are engaged in as well. Along with the recognition of being justified by grace through faith and standing in holiness before God, while at the same time struggling against temptations and falling and failing far too often, comes an understanding of Law and Gospel, not as abstract concepts memorized in confirmation class but as daily encounters with guilt and grace wrapped up in events, emotions, and relationships.

This isn't easy—it honestly takes a lifetime of maturing in Christ; and frankly, that's too short a time. Nevertheless, what grows out of this in our Christian lives is what I like to call "practical theological wisdom," the gift of understanding and applying Law and Gospel in our lives. Therefore, in a chapter entitled "Forgiven Youth," it's a good idea for us to explore the interaction of Law and Gospel in the teen years.

## How Do Teens Experience the Law?

Teens experience God's Law just like adults, only more so. Why do I say that? I say that because as any parent of a teen has come to learn, most everything with teenagers is more so—the highs are more high, the lows more low. The intensity of adolescence excludes moderation. To understand this phenomenon, we can either read up on the research (the study of First Article gifts) or run through our own memories. Let's do a little of both.

First, the memory: I can recall the events of the first dance, the first date, the first kiss. I can remember sitting in high school chemistry class devising a system by which I could write out her initials without lifting my pen from the paper—all in one clean stroke. How I ever managed to balance any chemical equations with a notebook covered with initials I don't recall, but I do remember the lump in my throat for three days when it seemed like she was going to be moving half a continent away and the utter relief when that didn't happen.[8] Living in the BCP era (before cell phones) meant that the scraps of phone time I got were precious, and a missed call was devastating. Everything seemed sharper, more serious, more severe, and more difficult in adolescence. Perhaps it is nothing more than the effect of having life happen for the first time in so many different ways that precipitates strong emotion and strong emotional swings. But it truly is more than that.

Now, for the research: It is a combination of internals and externals. Internally, the physical changes in the body and mind are of such a nature that mastering control takes time, energy, and practice. If the growth spurt creates physical awkwardness that we can easily observe, shouldn't we also consider the possibility that the growing cognitive abilities—self-awareness and interpersonal perspective taking creates an awkwardness of the mind that is more difficult to identify but nevertheless just as real?

Erik Erikson describes adolescence as the time in which change is most pronounced.[9] It is as if all the psychosocial stages of life up until that point are repeated. All the preceding "crises" that were previously resolved from infancy on (Trust vs. Mistrust; Autonomy vs. Shame & Doubt; Initiative vs. Guilt; Industry vs. Inferiority) are reworked during the Identity vs. Role Confusion years of adolescence. Why this might happen is obvious. The change in cognitive development, how teens think, is so great that the resolutions previously obtained no longer count; they were gained by means of thought processes no longer appropriate or workable. And so adolescents must devise answers for a whole series of significant questions one more time. Is the world a trustworthy place to be? Who am I? What can I do? How well can I do it? What does it mean to be me?

---

8 Not only did she not move away, but she has been my wife for thirty-five years! That was some first kiss.

9 Yount, 51–52.

Rehearsing these personal memories and reviewing psychosocial theory are important for this reason. They remind us of the difficulty teens may have in accurately comprehending the Law, and the personal wreckage and ruin of guilt and loss that often ensues for teens when they do understand God's Law. In its theological function of accusation, the Law attacks from two different angles, as a hammer and as a magnifying glass.[10]

## The Law as Hammer

A hammer is a great tool when wielded by a skillful carpenter. I'm not a skillful carpenter, so my thumb throbs when I accidentally hit it with a hammer. Likewise, my conscience hurts when I hit it by thinking lustful thoughts, by speaking cruel or untrue words, and by doing sinful deeds. Teen consciences work just the same way, perhaps not as sharply or accurately as the adult world might want; but the hammer strikes the teen conscience, too, sometimes very, very hard. The experience of one's own failings is guilt, and guilt means that one is accountable, answerable to somebody. In this case, that somebody is God.

Guilt operates on the heart and mind in ways both helpful and harmful. If guilt drives a person to confession, resolution, and restitution, then we might say it's a good thing. But when guilt has no outlet, no answer, it builds over time and destroys a teen's sense of value and self-worth. What hope is there when I'm dysfunctional, responsible for my mistakes, and God's out to get me? Or even worse, I begin to believe that I can't trust myself. If we listen closely to lyrics of popular music, we can pick up traces of self-rejection, giving up on oneself that comes from unrelieved guilt.

The Law as hammer tells teens as well as adults that they are hopeless—hopeless, that is, unless they know where to turn, unless they have been taught to confess their sins, unless they have learned the words of Psalm 51 as their own words.

---

10 Herman G. Stuempfle Jr., *Preaching Law and Gospel* (Ramsey, NJ: Sigler Press, 1990). Stuempfle uses the image of a hammer and a mirror for this distinction. Mirror is an illustration used in a different way in LCMS catechisms, so to avoid confusion, I've altered the illustration to that of a magnifying glass.

Have mercy on me, O God, according to Your steadfast love;
according to Your abundant mercy blot out my transgressions.
Wash me thoroughly from my iniquity, and cleanse me from
my sin! For I know my transgressions, and my sin is ever
before me. Against You, You only, have I sinned and done
what is evil in Your sight, so that You may be justified in Your
words and blameless in Your judgment. Behold, I was brought
forth in iniquity, and in sin did my mother conceive me.
(Psalm 51:1–5)

If this is the only way that the Law works on teens, it would be
enough. But we know from our own adult experiences that there
is more. Not only do we experience judgment as something that's
personal, but we also experience judgment as something that's
corporate. Not only am I a personal affront to the Almighty because
of my sin, but so is the world in which I live.

## The Law as Magnifying Glass

Grade school science class is never as interesting as the day we
learn the law of optics whereby a beam of light focused through a
magnifying glass heats up a piece of paper until it starts to smolder,
smoke, and then ignite. Wow! This is useful information, especially for
boys in class who discover what the same beam of focused light can do
to ants on the sidewalk.

"Ants on the sidewalk" aptly describes the feeling teens have
when the Law is working in their lives as a magnifying glass. If the
Law as hammer means that "I'm out to get myself," then the Law
as magnifying glass means that "the world's out to get me" too.
Unfairness, inequality, and injustice are the beams that focus in on
adolescent life experience. Parents, teachers, neighbors, the community,
all conspire to make life difficult. Disappointments mount. Successes
only bring pressure to do better. And then there is the world situation,
with wars and rumors of wars, earthquakes, and auto accidents, all
piling up to make the planet a very unsafe place to be. Whereas the
Law as hammer hits the conscience, the Law as magnifying glass heats
up the consciousness, and what is experienced is anxiety and fear.

Now, realize that this is just as true for adults as it is for teens. There
is a ready temptation available to every adult to let the imagination

multiply the dangers; and fears readily become debilitating. And it's not like this is all made up! There are genuine dangers and fears out there. Perhaps the difference for teens is that they now become aware of all the things there are to worry about, and worry about at an adult level, for the first time. "There, there, it will be all right" may have comforted the distressed child. It does nothing for the stressed-out teen. Unlike the hammer of the Law that accuses teens of being dysfunctional and hopeless, the magnifying glass informs them that the world is dysfunctional and they are helpless.

Sweating under the magnifying glass, teens—just like adults—develop magnificently contrived avoidance behaviors. We become fanatical sports fans devoting hours to listening and analyzing our leagues or we build an alternative universe for ourselves on the Internet or we become masterful gurus of video gaming or a hundred other things. Please note that I'm not condemning the various hobbies and interests we might have. I'm only pointing out that we, also, can use these as places to hide, as do teens, from the threatening realities that surround us. But there is really only one way to check the thermometer and lower the temperature under the magnifying glass, and once again we have an example from David.

> Be gracious to me, O God, for man tramples on me; all day long an attacker oppresses me; my enemies trample on me all day long, for many attack me proudly. When I am afraid, I put my trust in You. In God, whose word I praise, in God I trust; I shall not be afraid. What can flesh do to me? All day long they injure my cause; all their thoughts are against me for evil. They stir up strife, they lurk; they watch my steps, as they have waited for my life. For their crime will they escape? In wrath cast down the peoples, O God! (Psalm 56:1–7)

David chooses not to hide, but instead brings his complaint to God and in so doing trusts that God will vindicate him.

The Law affects the human heart from the inside (hammer) and from the outside (magnifying glass). Adolescence carries with it elements that can either intensify or muffle either one or both. The importance of relationships, particularly peer relationships; the self-consciousness that comes from believing the whole world is watching; the need to separate from parents while still being close to parents; the range of ages during which puberty can begin; and all the unmet expressed needs that begin to swell during adolescence create the context of our youth ministry. Where the Law is at work, sooner or later bad news is coming. Where do we find the Good News?

## How Do Teens Experience the Gospel?

Remember Moralistic Therapeutic Deism? Smith and Denton discover this default theological orientation among youth in America today in their *Soul Searching* research. It's a belief that God exists, wants us to be nice, and is there to help us out when in trouble while we live to be happy and feel good about ourselves; and good people go to heaven when they die.[11] Lutherans immediately note that a major flaw in Moralistic Therapeutic Deism is the lack of understanding of God's demands on us through the Law. After all, it doesn't take much effort on our part to be nice. It takes an enormous effort, an impossible effort, to be perfect and holy. The second thing we identify is that the Gospel is nowhere to be found in Moralistic Therapeutic Deism. That is, unless the gospel we are looking for is the good news that God really doesn't care that much to get involved in our lives except when there's trouble, and by the way, we are all pretty much nice enough to get ourselves into heaven anyway; thank you very much.

How can such weak concepts of Law and Gospel be so pervasive? Well, of course it is the natural reaction of fallen human nature to cover itself with fig leaves, and MTD is an attempt to do just that (Genesis 3:7). Nevertheless, there are statements, common aphorisms really, that when uncritically accepted reinforce a weak Gospel (read *non-gospel*). Let me share a few examples. Have you ever heard "The Lord helps those that help themselves" quoted as a verse from the Bible, probably from the Book of Hezekiah!? It actually is found in Benjamin Franklin's *Poor Richard's Almanac*, but he found it in one of Aesop's fables.[12] A minimal knowledge of Law and Gospel will alert us immediately that this statement can't come from the Bible. The one place where helping ourselves can't help at all is in our relationship with God. "For while we were still weak, at the right time Christ died for the ungodly" (Romans 5:6).

---

11 Smith and Denton, 162–163.

12 WELS Topical Q & A, http://www.wels.net/cgi-bin/site.pl?1518&cuTopic_topicID=47&cuItem_itemID=1958 1 / (accessed May 28, 2009).

An even more damaging, but often used, phrase by Christians is the statement "God hates the sin, but loves the sinner." How could this statement be a problem in understanding Law and Gospel? Doesn't it clearly show God's anger over transgression and doesn't it forthrightly proclaim the love of God for the lost? If we find ourselves defending the statement in this way, we need to look it again and realize that we are hearing the statement from within the context of faith; and within that context—in a believing community—the statement is really no problem at all because we are subconsciously filling in the blanks.

The blanks? Yes, there are blanks in the statement, and without those blanks filled in, what we have is not just a weak statement of Law and Gospel, but we have a deceptive statement that has the capacity to deceive the unbeliever into false security and misbelief. This misbelief is the very kind of understanding that supports Moralistic Therapeutic Deism and promotes a punchless Law and a useless Gospel.

When we say "God hates sin," we as believers automatically fill in the theological result of God's hatred for sin. David writes about God in Psalm 5, "You hate all evildoers. You destroy those who speak lies" (5b–6a). Jesus warns those who wonder if the victims of the Siloam tower collapse were worse sinners than others by saying, "No . . . but unless you repent, you will all likewise perish" (Luke 13:5). Jesus explains that perishing involves being "thrown into the outer darkness. In that place there will be weeping and gnashing of teeth" (Matthew 8:12). You see, in our minds we fill in the blank. This sentence with the blank filled in reads, "God hates sin and condemns the sinner to hell." That is the Law in all of its severity. The natural consequence of God's hatred of sin is eternal damnation.

When we say "But God loves the sinner" we, as believers, automatically fill in the action that results from God's love for the sinner. We know what Jesus says to Nicodemus in John 3, "For God so loved the world, that He gave His only Son, that whoever believes in Him should not perish but have eternal life. For God did not send His Son into the world to condemn the world, but in order that the world might be saved through Him" (John 3:16–17). We include within God's love the reality of the cross. So when we hear "God loves the sinner" we automatically fill in the blank with "But God loves the sinner and sent His only begotten Son to die on the cross and rise again on the third day for the sinner so that the sinner might by believing in Him be saved." Now, granted, that's a long fill-in-the-blank; but that's what we are really doing and that is what we really mean.

So, used within the context of a believing community that subconsciously fills in the blanks when the phrase is used, we have an efficient form of shorthand. But when used outside the believing community, the statement takes on a falsehood all its own. Try this for yourself; what is communicated to you by "God hates sin, but loves the sinner" if you consciously and forcefully remove the filled-in blanks that you are so accustomed to? And remember, the unbeliever does not have the information necessary to fill in the blanks on his or her own. Do you see what we communicate? The unbelieving world hears us say "God's upset about sin, but don't worry about it; He loves you anyway."

God loves you anyway? "Well, if He loves me anyway, what are you Christians so upset about? I can go about doing whatever I would like, because God just overlooks it—because He loves me!" The discounted Law results in no Gospel. The cross of Jesus Christ is excluded. There is no place to insert the cross of Christ or the empty tomb because there is no reason for it. God just overlooks sin through His overly compliant and permissive love. At least, this is what the culture around us hears us saying by "God hates sin, but loves the sinner."

Do you see how careful we need to be in how we speak the Law and the Gospel? We might think we are offering an attractive invitation to the adolescent who has been hammered by the Law and baked under its magnification, but what we have really done is made ourselves irrelevant. Nevertheless, there is a way we can use the statement, but we have to change the subject of the sentence. Rather than saying "God hates sin, but loves the sinner," we can say as Christians "We hate sin, but love the sinner." When we have made ourselves the subject of the sentence, there are no blanks to fill in. We don't condemn, and we don't save. We do reject sin, and we do want to bring the same message to others that has saved each of us. This we are empowered to do through the work of the Holy Spirit through the Means of Grace. Loving the sinner is part of our Christian vocation, a topic we will look at in greater detail in another chapter.

But is the contrast between the Law and the Gospel really that sharp? Can we put the two clauses of the statement together when the blanks are filled in? On the one side, God hates and damns; on the other, God loves, sacrifices His Son, raises Him from the dead, and forgives? Yes, the contrast is really that sharp. And no, as human beings we can't reconcile holiness and justice as pure as God's with self-giving love and sacrifice as complete as God's. The resolution of this paradox is within God. What we confess by faith is that both justice and love intersect at the cross.[13]

## The Gospel of Christus Vicar

Let's say that the teens with whom we, as Third Article gifts, are working are grasping the Law according to their capacities by virtue of their First Article gifts. We think they are getting it; there is the experience of genuine (as opposed to neurotic?) guilt and the sense that the created order is messed up and busily trying to mess them up too. But of course, the Law brings no comfort or hope. Where is the Good News and how is the Good News experienced by teens?

The Good News for teens under the falling hammer is that the hammer doesn't hit us; it hits Jesus instead. He takes our place under the judgment, the condemnation, and the damnation of the Law. This is what the cross is all about. The technical term used for centuries in the Church for the hammer blow missing the guilty and striking the innocent Jesus Christ is *Christus Vicar*. The word *Vicar* means substitute. Jesus Christ is our substitute. This is possible under the hammer of the Law because He is truly human. His is real Man in every sense but one—He lacks sin (2 Corinthians 5:21; 1 Peter 2:22).

How does the teen experience the Gospel? The Gospel is the unexpected acquittal when conviction is dead certain. The Gospel is the great escape from earned and certain punishment when no escape is possible. The Gospel is the great act of self-sacrificing love that willingly gives up all for the loved one. Teens are the loved one, just as you are the loved one and I am the loved one. If doubt surfaces that any of us are worthy of such love, as it really ought to, the prophet Isaiah responds with a testament to God's unfathomable love.

---

13 Here are some more resources on Law and Gospel. C. F. W. Walther, *God's No and God's Yes: The Proper Distinction between Law and Gospel*, condensed by Walter C. Pieper (St. Louis: Concordia, 1973); C. F. W. Walther, *The Proper Distinction between Law and Gospel*, trans. W. H. T. Dau (St. Louis: Concordia); Robert J. Koester, *Law and Gospel: The Foundation of Lutheran Ministry* (Milwaukee: Northwestern Publishing House, 1993).

He was despised and rejected by men; a man of sorrows, and acquainted with grief; and as one from whom men hide their faces He was despised, and we esteemed Him not. Surely He has borne our griefs and carried our sorrows; yet we esteemed Him stricken, smitten by God, and afflicted. But He was wounded for our transgressions; He was crushed for our iniquities; upon Him was the chastisement that brought us peace, and with His stripes we are healed. All we like sheep have gone astray; we have turned—every one—to his own way; and the Lord has laid on Him the iniquity of us all. He was oppressed, and He was afflicted, yet He opened not His mouth; like a lamb that is led to the slaughter, and like a sheep that before its shearers is silent, so He opened not His mouth. (Isaiah 53:3–7)

Don't underestimate the ability of a crucifix to bring meaning to the internal confusions of adolescent life. Holy Week can be especially meaningful for teens. Challenge teens during Holy Week to meditate on Jesus on the cross, and then ask what emotions they feel. What happens to their spirituality; how close do they feel themselves to be to the One who took their place? Let them discuss what they experience in their contemplation, and see if Good Friday isn't a Better Friday, or even the Best Friday as the Good News of *Christus Vicar* soaks in.

## The Gospel of Christus Victor

A different scenario presents itself when the teens are under the magnifying glass. It isn't necessarily Good News to see Jesus hanging from the cross when feeling that sin, death, and the devils of this world have the upper hand. In that over-heated frame of mind, the crucifix may be less than comforting as the sufferer imagines the Lord suffering the agonies of shameful death. Rather than comfort, despair may set in. "What hope do I have? Look what they did to Jesus!"

No, this is the time to look at the empty cross and the empty tomb. *Christus Victor* is the power of the Gospel when it is circumstance and consciousness, rather than guilt and conscience, that alienate from God and distance us from our Father. If *Christus Victor* focuses our attention on the cross of Good Friday, then *Christus Victor* focuses our attention on the empty tomb of Easter morning. "But in fact Christ has been raised from the dead, the firstfruits of those who have fallen asleep"

(1 Corinthians 15:20). Jesus Christ wins the victory. Each and every one of the enemies that seeks to destroy us is conquered, and the most terrifying of all, death, is done to death. The captives are released. The dead are raised, and teens have Good News preached to them.

Do teens hear this Good News? Do they see it in us? The victory over sin, death, and the devil won by Jesus Christ removes fear and in its place brings peace. "I have said these things to you, that in Me you may have peace. In the world you will have tribulation. But take heart; I have overcome the world" (John 16:33). "Thanks be to God, who gives us the victory through our Lord Jesus Christ" (1 Corinthians 15:57). Jesus has overcome the world, and through Jesus we have received victory over the enemies.

The challenge for us in youth ministry is to model the victory that is ours by living lives in the victory of the resurrection. You see, the teens that we serve need to see that victory in the adults around them, in us, in order for them to grasp the victory's reality. Every adult in youth ministry needs the victory and has the victory, just as the believing youth do under our care. This requires spiritual maturity on our part, and we will look at that maturity in a later chapter. But here let's be clear that we understand the victory doesn't mean we have no trials and tribulations in this world. We do—but they don't separate us from God (Romans 8:19–31), and we live through them sustained by God through the Means of Grace. This is what we model for our youth.

## Clarity and Charity

Practical theological wisdom—the ability to correctly divide Law and Gospel in the Word of God and apply it to life—is not gained quickly. Such wisdom takes a lifetime of experience to acquire. Nevertheless, the Holy Spirit is working through the Word, bringing us further in our understanding and our application of Law and Gospel in our own lives and in our service to others. Two aspects of our growth need special recognition: clarity and charity—that we are clear in what we communicate and that we communicate our message with love.

Clarity means that we don't give mixed messages to teens about what is sinful behavior and what is not. By doing this, we of course put ourselves in opposition to the direction North American culture has taken on a whole bushel full of issues: human sexuality, the definition of marriage, the beginning and the ending of human life. Culture loves the mixed messages because in the ensuing confusion, the individual is free to do what he or she wants and make up the rules as the game goes on. Then the big question each needs to answer is nothing more than "What do I think about sex before marriage? What behaviors do I believe constitute sex? Do I think abortion is taking a human life or not? Should I really bother to care if two people of the same sex marry each other? If I am deathly ill with no hope of recovering, won't I want someone to put me out of my misery?" You see, the real ethical issue behind each mixed message given is that the individual is both competent and empowered to give an answer, to declare what is right or wrong.

Avoiding mixed messages to teens (and to ourselves for that matter) starts with the admission that we do not set the standards. We have neither the authority nor the competency to do so. God establishes the boundaries; He sets the parameters; and He does so through the avenue of the conscience (which may err) and the Word (which never errs). Therefore, what we say about sin will not come as a surprise to our youth. If they have been growing up in the congregation, the positions that we take governed by Scripture is what they will expect to hear. If they have not grown up on a steady diet of Sunday School, worship, and then confirmation, the clear and honest presentation of the Christian life will be met with appreciation. Finally, somebody in the adult world cares enough to tell the truth. Consistency in the message is the handrail on the steps leading teens into the adult world.

But the message consistent with Scripture is governed by charity, because the manner in which teens hear the message will make a huge difference for them. The very last thing most teens today want to be is judgmental. In the perception of many, to confront another over misbehavior (sin) is worse than the misbehavior itself, because to do so it to be judgmental. So here is the challenge that we have: we want to communicate clearly God's Law, but God's Law—when communicated clearly—accuses, condemns, and kills. Charity, in this context, means that our communication of God's Law is not done from a position of self-righteous superiority, as if somehow we enjoy pointing our finger at others because we are, after all, such excellent examples of moral rectitude, but is done out of genuine concern and love for the sinner.

It is that love for the sinner demonstrated by Jesus time after time that becomes the connotation behind our denotation of God's Holy Law.

Sometimes subtle approaches can teach with great effect. A case in point is the recent film *Juno*, in which Juno, a teenager who is pregnant, considers getting an abortion. She is not at all thinking about her pregnancy as another human being until she visits the abortion clinic. In the parking lot is a classmate with a pro-life sign chanting pro-life slogans. This has minimal effect on Juno. What does have an effect is when her classmate tells her that "it" has fingernails. Juno draws the conclusion that if "it" has fingernails, then it must not be a blob to be removed. "It" must be something more. From that point, Juno's strategy changes, and she decides, showing remarkable maturity, that adoption will be her course of action.

The point I'm drawing from the film is really a point made by Smith and Denton's fifth conclusion in their "unscientific postscript" from the book *Soul Searching*. They suggest that:

> Religious communities might themselves think more carefully and help youth think more carefully about the distinctions among (1) serious, articulate, confident personal and congregational faith, versus (2) respectful, civil discourse in the pluralistic public sphere, versus (3) obnoxious, offensive faith talk that merely turns people off.[14]

Smith and Denton don't want to be critical of strong statements of belief, but they do realize that often strong statements of belief are made in ways that cut off communication and actually work against the intended goal of sharing Jesus Christ with the people who need Him.

## The Power of Absolution

It is the person, teen or adult, understanding what it means to be forgiven, who knows what it is that he or she is offering when sharing the Law and the Gospel. I find it very awkward to be self-righteously superior with someone else when I have been the penitent whose sins have been heard and absolved by another. Confession and Absolution

---

14 Smith and Denton, 268.

is training in Christian humility and a basic introduction into practical theological wisdom.

Why does Confession and Absolution do this, especially for teens? It does so because it places us under the shadow of the cross of Jesus Christ. In a culture that wants to cut Jesus out of the Good News, that wants to make the Good News the promise of wealth, health, or living the best life you can live right now, Confession and Absolution corrects our twisted worldview and turns us to God's mercy. In adolescence, when everything is made up of extremes and so much isn't the way we want it to be and we feel so bad about ourselves, the real Good News is a Savior who takes our place and wins for us the one real victory we need.

Forgiven youth live in a world of promises—promises fulfilled every day. What can you tell them about these promises? You can tell them this: Your parents might not understand you, but God knows your heart. Your friends might abandon you, but Jesus is always there. You don't like yourself and the pressure under which you live, but you have the Holy Spirit dwelling in you with holiness and purity that will one day shine like the stars.

The law that applies directly to Eutychus in Acts 20 is the Law of Gravity, and like the Law of God, it is merciless. The Gospel for Eutychus is the pure grace of life restored, and like the Gospel of God, it restores life where there was only death. The more we think about forgiveness through Jesus Christ, the more we understand and communicate what the family of Eutychus felt when, according to the words written by the boy's attending physician, "They took the youth away alive, and were not a little comforted" (Acts 20:12). That's an understatement! All forgiveness is.

# CHAPTER 7

# Healthy Youth

The kitchen door slams behind me as I run in from outside, leaving a trail of sand wherever my bare feet touch the linoleum floor. "Mooommm!" I am shouting. My younger brother and I are in the middle of an argument that has not yet come to blows, but soon will if there is no adult intervention. Our morning of peacefully playing together in the sandbox under the lilac bush near the garage has abruptly ended, and he's right behind me, spreading more sand and not a little mud, ready to provide his defense of whatever it is that's got me incensed. "Mom, Larry's wrecked my road and he stomped on the house I was building," I whine, trying to exaggerate just enough but not too much. "Did not!" is all Larry can muster, but he's starting to giggle, and his pleasure at my displeasure proves his guilt beyond all doubt, at least to me. "Yeah, you did. You always do."

"Stop it!" Mom says firmly, cutting off Larry's second attempt at a lame excuse. "Just look at the two of you. You are filthy!" We stop and look at ourselves. Mom's right. Boy is she ever right. We are dirty the way only little kids can get when they've been civil engineers all morning with water and sand in a sand box. We have those splotches of pale cleanliness dotting our otherwise dirty legs and arms. We have particles of sand in our hair, in our ears, in our eyebrows. "And I don't suppose you cleaned out the sand box before you started playing, did you?" Oops, we keep forgetting that we share the sandbox with several farm cats. Who has time to sift sand, anyway?

"You have to quit anyway; it's time for lunch," Mom informs us. Her words trigger a switch hidden inside our abdomens. We are suddenly famished, weak with hunger. Our irreconcilable conflict fades from consciousness as our looming starvation takes hold. "You are such a mess. Here, let me get you cleaned up." Off to the laundry room sink we are marched, where the scrubbing begins in earnest. Once we get cleaned up, we proceed to the table where our appetites have been waiting for us. The feast begins as each fork finds first the macaroni and cheese and then our mouths. Life is good.

This is a chapter on the Means of Grace, which in Lutheran theology consist of the Word of God (Scripture) and the Sacraments (Baptism and the Lord's Supper). The theological question we deal with in this chapter is twofold. First, how do the Means of Grace function in the lives of believers? Second, how is the truth of the Means of Grace communicated to teens?

A good place to start in order to grasp the significance of the Means of Grace for both youth and adults is childhood. We are, after all, children of God. "The Spirit Himself bears witness with our spirit that we are children of God" (Romans 8:16). We are His sons and daughters through faith in Jesus Christ. What do children need in order to be healthy and grow as Christians? As children grow and mature through their teen years, they will need clear definitions to aid their understanding of their faith and their own participation in the practice of that faith. But early on, before definitions will make much sense, children need someone to tell them "yes" and "no," someone to wash them when they get dirty, and someone to feed them with a healthy diet. Likewise, years later when we look back with comprehension, we confess that the Holy Spirit, working through the Means of Grace, has been guiding, washing, and feeding us all along. Even though we consider ourselves more mature in the faith, we don't liberate ourselves from the guiding, washing, and feeding of the Holy Spirit as if we can handle these vital functions quite well by ourselves now that we are adults. Absolutely not! As adults, we discover our need for the Means of Grace is just as great as when we were infants. Mixed messages are more confusing, the dirt we get into much deeper, and our spiritual hunger pains much sharper. In this way, we, as Lutheran Christians, confess the absolute necessity of the God's Word, God's cleansing, and God's banquet in our lives.

# Children Guided, Washed, and Fed

Children need guidance. They need to be washed. And they need to be fed. The Bible time and time again calls all of us, regardless of our age, children. John addresses us as children because we can be naïve and easily deceived (1 John 3:7). He also calls us children because we are dearly loved by the Father (v. 1). Peter describes us as "obedient children" who no longer live in ignorance, but in holiness (1 Peter 1:14). The author of Hebrews reminds us that because we are children, we can expect to be disciplined—that is, if we are legitimate children of God (Hebrews 12:8). Paul is less prone to use the word "children" in this theologically real but nevertheless metaphorical sense. But when he does it is with profound effect. He tells us that we are not "children of the slave but of the free woman" (Galatians 4:31) to emphasize we are under grace, not law. To the Romans, he reveals[1] that the Holy Spirit is the one who testifies that we are not only children of God, but heirs (Romans 8:17), and therefore eligible to inherit everything that belongs to Jesus Christ. As adults trying to think of ourselves as children, we often think of the sentimental positives rather than the practical negatives—like being argumentative, dirty, and hungry.

The significance for believers in being addressed as children always pivots back to the words of Jesus, who said, "Truly, I say to you, unless you turn and become like children, you will never enter the kingdom of heaven" (Matthew 18:3). In what way are we to be like children? Are we to be like children in their innocence? No, don't go there. That "childhood innocence" is a falsehood we were freed from a long time ago. Lutheran Christians believe in original sin, and we believe we have sufficient empirical evidence on our side to prove it.[2]

---

1 Of course, it isn't Paul who is revealing this, but the Holy Spirit who is revealing this about Himself through the apostle Paul—just want to be clear about who is doing what here.

2 For Scriptural support see Psalm 51:5; John 3:6; Romans 5:12; Ephesians 2:3.

Then how are we childlike? We are childlike in our dependence. Our sin trashes our relationships. We need God's Word to prompt our repentance. In our sin, we are filthy, tarnished with stains that none of us can remove and much of which we are completely unaware.[3] We need the Holy Spirit working through water connected to the Word to wash us clean, to bury us with Christ and raise us to new life, to strip the rags of unrighteousness from our souls and to clothe us in white robes. Having been cleaned up, we discover how hungry we really are, hungry for purity and holiness, hungry for genuineness and authenticity, hungry for truth, and hungry for God. We need to be fed, and because we have been washed in the blood of the Lamb, we are invited to the only table that will fill our spiritually empty bellies and quench our spiritually crackling thirst. At every stumbling step we take along this path as spiritual infants, toddlers, teens, and adults, we are reminded that behind every action is the cross, and inside everything we receive is the forgiveness of the Father.

## The Guiding Word

"Stop it!" Mom exclaimed "Just look at you. You are filthy!" Before anything else can constructively take place, the Word of God in its Law function shocks us into realizing what our condition is. "You are filthy," the Law says. We stop our complaining, look at ourselves, and discover we are clothed in shame. Guilt is written all over us. Consider for a moment the common confession of sins, "I, a poor, miserable sinner." (*LSB*, p. 213) Now, truth be told, frequently when I speak these words, or similar words of confession printed in the bulletin on a Sunday morning, I don't feel poor and I don't feel miserable. Sometimes I feel pretty comfortable and pleasantly complacent with myself. The words of the Confession cut through the false reality with which I've surrounded myself and open my eyes to the true reality—before Almighty God I have once again failed to be holy, just as God is holy (Leviticus 19:2). My complacent feelings don't make any difference and certainly are no defense. No, I've managed *not* to love my neighbor as myself and I've conspired *not* to love God above all else. The guiding Word of God never lets me off the hook by saying, "Well, at least you tried. Your heart is in the right place." No, the guiding Word of God

---

3 Sometimes we discover we are sharing the sand box with critters larger than cats.

tells me my heart is in the wrong place, even if my own feelings can't figure that out.

The guiding Word does its work when I realize that I'm filthy, but it doesn't stop there. Like the mother who, evaluating the messes that are her children, says "Let's get you over to the sink and clean you up!" the guiding Word of God cleans us up. And like the children who can't get themselves clean, the word of Absolution—claiming the saving blood of Jesus Christ—cleanses us of shame, guilt, and sin (1 John 1:8–9).

Now, the previous paragraphs seem to be doing nothing more than repeating the major themes of the previous chapter—the work of the Law in accusing us and the work of the Gospel in saving us. And, to a certain extent, this observation is correct. However, we are now looking at the work of Law and Gospel from a slightly different angle. We are raising questions about the purpose of God's Word in our lives and sensitizing ourselves to the operation of God's saving grace through the Word of God as a means of our receiving that grace. You see, in Lutheran theology, the Word of God—Scripture—isn't merely a source of information; in Lutheran theology, the Scripture is a source of power: and not a power that we wield in the name of God, but a power that wields us. The Holy Spirit works through the Word, not only to give us information about Jesus, but to give us Jesus as well. The Holy Spirit works through the Word, not only to describe the forgiveness of sins, but also to forgive us our sins.

Do you see the significance of this? It means that when the Word of God is preached, taught, read, memorized, contemplated, and recalled, we are in the presence of the Holy Spirit working in our lives. You see, Lutheran Christians just can't pick up a Bible like it is any other book; it isn't any other book. This is a book that has the power to do things to us.

Many young adults today remember seeing the movie *The Never Ending Story* as children, and many children continue to see this movie today, though it was released in 1984. In the film, a boy, Bastian, is being bullied, and to avoid the bullies he runs into Koreander's used bookstore. There he encounters an old man, Koreander, reading a book. In the dialogue that follows, Bastian tells Koreander about all the books he's read, *Robinson Crusoe, Lord of the Rings, 20,000 Leagues Under the Sea*. "Your books are safe," Koreander tells Bastian. "When you are done, you get to be a boy again." "And that one isn't?" Bastian asks, now incredibly curious about Koreander's book. "That's what I mean. The ones you read are safe," and then he tells Bastian, "This book is not for you." The phone rings and Koreander is distracted. Bastian grabs the book, leaves a note saying he'll return it, and runs off to read the dangerous book. And dangerous it is! By the end of the film, Bastian discovers that he is part of the story in the book; in fact, he must make a decision upon which the entire story hangs!

I've used this clip a number of times in classes when illustrating what Lutherans means when they say that the Bible is "efficacious." The Bible is a dangerous book. The Bible is not "safe." It has the power to change a person's perspective, worldview, and life—both now and for eternity. The Bible, because it is a Means of Grace through which the Holy Spirit works, gives not only information, but also what the information promises: saving faith in Jesus Christ. We cannot read the Bible as we would any other book because, viewed in this way, we know the Bible to be a living document unlike anything else. Like Koreander's book, the Bible places us within the story, God's story.

Believing this about the Bible has, as you might guess, significant influence for us in youth ministry. We use every appropriate opportunity to incorporate Bible study into our ministry events. Our own manner toward the Scripture models respect and a sense of awe, going even so far as to take care how we store and shelve God's Word in the youth room. We do not use the Bible in a careless manner, and by that I mean being ill-prepared or not prepared when we are leading or teaching from the Scripture. Treating the Scriptures with respect also means that our preparation includes prayer and study. We won't take Bible passages out of context or try to make the Bible say what we want it to say and ignore the meaning the Bible intends from a given passage.

Finally, we are open to discussion and we encourage youth to share insights they discover as they read the Bible. These conversations increase teens' familiarity with the Bible and enhance their sense of competence in reading the Bible. While affirming the validity of teens' readings of a Bible passage, alongside their readings we are ready to share how the passage has been understood and is understood by the Church through history.[4] We do this because we realize the ease with

---

4 *The Lutheran Study Bible* is an excellent resource containing devotional and study notes,

which God's Word is distorted, manipulated, and falsified in the world today. The Bible itself warns how easily this can happen (2 Peter 3:16). Our goal is not diversity of interpretation but unity of belief, brought about by the Holy Spirit working through the Word.

This principle applies not only to individual Bible passages, but also to key doctrines. For example, something as important as the definition of the Good News, the Gospel, can get lost or subverted though it is contained within some very positive sounding statements; and if we are not careful, we may not even notice. Take for example an article I once read from a mission organization's newsletter. The title of the article was "Just what is the Gospel?" This is a great question, and one about which we desire to be crystal clear.

What is the Gospel? What "good news" is brought to humankind through God's Word? Oddly enough, though this newsletter came from a Christian organization that emphasizes mission, the good news as defined by their article consists of our capacity to actualize our human potential. According to this organization, the good news is the message that Jesus Christ clears the way for us to maximize doing what is good and hasten the presence of the kingdom of God on earth. Read this carefully. I do not question the sincerity of the authors or their intention to do good. Nor do I doubt that doing good is to be the lifestyle of the believer in Jesus Christ. The number of Bible passages that encourage us in this regard is simply overwhelming. But the good news of the Gospel is not the unleashing of our human potential. The Good News is the life, death, and resurrection of Jesus Christ through which we have received the forgiveness of our sins and life everlasting. The Good News is what God has done for us, not what we do for God or for our neighbor. This doesn't mean, of course, that what we do for God or our neighbor is unimportant. It is very important because it is our vocation as Christians, as faithful followers of Jesus Christ. It just isn't the Good News of the Gospel.

## The Cleansing Water

At a transdenominational conference on children's spirituality, I listened to a Baptist theology professor from a western seminary describe the history of Baptism from the Early Church to the present.

as well as brief explanatory essays.

I was impressed with his overview, not least of which because he told the story fairly, dispassionately, and in much the same way I have in seminary courses on confirmation. His goal was to describe how different denominations engage children in faith formation based on their doctrines of Baptism and conversion. He concluded that there are three basic approaches, all dealing with how one becomes an "insider."

Some denominations (Catholic, Lutheran, Anglican, and Orthodox) approach the spiritual growth of children believing that they are, by virtue of their Baptism, already insiders. Children are therefore instructed in the faith into which they were baptized. Other denominations (Reformed, Presbyterians) assume that children are insiders; nevertheless children are instructed in the faith so they can confirm that faith, apparently allowing for some uncertainty as to whether the children are inside or outside. Finally, there are other denominations (Baptist, many Evangelicals) who view the spiritual growth of children as an invitation to become an insider. They are instructed in the faith with the goal that they might embrace it and become believers and then in obedience be baptized.[5]

I share this because it illustrates how doctrine really does drive practice for a subject as significant and controversial as Baptism. But I'm also sharing this because of something the professor said in his presentation about Lutherans. He said, "When Lutherans talk about Baptism, they often emphasize remembering one's Baptism." He must talk with Lutherans with some frequency because, though he denies the power of Baptism as a Means of Grace, he's absolutely right that Lutherans encourage believers to remember their Baptisms. Why do we do this often enough to be noticed by a Baptist theologian?

Why do we emphasize remembering our Baptism? We emphasize remembering our Baptism because that's when we became insiders. We instruct children in the faith into which they have been baptized—assuming that they have been baptized, which is not always the case for youth in our youth groups—because we believe that at Baptism, God actually does something, something wonderful. Lutheran Christians remember their Baptism because their Baptism has application day after day throughout our lives. Luther put it this way:

---

5 Kevin Lawson, "Baptismal Practice and Spiritual Nurture" (lecture, Concordia University, Chicago, Children's Spirituality Conference, June 15, 2009).

*What does such baptizing with water signify?* Answer: It signifies that the old Adam in us should, by daily contrition and repentance, be drowned and die with all sins and evil lusts. And also it shows that a new man should daily come forth and arise, who shall live before God in righteousness and purity forever. (SC Baptism, Fourth)

Remembering our Baptism brings two past acts into the present experience of our lives The first act is of Jesus' death and resurrection; and the second act is of water and the Word bringing about the death of our old Adam and the rising to new life of ourselves as pure, washed, and holy people. It's not that we as Lutheran Christians are remembering because we don't want to forget some important past event, like our anniversary, because otherwise we would miss all the sentimental value the event might have. It's that we as Lutheran Christians remember our Baptism because it is the promise made and the promise being kept every day of our lives that gives us new life!

Go back to my memory of two dirty children in the kitchen. Having given us the guiding word to march to the laundry room sink, Mom met us there armed with soap and washcloth. "I don't know how you ever get yourselves so dirty," she said. "You'll never get yourselves clean. How did you get dirt all the way up there?" Up and down each arm and leg to the tan line, short cropped hair washed and brushed, faces pressed against the washcloth—in short order, we were scrubbed clean.

Baptism scrubs us clean. I particularly appreciate the passages of the Bible that talk about Baptism as getting cleaned up. Take Titus 3:5–6 for example. "He [God] saved us, not because of works done by us in righteousness, but according to His own mercy, by the washing of regeneration and renewal of the Holy Spirit, whom He poured out on us richly through Jesus Christ our Savior." Or Hebrews 10:22, "Let us draw near with a true heart in full assurance of faith, with our hearts sprinkled clean from an evil conscience and our bodies washed with pure water." Three water words are used in those verses: poured, sprinkled, and washed. Before our Baptism, we were dirty, and it wasn't just a sand box we were playing in. After our Baptism, we are clean.

When we remember our Baptism, we are remembering that the Holy Spirit actually did something to us through the water comprehended with God's Word in our Baptism. We recall the promise that comes with Baptism—the same promise Peter uses to invite the Pentecost audience ten days after the Ascension of Jesus.

> Repent and be baptized every one of you in the name of Jesus Christ for the forgiveness of your sins, and you will receive the gift of the Holy Spirit. For the promise is for you and for your children and for all who are far off, everyone whom the Lord our God calls to Himself. (Acts 2:38–39)

We could not wash ourselves, because we could not get to where the dirt was piled in our lives. Only the Holy Spirit, working through the Word, could get us clean.

Now, there are other ways in which the Bible communicates the blessings of Baptism. Another wonderful image is that of being buried with Christ into His death through Baptism and then being raised up to new life with the promise of Jesus Christ's own resurrection (Colossians 2:12). Another meaningful description comes from Paul's letter to the Galatians (3:27), where Baptism is like taking off the soiled garments of sin and putting on the pure robe of Christ's perfect life.

Our understanding of God's action in our lives through Baptism can be enlightened through any one of these helpful images, but I suggest that in youth ministry the cleansing concept may be most helpful for this reason. Few teens if any have had an experience that comes close to being buried and then raised. All teens have had an experience of being dirty and needing to be clean, and perhaps they can recall a time when they were so dirty—perhaps even on the inside—that they knew very well they could not get themselves clean no matter how often they changed clothes or how hard they scrubbed themselves.

Now, I still haven't quite answered the question why a Baptist theologian would connect the two words—*Baptism* and *remember*—with Lutherans. Nor have I made the all-important leap to what this means for youth ministry. Believe it or not, the way to a clear answer to both these concerns comes by way of an Episcopalian.

I'll first give you the answers and then explain how we get there. Lutherans emphasize baptismal remembrance because Baptism removes all doubt from the believer about his or her salvation. Moreover, since adolescence is a time of life filled with doubt about all kinds of things, not the least of which is the presence of God and God's love in one's life, a clear understanding of Baptism provides a rock the teen can stand on. Or, to use a more ancient analogy, an unsinkable ship that can cross the stormy seas.

I regret that I did not have this clear understanding of Baptism when I was a teen. In college, as I was preparing for a life of ministry, a classmate of mine seemed to have a fixation on Baptism. He didn't talk about his Baptism all the time, but every time it was his turn to pray in dorm devotions or when we were on a retreat doing a "popcorn" prayer or an open prayer time was taking place in chapel, all he need do was open his mouth and the rest of us knew what would follow. "Dear God, help us to remember our Baptism. Help us to have joy in the gifts we received in our Baptism." It was automatic—always something about Baptism. At the time, we thought it was funny.

I wish I knew then what he knew then—rather than learning it years later. I need to remember my Baptism daily and hold on to it for dear life through the storms of this world, because that all-too-simple act done by Pastor Wahl on May 25, 1952, washed me and cleansed me and forgave me and made me a child of the Creator of the universe whose very Spirit dwells in me. Do you think knowing this could have an effect on my outlook toward life? Could knowing this have an effect for a struggling teen? Could something like this be what brought Eutychus to Paul's midnight preaching festival?

About the Episcopalian: his name is Phillip Cary, he teaches at Eastern University (a Baptist school!), and he has written a very helpful article for the journal of Concordia Theological Seminary, Fort Wayne.[6] I'm sharing the argument he presents because it illustrates in a profound way the manner in which our theology affects our daily lives and the lives of those we serve.

Cary argues that Protestants, generally speaking those following the reformer Calvin, will answer a very important question differently than the followers of Luther. And the question is this: How do I know that I am saved?

The Protestant will reason in the following manner. I know from the Bible that whoever believes in Christ is saved. I believe in Christ. Therefore, I am saved. This gives every appearance of an airtight

---

6 Phillip Cary, "*Sola Fide*: Luther and Calvin," *Concordia Theological Quarterly* 71 (2007): 265–281.

argument. In fact, it wouldn't surprise me if many of us, myself included, would look at that syllogism as a fairly accurate description of our understanding of justification by grace through faith—the keystone doctrine of Lutheranism.

And yet, there is a problem. If this syllogism is to provide me with certainty about my salvation, then I must know beyond a shadow of a doubt that I truly believe, and that I believe truly. So the syllogism requires an additional question. Do I really believe? Do I really have faith? In order to answer that question, I must gather supporting evidence. Do I worship regularly? Do I pray fervently? Do I read the Bible frequently? Does my life give evidence through my acts of charity, through kindness in my relationships, through diligence in my vocation that I really believe? So I gather together all the necessary information and all the while I am encouraged more and more by my church to do more and more. Nevertheless, I am still plagued by the doubt in the back of my mind—am I doing enough? How can I know? How can I be sure? Cary gives this view the name "Reflective Faith" because it reflects back on the self as the source for certainty—a commodity the self is incapable of providing.

The Lutheran, the discussion goes, reasons in a different manner, though just as committed as the Protestant to the doctrine of justification by grace through faith. The Lutheran reasons this way. How do I know that I am saved? Well, Jesus Christ has given the command to baptize "in the name of the Father, and of the Son, and of the Holy Spirit." Jesus Christ never lies but always tells the truth. Therefore, whoever has been baptized receives the gifts promised in Baptism. Like the syllogism above, this line of reasoning also has a necessary follow-up question that I must ask, but it is a much simpler question. The question is, "Have I been baptized?" If I can answer yes to that question, then I can be sure that I have all the gifts given in Baptism—not because of my capacity to receive those gifts, but because of God's promise—and it is impossible for God not to keep His promise—to grant these gifts in Baptism. This view Cary gives the name "Confident Faith" because it derives certainty of salvation from the promises of God.

Remember the question with which this comparison began, "How do I know that I am saved?" Do you see the difference between the Reflective Faith and the Confident Faith? With the former, I must provide the evidence that will let me have assurance of my salvation.

With the latter, I only need trust the action of God in providing me with promises He is already fulfilling. With the former, I remain in the shadow of doubt; with the later I'm standing on an unbreakable rock.[7]

Youth need an unbreakable rock to stand on. Baptism, within Lutheran theology, is just such a rock and is why Lutherans emphasize God's promises in Baptism. Rather than focusing on whether or not I'm living up to expectations (and how will I ever know that?), Lutherans attend to what God has already done and continues to do for us daily. Luther describes the confidence given Christians through their Baptism:

> We must think this way about Baptism and make it profitable for ourselves. So when our sins and conscience oppress us we strengthen ourselves and take comfort and say, " Nevertheless, I am baptized! And if I am baptized, it is promised to me that I shall be saved and have eternal life, both in soul and body. "
> (LC IV 44)

Youth, remember your Baptism! Why? Remember your Baptism because God keeps His promises; because no matter how dark the days get, how many friends betray you, how little communication, affection, or love there is with your parents, how deep into sex and drugs and online pornography you have gotten, or how often you have found yourself feeding pigs in a foreign land (Luke 15), you have a heavenly Father who is ready and waiting to run down Main Street and throw His arms around you. And how do you have this unreal yet super-real faith? You have it because God made a promise to you with some water and some words, and God will keep His promise. You were filthy and dirty. But you were washed by the blood of Jesus Christ. That blood has been scrubbed into every pore of your being. You are clean.

Can we communicate this love to youth? There are obstacles, surely. But none of the barriers is impossible to cross, not for the Holy Spirit. After all, crossing barriers is what Means of Grace are all

---

7 If you are following this argument closely, you probably are asking if this means that once a person is saved through the gifts given in Baptism, that person is always saved no matter what. To answer this concern we need to remember who is asking the question in Cary's illustration—a believer. In fact, only a believer would ever ask the question, "How do I know that I'm saved?" A person who does not believe though once having been baptized isn't concerned about the gifts that have been thrown away or lost. Such a person does not have saving faith and is in need of the Good News of Jesus.

about—crossing the boundary between creation and Creator, human and divine, lost and found, dirty and clean. And now that we have been made clean, washed thoroughly, what's the next stop? Why, the table of course. It's time to eat.

## The Satisfying Meal

My brother and I have made it to the kitchen table. Before us there are plates and cups, forks and knives, but no food. We are ready to eat, and we want to eat NOW! "Just wait a minute," Mom says, as she pours the cheese out of the packet onto the macaroni and begins to stir. "It will be ready in just a minute." She's right again, and in just a minute the delicious lunch is spooned on our plates, and we dig in.[8]

We know something about feeding the body. A nutritional diet is one that comprises all the major dietary necessities—carbohydrates, proteins, fats, fiber, and so forth—found in grains, fruits, vegetables, dairy products, meat, and nuts. Knowing something about our dietary necessities doesn't guarantee a good diet, however. Most of us are susceptible to junk food and only those who really monitor their intake maintain a balanced diet. Though we might wish it were so, we know that chocolate and corn chips aren't really major food groups, though pizza and ice cream just might qualify.

What do we know about feeding the soul? We know more than we think, primarily through our practice as words are spoken and elements distributed. In worship service after worship service, we hear the words "This is My body. . . . This is My blood." We are reminded that these elements have been given and shed for us for our forgiveness. If nothing else, the repetition of this sacred-looking, ritual-like behavior inculcates within us a sense of humility before God by giving us something we must really need but cannot supply for ourselves.

Not only are we humbled, but we come face-to-face with our own dependence on God. Our souls get hungry and our spirits faint; and have you noticed? Nothing we consume from this world's larder satisfies. Each new possession, every new relationship, all our best laid plans break, grow stale, and unravel. God must feed us and not we ourselves. When He does, we leave His altar spiritually satiated, which means we have a peace that passes our own understanding.

---

8 It wasn't until several years later that we began the practice of regular table prayers.

Not only are we humbled and made dependent at the Table of our Lord, but we also submit to His Word. Confronted with the mystery of Christ's words at the Last Supper, Lutheran Christians do not use their reason in order to dissect the elements but instead use their reason to discern the love of Christ that would give us such a gift. What is it about my spiritual condition that prompts Jesus Christ to give me His body and blood? Could it be that this spiritual food is the God-given diet that strengthens faltering faith, nurtures growing faith, and sustains mature faith?

Not only are we humbled, made dependent, and find ourselves submitting to the words of Christ, we are also filled with hope—the kind that doesn't disappoint (Romans 5:5). This hope is—to fall into using theological jargon—eschatological. The word comes from the Greek ἔσχατος, which means "last." The Sacrament points us to what is coming, to the culmination of all things, to the end-of-time banquet when eternity begins. Truly, this bit of bread and sip of wine comprising the body and blood of our Lord is a foretaste of the feast to come.

For years, a picture was hanging in our dining room. It is a view of a table set for a magnificent banquet. The scene is set in such a way that you have the perception of standing at the head of this very long banquet table. In fact, the table recedes into the distance so far that you can't see the end—as if it goes on for eternity. There are candelabra spaced every so often into the distance, with a full set of dinnerware at each place setting, with beautiful stemware ready to be filled, and multiple spoons, forks, and knives in all the right places.

I appreciate this picture for a number of reasons, not the least of which is that for years it provided me with a pattern to follow whenever I was setting the dining room table for a formal dinner—a perfect template for the plate and its silverware. But the real reason I value it is that when I look at it long enough, I can't help but recall the words of the prayer from the Communion liturgy that goes, "With angels and archangels and all the company of heaven, we laud and magnify Your glorious name, evermore praising You and saying . . ." (*LSB*, p. 208). Doesn't it seem to you that the Lord's Table is the place where the membrane between time and eternity, heaven and earth, the humble now and the glorious then, is most permeable? The time when I could sit at a table with the woman who made such great macaroni and cheese for Larry and me ended half a decade ago. But all the company of heaven is there at the Altar of our Lord, and together we are being fed.

The Sacrament of the Altar/Last Supper/Holy Communion/Lord's Supper/Eucharist gives us the last thing we might have expected from Jesus: His true body and blood in with and under the bread and wine. Nevertheless, we receive the first thing Jesus wants us to have as maturing Christians in a fallen world: Himself. If the washing of Baptism makes us clean, then surely the meal we receive makes us strong.

# God Connecting to Teens

Do the Means of Grace empowered by the Holy Spirit address the needs of teens differently than for adults? From the perspective of youth ministry, this is not an insignificant question, though the answer may seem at first obvious. Looking at these gifts as Third Article gifts, we affirm that the grace of God given by these means is the same for Jew and Greek, slave or free, male or female, teenager or geriatric, to paraphrase Paul. Water and Word are the same; body and blood/bread and wine are the same; sure Word is the same; as is the forgiveness of sins and life everlasting.

Nevertheless, each teen is, according to her or his First Article gifts, different and is addressing life issues from an early phase of life's trajectory without the benefit of life experiences available to parents, grandparents, and youth leaders. For this reason I believe that God, in His abounding mercy, *communicates* through the Means of Grace in ways especially meaningful for teens. Let me suggest four ways in which this happens.

## EPIC Teens

Much is made in youth ministry literature about the postmodern nature of adolescents today. If indeed teens are (E) Experiential, (P) Participatory, (I) Image-Driven, and (C) Connected, as Leonard Sweet has described,[9] consider how well the Means of Grace fits the need. Knowing the gifts being received in the Lord's Supper, what could be

---

9 Leonard Sweet, *Postmodern Pilgrims: First Century Passion for the 21st Century World* (Nashville: Broadman & Holman Publishers, 2000).

more experiential than kneeling before an altar with family and friends and receiving the bland taste of the wafer followed by the sharp tang of the wine? Group Bible study that makes use of God's Word by drawing each youth into the discussion is nothing if it is not participatory. God in His wisdom has not chosen complicated rituals to give us His gifts, but simple actions that fix a repeatable image in the mind. Baptism is simple water with the Word; but every time another infant or adult is baptized, the image of our own participation is recalled—if not through our own memory (because we were too small), then through the gathered memory of the Christian community worshiping together and reciting the Creed. All of this makes us connected at a level deeper than digital technology. We lose nothing in ministry to youth if they are EPIC; in fact, we are probably making gains.

## Tuned-in Teens

Remember the research being done on adolescent spirituality mentioned earlier? Teens around the world were asked what kinds of activities make it easier or harder "to find meaning, peace and joy." The researchers wanted to know what teens thought made spiritual development easier or harder. The top five things that made it easier in order of influence in the study were (a) spending time outside or in nature; (b) listening to or playing music; (c) spending time helping other people in the community; (d) being alone in a quiet place; and (e) the influence of parents.[10] As I look at this list, I realize that there is a very wide bandwidth of spiritual information and spiritual contact in the life of the teen. I'm not surprised that teens look for spiritual insight from multiple sources. (There are eight I didn't even mention from the research). Teens are searching for God. Where is God to be found? God is to be found where He has promised to be; and where has He promised to be? He has promised to be in Word and Sacrament. All the other sources of spiritual information can be helpful and give a spiritual feeling, but only through the Means of Grace is there spiritual truth. In youth ministry, we do not ignore the awe that overcomes us when we are in nature or the spiritual feelings that might arise while listening to inspiring music, but we never stop there. Instead, we direct our attention and the attention of youth to where God has promised

---

10 Eugene C. Roehlkepartain et al., *With Their Own Voices* (Minneapolis: Search Institute, 2008), 31.

to be for us. The broad bandwidth of spirituality may help a teen start looking for God, but it is in the narrow bandwidth of the Means of Grace where God is certain to be found.

## Tracking Teens

If teens have been tracking along in their catechetical instruction, they may have no difficulty in comprehending why the Lord's Supper is handled with such care, and why it is important to practice close Communion. On the other hand, they may find themselves struggling to understand why some should not participate. Isn't that being unfriendly and inhospitable? The pertinent passages from 1 Corinthians 11 guide us in our explanations—pointing out the importance of self-examination and recognizing the true presence of Christ, which the uninstructed and those too young are unable to do. We emphasize repentance as part of preparation for the Lord's Supper so that no one comes to the Table unrepentant and then leaves thinking all is well between himself or herself and God when in fact the gift of the Supper has been turned into judgment against the one receiving through their lack of repentance. We don't want to scare anyone away, but we do want the Supper to be treated with proper respect.[11] I like to use the analogy of the Sacrament as strong spiritual medicine, and like any powerful medication, it is to be received by those for whom it has been prescribed. I take medication for high blood pressure that does me a lot of good. Because it helps me, should you take it? It isn't hard to get the point.

## Child/Adult Teen

Finally, the Means of Grace have the unique capacity to address the teen in the middle of their transition from child to adult. For

---

11 I recall a situation in which the parent of a child I had instructed and confirmed called me several years later out of concern for his son, who had stopped communing though he was still attending church. As I inquired about the circumstances, I learned that there was a conflict brewing at the congregation, and his son's rationale for abstaining was Matthew 5:23–24, "So if you are offering your gift at the altar and there remember that your brother has something against you, leave your gift there before the altar and go. First be reconciled with your brother, and then come and offer your gift." I was impressed with the son's understanding of Scripture and the seriousness with which he regarded the Lord's Supper, and I shared that with the father, assuring him that there would be a time when the son would return, but that the boy shouldn't go against his conscience. He had really been listening in confirmation class!

children who have grown up in the Church, Baptism reminds them they have been children of God since they were infants. At the same time, early teens being catechized in preparation for first Communion are anticipating entrance into the spiritual world of adult believers, and there is excitement in that. Likewise the youth group members, though they may not realize it, are taking steps toward a more mature faith as they regularly come to the Lord's Altar and receive the gifts prepared for them.

## Healthy Youth

The following experience happened to me at a transdenominational gathering of youth leaders being held in a convention center. As each of us entered the meeting room and struggled to adjust to the dim light and the configuration of chairs, we were handed a plastic resealable bag. In the bag were three small plastic squeeze containers, the kind one gets at the fast food drive-up window, containing ketchup, mustard, and mayonnaise. Also in the plastic bag were a small paper salt container and another one with pepper. I stumbled into a seat toward the rear of the hall, primarily because the band is often louder than my aging ears can tolerate.

After announcements and some praise songs, a presenter began a devotional time. He asked us to open our bags and taste each of the flavors in the bag. I found this more difficult than it sounds because I didn't want to get ketchup or mustard all over myself. With care, I opened each one and tasted them. The leader told us to think about each flavor and then choose our favorite. It didn't take me long to choose mayonnaise as my preferred food experience. Our leader asked us to contemplate how God is like our favorite flavor. I struggled a bit with my assignment. God and mayonnaise—let's see, how could I compare them? Thankfully, my imagination hasn't atrophied with age, and I begin to think about how mayonnaise adds so much culinary delight to an otherwise drab sandwich and how knowing God's presence in all our life activities provides profound meaning to an otherwise mundane existence. Not a bad comparison—as lame as it might sound, I thought it could do. Our leader then shared a verse from the Psalms, "Oh, taste and see that the LORD is good! Blessed is the man who takes refuge in Him!" (Psalm 34:8), and followed it up with some interesting words that encouraged us to think on the goodness of God whenever we apply condiments to our diet.

After the devotion and while the main speaker was onstage, I found myself contemplating the devotion on several different levels. Given my conservative nature, I began to wonder if I had inadvertently participated in some kind of illicit condiment "fellowship" across denominational lines. But I put that idea away as another incidence of my overactive conscience. As an educator, I analyzed the devotion and admired how the author brought together the experience of taste and the feeling of the different textures—the grainy-ness of salt and mushy-ness of mustard—and connected it with a Bible passage, providing a clear and effective example of experiential learning. On a different level, however, I became concerned. Maybe the devotion in which I just participated *had* functioned like a sacrament, though it surely isn't one. Perhaps it functioned like as a *pseudo-sacrament*, and here is why. The activity brought me just so far along the sharing of the Gospel, but it didn't close the loop. It took me through a comparison, but never got me to the reality. It helped me in the search for God, but didn't tell me where God can be found.

I need to be very careful in making this constructive criticism, because some may interpret what I'm writing as a condemnation of experiential learning strategies, and nothing could be further from my intention. What I am cautioning us about is that when we use experiential learning strategies, as Lutheran youth leaders, we will want to close the loop—that is to say, get from the comparison to the reality and move us from the "Where is God?" to "Where God is."

How might that have been done in my example? I'm not sure it could have been done in such a mixed group. But for a Lutheran group of young people, the move is pretty obvious. We go from Psalm 34:8 to 1 Peter 2:2–3, "Like newborn infants, long for the pure spiritual milk, that by it you may grow up into salvation—if indeed you have tasted that the Lord is good." From 1 Peter it is a short step to Psalm 116:13, "I will lift up the cup of salvation and call on the name of the LORD." Now we recall the comparisons we have made between our condiments and God, explaining why one rather than another is our favorite flavor, but then as the discussion is drawn to a close bringing the attention of the youth to the chalice and the paten and the taste and flavor that is beyond anything we can compare. Yes, we do taste and see that the Lord is good. We do it at His invitation, at

His Table, to receive His forgiveness, where He has promised to meet us with His blessing.

I can think of several other learning experiences that I've done over the years that could have been pseudo-sacraments because they didn't close the loop. One time, we all wrote one of our sins on a slip of paper, slipped the slips in helium balloons, and sent them up into the air; one time, we wrote sins on rocks and threw them into the lake, reciting Psalm 103:12 "As far as the east is from the west, so far does He remove our transgressions from us;" and then I didn't close the loop. I didn't take the group from their Confession of sin to the Word of God—the Words of Absolution, where God has promised to be for each of us for Jesus' sake.

I understand and appreciate very much the emotional connection and the spiritual encounter that takes place with a well-conceived experiential learning activity. But I want that connection to be made with the reality, not the comparison. Otherwise I run the risk of offering a pseudo-sacrament, which then becomes like junk food when what is needed is a strong healthy diet. The Means of Grace is just such a healthy diet.

A guiding word, cleansing water, and a healthy meal: this kept me physically healthy as a child. Should it be surprising that the Holy Spirit keeps teens spiritually healthy through these same means? I wonder, could this have been what drew Eutychus to the third floor lecture hall? Was it there, listening to Paul, that his spiritual hunger was filled?

# CHAPTER 8

# Christian Youth

A re you going to grow up to be a pastor like your dad?" the friendly member of the congregation I'm serving asks my son, who is five years old at the time. "NO!" is the emphatic response of my offspring. He provides no explanation, just a categorical denial of the possibility that some day he should occupy the Office of the Public Ministry. He has no interest in it, feels no calling toward it, and even at an early age fends off the pressure to follow in his father's footsteps. The friendly congregation member, somewhat taken aback by the forceful reply, prudently changes the subject. The child, in the meantime, grows up and becomes an attorney. Did he already know something at age 5?

What does Eutychus want to be when he grows up? Not knowing his age precisely from the account in Acts 20, we aren't exactly sure how close Eutychus is to being grown up in the culture of his day. Though only a teen, he may very well already have a clear course laid out ahead of him. If his father is a tradesman, he may be completing what we might call an apprenticeship. He may feel drawn toward the sea to be a sailor or merchant. No doubt the Legions are looking for recruits, and if he's physically capable, the military might be a possibility. Educational opportunities are rather hit or miss in those days, so we don't know if he is in a position to consider a profession—medicine, law, or politics; and his social position could make those options either probable or impossible. We do know, however, that for Eutychus, decisions of this nature are unavoidable. He will need to find something to do, and given the divine, miraculous intervention in his life, it wouldn't surprise me if Eutychus finds himself very much drawn to the gathered group that is called Christian. Perhaps he might even become an evangelist, like the man who prayed over his lifeless body as it lay in the street.

## Growing Up Christian

God-fearing parents and faith-nurturing congregations pray that when their children grow up, in whatever vocation they find themselves, they are also found to be Christians. We want them to grow up to be Christian adults who manifest their faith in simple and profound, common and extraordinary ways—thereby giving testimony to Christ in them (Colossians 1:27).

But will they want the name "Christian"? We all know from our grade school experiences that "sticks and stones may break my bones, but names will never hurt me." But we said that in self-defense because names *did* hurt. Names mean something. Unfortunately, the name "Christian" doesn't always mean what we think it means.

Our desire is that our offspring grow up to be Christian and that they exercise their faith in the Christian community of their Lutheran church. But we are discovering that in North American culture today, not only is the word "church" a turnoff to those outside the Church, but the name "Christian" is a turnoff as well. This change in perception has happened over the last several decades and has been largely unnoticed by those of us deeply embedded in what sociologists call "the Christian subculture."

Those outside the Christian Church, along with many in their twenties and thirties who are inside the Church, do not have a positive perception of Christianity. So when earlier I raised the question of whether or not the next generation will want the name Christian, the question anticipates several potential outcomes. The first, and most hopeful, is that our youth will claim the name Christian and give thanks to God that they are part of a Lutheran church body that unashamedly confesses Jesus Christ. The second possible outcome is that much of the next generation will believe, but not within the confines of organized congregations. The third potential outcome, and the most tragic, is that much of the next generation will, based on their negative perceptions, reject the faith and seek their spirituality elsewhere.

In this chapter, I will present an overview of the research that substantiates the negative perceptions I've introduced above. In the trinitarian model I shared earlier, this information falls under the rubrics of the First Article. We are observing what is happening within the *fallen* created order, an order that is susceptible to the enticements and deceptions of the evil one, who attacks each successive generation with the same old temptations, although delivered within the changing cultural context of each. Remember that we are not looking at Christianity as it actually is—the pure love of God shed on us through the life, death, and resurrection of Jesus Christ and received by faith, but instead we are examining some of the most effective frauds the father of lies has concocted for our time and place. After reviewing this information, I'll suggest three doctrines from Lutheran theology that are particularly helpful in guiding youth within our church, as well as those outside, through the objections, misperceptions, and caricatures of Christianity that are so readily observable in our culture.

A recent news article provides an example of our culture's new attitude toward Christianity. The headline reads "Christian Drifter May Have Killed Two Couples in Separate Beach Murders, Police Say."[1] Is it just me, or does it strike you as odd the way the accused murderer is identified as a "Christian"? The article identifies the man as "part of a Christian commune that disapproved of relationships between unmarried couples." Why is this headline significant? It is significant because the author feels the key descriptor to help readers understand the crime is the word *Christian*. The perpetrator isn't any ordinary drifter; he is a "Christian" drifter.

---

1 Associated Press, "Christian Drifter May Have Killed Two Couples in Separate Beach Murders, Police Say," *Fox News*, July 24, 2009, http://www.foxnews.com/story/0,2933,5 34765,00.html?test=latestnews (accessed July 25, 2009).

When Jim Jones's suicidal Guyana community made the phrase "Don't drink the Kool-Aid" a part of our language or when the smoke from David Koresh's Waco holocaustic compound was on the evening news, there was recognition on the part of the media that these were fringe groups not to be confused with mainstream Christianity. Their activities were not likely to be replicated at the local Methodist or Presbyterian church down the street. The headline quoted above is evidence that the media now struggles to make that distinction. The author of the headline appears unaware that this behavior, killing couples on beaches, would be frowned upon by average run-of-the-mill Christians. In the reporter's mind, the characteristic of the drifter that stands out is not his prior criminal record, his move to Canada to escape the draft, or that the "Christian" commune to which he belonged kicked him out because of the weapons he carried—all of which is explained later in the article. The key element worth displaying in the headline was that he was "Christian."

There is a subtle change in the use of language within our culture that has a huge impact on perceptions. To be fair, however, how would the reporter know that Christianity is not a threat? The probability is high that the author knows few if any average Christians. Through the lens of a skeptical and ill-informed media, Christians are suspect.

## Perceptions of Christianity

There was a time in the history of the Church when to be called a Christian was to be put under suspicion of terrible crimes. I'm not suggesting that we are anywhere near a return to persecution like that of the Roman Empire. I am suggesting that we are in a culture that knows less and less about the Christian faith with the result that it struggles to distinguish the genuine article from warped and distorted caricatures. Without the capacity to discern, all are lumped together.

Two authors paint nearly identical pictures of Christianity's perceptual problems, though they draw their colors from different palettes. David Kinnaman is a researcher who conducts surveys, while Dan Kimball is a pastor who hangs out in coffee shops a lot. Their observations are worth noting because they describe the social and intellectual climate in which today's adolescents are forming their own worldviews. This is what Kinnaman found.

In our national surveys we found the three most common
perceptions of present-day Christianity are antihomosexual
(an image held by 91 percent of young outsiders), judgmental
(87 percent), and hypocritical (85 percent). These "big three"
are followed by the following negative perceptions, embraced
by a majority of young adults: old fashioned, too involved
in politics, out of touch with reality, insensitive to others,
boring, not accepting of other faiths, and confusing. When
they think of the Christian faith, these are the images that
come to mind. *This is what a new generation really thinks about
Christianity* [italics in original].[2]

Kimball's main theme differs little from Kinnaman's—the new
generation really likes Jesus but is put off by the Church, which it sees
as having abandoned the principles taught by Jesus. Though we find
the perceptions of the new generation to be inaccurate, inadequate,
and ignorant of the Jesus revealed in the Bible, Kimball builds a strong
case that the Church—understood as any organization claiming a
connection to Christianity—has done much of the damage to itself,
and the responsibility belongs to every branch, whether mainline,
conservative, or evangelical. Kimball points out that the outsider makes
no distinction.

Criticisms and misperceptions of the Church should matter
to all of us, even if the criticisms are against a branch or
denomination of the church that we have nothing to do with.
The criticism is still about the church, and we are all part of
the universal Church. When part of us misrepresents Jesus, we
are all misrepresented. If part of us is misunderstood, we all
are misunderstood.[3]

Kimball organizes the perceptions and criticisms of the Church
around six major headings: (a) the Church is an organized religion
with a political agenda, (b) the Church is judgmental and negative,
(c) the Church is dominated by males and oppresses females, (d) the
Church is homophobic, (e) the Church arrogantly claims all other

2 David Kinnaman, *UnChristian: What a New Generation Really Thinks about Christianity
  . . . and Why It Matters* (Grand Rapids: Baker, 2007), 27.

3 Dan Kimball, *They Like Jesus but Not the Church: Insights from Emerging Generations*
  (Grand Rapids: Zondervan, 2007), 68.

religions are wrong, and (f) the Church is full of fundamentalists who take the whole Bible literally.[4]

| Kimball<br>The Church Is | Kinnaman<br>The Church Is |
|---|---|
| Organized religion with political agenda | Too involved in politics |
|  | Out of touch and insensitive |
| Judgmental and negative | Judgmental |
|  | Old-fashioned |
| Dominated by males and oppresses females |  |
|  | Boring and Confusing |
| Homophobic | Anti-homosexual |
| Arrogantly claims all others are wrong | Not accepting of other faiths |
| Full of Bible-thumping fundamentalists |  |
|  | Hypocritical |

We can understand how those outside the Church, watching the media and listening carefully, have come to these conclusions. Is the "Church" politicized? Is the "Church" hypocritical? Is the "Church" judgmental? Is the "Church" homophobic? If all I know of the "Church" are the political maneuverings of a moral majority or the evasive practices that allowed predatory priests to move from parish

---

4 These are the chapter titles for chapters 5–10 of Kimball's book.

to parish or the conversation I have at an airport where the person handing out tracts informs me that my eternal destination is hell[5] or that a certain group of "Christians" attend funerals of soldiers killed in action in order to picket with signs saying the death is punishment from God against the United States for its openness to gays, then the answer to the questions has to be yes. Each one describes the "Church."

*And* if there is little difficulty in identifying sources for misperceptions about the Christian Church, then there is also no problem in comprehending the challenges these misperceptions present for the Church, any church, to reach out with its message. Those outside the culture don't trust the Christian Church and don't believe the Christian Church when it speaks.

*And* if those outside the Church regard the Church with disdain, neither trusting its actions nor respecting its words, then in what position do youth within the Church find themselves as they grow in awareness and interact with the culture through relationships with peers, through messages gleaned from the media, through challenges to faith as they enter higher education, and through interactions with others where they work? Will they want to be identified as one of those "Christians"?

Do you see the double jeopardy for the Church? Kimball describes the problem from the perspective of the outsider. "Based on outside observations of Christians, there's no way I would want to become one of them. I wouldn't want to become an angry, judgmental, right-wing, finger-pointing person."[6] Kinnaman reveals that it's not just an outsider problem. "Christianity's image problem is not merely the perception of young outsiders. Those inside the church see it as well—especially Christians in their twenties and thirties. I was unprepared for the research showing that Mosaic and Buster Christians are skeptical of present-day Christianity."[7]

---

5 This recently happened to me when I was confronted by a fervent Baptist at an airport who informed me that my confession of faith in Jesus Christ as my Savior through the forgiveness of sins won for me at the cross and through the empty tomb was insufficient because my Baptism as an infant was invalid. Not only was I on the way to hell, I was leading others there too. Shame on me!

6 Kimball, 32–33.

7 Kinnaman, 18.

Kimball tells of a youth pastor who was asked by a non-Christian teen at a youth meeting, "You Christians really hate homosexuals, don't you?" Kimball observes,

> That's the first impression this seventh-grader had of the church. He didn't say, "You Christians really know how to love other people," or, "You Christians really take seriously caring for the widows and the poor," or, "You Christians really have strong marriages." Nope. Once again the impression is about something we stand against, rather than what we stand for. And if the impression people get is that we are negative, complaining, judgmental people, no wonder people don't want to become Christians.[8]

What may seem odd, and at the same time hopeful, is that while the caricature of the Church held by many outside the Church is negative, both authors say the perception people have about Jesus is not. Jesus remains an attractive figure known for His kindness, His thoughtful teachings, His forgiving attitude, His social ministry, and the mystery around the meaning of the cross.

## Our Image of the Church

Are we negative, judgmental, complaining people? After attending our men's Bible study group one Sunday morning during his high school years, the same child who didn't want to become a pastor like his father declined to attend any more of our sessions. "All you guys do is complain" was his justification. Reflecting on his experience, I realized he was right. We had spent an inordinate amount of our Bible study time grousing about the decline of morals, the disintegration of entertainment, the rise of atheism, the flatline of church attendance, and the quality of our donuts. "Things aren't that bad," my son said, with the optimism that youth often provides.

Well, are all the charges these two authors lay at the feet of the Church true? "No," I responded, assuming a solidly defensive posture. "Absolutely not; it's the fault of the cults, the media, and sinners outside the Church who deny their sin and want to remain in their sin." And of course, to some extent my defense is true. The Church

8 Kimball, 103.

calls sinners to repentance, but sinners don't want to be called to repentance. Repentance hurts. In my defensive posture I can shift all the responsibility for the perceptions of the Church onto others.[9]

But that answer falls far short of Lutheran theology. As Lutherans, we apply Law and Gospel to ourselves as God's Word gives it, and we discover that the charges are not without foundation. The Church is the Bride of Christ, but she is a bride that must be washed in the blood of her Bridegroom to be cleansed of her sin. We who are the Church are both saints and sinners; and while we live in the hope and the certainty of our sainthood—our justification through the cross of Christ displayed in a life of sanctification—it is we as sinners who too often are visible to those around us. And so we confess our sin.

Our confession before our culture must be carefully made. To be authentic, which is to say spoken in humility and accuracy, this confession must be honest, genuine, and biblical.

We ask no forgiveness for upholding the sanctity of marriage as a union of male and female, for none is needed; but we do ask forgiveness for whenever our words, attitudes, and actions have not demonstrated Christ's love for those who see themselves to be gay, lesbian, bisexual, or transgendered.

We ask no forgiveness for exercising our rights and privileges as citizens by voting for candidates whose values and intentions match those of biblical morality, for none is needed; but we do ask forgiveness if ever we have thought that we could bring about righteousness through legislation rather than through a changed and repentant heart.

We ask no forgiveness for preaching the truth given to us in the Scriptures that Jesus Christ is the only Son of God and that salvation comes exclusively through Him, for no forgiveness is needed; but we do ask forgiveness for failing to respect or appreciate the truths that are found in the religions of the world, even as we seek to introduce the adherents of those religions to Jesus Christ—following Paul's example in Acts 17.

What I'm suggesting here is nothing less than that a Lutheran response to the issues raised by Kinnaman and Kimball is a thorough

---

9 For a more extensive discourse on the problem of preaching the Law to society today, see John Oberdeck, "Speaking to Contemporary American Culture on Sin and the Wrath of God," *Concordia Journal* 31:4 (October 2005), 398–410.

rereading of Matthew 7:3 "Why do you see the speck that is in your brother's eye, but do not notice the log that is in your own eye?"

If there are logs in our own eyes, they need the removal offered by the divine ophthalmologist—the Holy Spirit, who convicts the world of sin (John 16:8). We want the logs removed first because of our own need for forgiveness when our witness has been callous, loveless, and self-serving. We want the splinters excised second for our witness to the world so that we see ourselves as others see us, with the hope that through those eyes we might observe a self-sacrificing community of love: the Church. Finally, we want the motes washed out as a testimony and model for our youth. Why for our youth? So they see their Church as the humble servant of God in the world that God has called it to be; so they can see how lovely and attractive the Bride of Christ really is; so that "Christian" is a name they bear with humility, appreciation, and a sanctified pride.

## A Theological Vaccination

So far in this chapter, we agree that we want our youth to grow up Christian, and we are witnessing how often the term "Christian" is coming to mean something very different in our culture than what we think it means. We also note how much this negative perception creates barriers for the Gospel to those outside the faith, and how it also challenges the maturing faith of younger generations within the Church.

It's as if the younger generation is swimming in a germ-infected atmosphere. The pathogen's goal is either the prevention or the destruction of faith by rendering the foundations of faith—the Word of God and the Church that preaches the Word of God—at best irrelevant and at worst evil. If our young people are at all intellectually gifted, they will sooner or later run into the works of contemporary militant atheists, who sense a weakened church boldly deny the existence of God.[10] If they spend a lot of time in front of the flat

---

10 The most prominent are Christopher Hitchens, *God Is Not Great*; Richard Dawkins, *The God Delusion*; Sam Harris, *Letter to a Christian Nation* and *The End of Faith: Religion, Terror and the Future of Reason*; and anything written recently by Bart Ehrman. Christianity has not been without defenders, however, and popular apologists include Timothy Keller, *The Reason for God: Belief in an Age of Skepticism*; Dinesh D'Souza, *What's So Great about Christianity?* and David Bentley Hart, *Atheist Delusions: The Christian Revolution and Its Fashionable Enemies*.

screen (television or computer), they will sooner or later be engulfed in American civic religion, which we learned about earlier under the name of *Moralistic Therapeutic Deism*. If they are hitting puberty and beginning the exploration of themselves as embodied created beings, they will sooner or later run headlong into questions about sexual orientation, if not about themselves then about their friends.

How can we as Lutheran Christian leaders and parents prepare? Is there something we can do as we listen to our young people, teach our young people, and model Christian lives? Yes, there is. We have already established a trinitarian framework through which we receive God's gifts from above and from below. We have also explored how sin and grace, Law and Gospel, function in the Christian life—particularly in the lives of adolescents. And we have recognized through the Means of Grace how the Holy Spirit "calls, gathers, enlightens, and sanctifies" us in our Christian walk.

Each of these Lutheran theological teachings is of value in applying theology to Christian youth. All the same, I suggest that there are three doctrines in Lutheran theology that are of particular significance in helping youth understand the nature of the Church in the world and their place in the Church. These three doctrines provide us with a biblical understanding for the inexplicable fact that the Church consistently appears to fail but nevertheless succeeds. Only by comprehending the paradoxical nature of the Church can we comprehend how the Church succumbs to hypocrisy and all the other failings, but nevertheless maintains its authenticity and integrity. These teachings are, of course, gifts from above—Third Article gifts—that we have received through God's Word, and they have the power of the Holy Spirit working through God's Word to bring us and adolescents to a strong and healthy understanding of God's work in the world and in our lives. Like a vaccine, they have the power to deflect the more deleterious effects of Satan's schemes.

So what are these doctrines? The first is the doctrine of the two natures of Jesus Christ. The second is the doctrine known as the theology of the cross, and the third is the doctrine of vocation. Let's look at the source of each of these teachings and how it applies to youth ministry. In so doing, we will discover why an emphasis on these doctrines assists youth and adults in their inevitable confrontations with an unbelieving world.

# The Two Natures of Christ

What does Christology—the study of who Jesus is—have to do with youth ministry? To put it succinctly, it is foundational, just as it is for every other kind of ministry in the Church. A brief review is helpful.

It might come as a surprise that any would doubt that Jesus was a human being, but in the early centuries of the Christian faith, the humanity of Jesus was challenged by Gnosticism. Gnosticism is a belief system that takes Jesus and turns Him into the bringer of secret knowledge who reveals the secret of salvation only to the initiated. Gnostic scriptures teach a Jesus who is not human: He is a god, and probably a lesser god at that.[11] To understand how much the biblical account of Jesus' life is distorted by Gnosticism, imagine that I take another historical person, say Thomas Jefferson, and write a whole new chapter of his life, such as when he succeeds George III as King of England. This secret knowledge of Jefferson's life has been revealed to me, but hidden from ordinary people. But I'm willing to share it with my followers, my group of "insiders." From early on, the humanity of Jesus was under attack by similar types of secret knowledge.

Lutherans believe that Jesus Christ is true man, a true human being. The Bible explains why it is necessary that the savior be a human being. Reconciliation between the holy God and sinful humanity requires a human to participate. Jesus was truly human, born of the Virgin Mary. Reconciliation between the holy God and sinful humanity requires a participant who is under God's holy Law. Jesus is under the Law, meaning that if He would transgress God's Law, He would be a sinner. Third, the plan of salvation requires that the perfect sacrifice for sin be made on the cross, meaning that Jesus would have to die. Paul summarizes Jesus' work as true man for all these reasons when he writes to the Galatians, "But when the fullness of time had come, God sent forth His Son, born of woman, born under the law, to redeem those who were under the law, so that we might receive adoption as sons" (4:4–5).

Not so surprisingly, in the early centuries of the Christian faith, the divinity of Jesus Christ was also hotly debated. Many followed a man

---

11 For a more complete description of what are known as the "Christological Controversies," see Douglas W. Johnson, *The Great Jesus Debates: Early Church Battles about the Person and Work of Jesus* (St. Louis: Concordia Publishing House), 2005.

named Arius. "Arius insisted that the Word [Jesus] was not of the divine nature but a creature—perhaps the first and best of all creatures, but a creature still."[12] In addition to Arius's denial of the divinity of Christ, others who affirmed His divinity to some degree created controversy in the Church over the nature of the relationship of Jesus' divine and human natures. Was He more one than the other? Did they mix within Him to create a third type of being? The Church's acceptance of the three ecumenical creeds, the Apostles' Creed, the Nicene Creed, and the Athanasian Creed, testify to the consensus that was ultimately achieved at several ecumenical councils. In these creeds, both the Trinity and the person of Jesus Christ are confessed—with Jesus Christ being true God and true man, without separation or mixture of the two natures.

Lutherans accept and confess these creeds and believe that Jesus Christ is also true God. The Bible explains why it is necessary that the Savior be true God. Reconciliation with God requires that God's Law be kept perfectly (Leviticus 19:2; Matthew 5:48), and no son of Adam or daughter of Eve can do that. Reconciliation with God requires that the perfect sacrifice given on the cross be of such value that it covers the sins of the whole world (1 John 2:2). Even if you or I could be a sacrifice for sin, we could only at best atone for ourselves, much less for anyone else or the transgressions of our race for all time. The perfect Son of God is a sacrifice of sufficient worth that no doubt is left—all sin has been paid for. How do we know this? We know the reconciliation is complete because Jesus is risen from the dead. Only God has power over sin and death. Paul explains in his second letter to the Corinthians, "In Christ God was reconciling the world to Himself, not counting their trespasses against them. . . . For our sake He made Him to be sin who knew no sin, so that in Him we might become the righteousness of God" (5:19, 21). As a standard theology textbook we use in biblical theology class puts it, "We needed a human Savior. We needed a divine Savior. All of our needs are perfectly met in Jesus Christ the God-man."[13]

This review of the two natures of Christ only skims the surface of the topic, as any well-trained systematic theologian will tell you. Nevertheless, that Jesus is true God and true man is accepted

---

12 Johnson, 85.

13 Steven P. Mueller, ed., *Called to Believe, Teach and Confess: An Introduction to Doctrinal Theology* (Eugene, OR: Wipf & Stock, 2005), 189.

teaching by all who share a connection to orthodox Christianity. There are differences in how this is understood, of course. We ought not to be surprised by that, and if you want to dig deeper into these distinctions—and they aren't insignificant—Johnson's book noted earlier, *The Great Jesus Debates*, will be very helpful. But what is common among Christians is the belief that the incarnation of Jesus Christ involves a miracle: God and man in one person with two natures.

How does this doctrine assist youth as they encounter the skepticism and secularism of our culture? What can Lutheran theology add to their understanding? The doctrine of the two natures of Christ prepares youth and adults to encounter our culture in three ways.

> • Just as Jesus Christ is a miracle of two natures—God and man—in one person, we know ourselves to be miracles of two natures in one person—saint and sinner.[14]

> • Knowing that we are both saints and sinners, we are better equipped to understand ourselves.

> • Knowing that the Church consists of saints and sinners, we don't expect perfection from ourselves or from the Church, but only from Christ.

## We Are Both Saints and Sinners

The practical effect of being baptized into the death and resurrection of Jesus Christ (Romans 6:3–5) is the creation within the believer of the new person in Jesus Christ. Christian teens need to learn from us that they are miracles, not of their own doing but by the work of the Holy Spirit in their lives. They were born sinners and would have been just as pleased to remain sinners, except that the Holy Spirit worked through water and Word, or perhaps through Word leading to the water, creating in them a new nature, so that now they have two natures. If it seems strange to them that they are both new persons in Jesus Christ who have been born again (1 Peter 1:23) and at the same time sinners who struggle daily with their fallen human

---

14 The point of comparison I make here is that both Jesus and those who believe in Jesus are a miracle involving two natures, but the miracles are very different from each other: Jesus is God/man; we are saint/sinner.

nature, their old Adam (Romans 7:14–17), they can recall that Jesus Christ also has two natures, though very different from their own. Yet, different as those natures are from each other, they describe the common link, a bond tighter than any of them might imagine.

I like to think in outlines and diagrams, which has led me to believe that at heart I am more a visual learner than an auditory learner. It wouldn't surprise me if other visual learners might try to construct a diagram to illustrate the relationship I'm suggesting. For a long time, I thought the diagram looked like this:

| Jesus Christ – True God | |
|---|---|
| ⇨ Jesus Christ – True Man | Me the Saint |
| | Me the Sinner |

Jesus is a perfect human, and in Jesus I'm a perfect human. The shaded region doesn't indicate equality, but rather a transfer, and so the arrow shows that the sinlessness of Christ is given to me. The righteousness that makes me a perfect human (saint) isn't mine, but is the righteousness of Jesus I have received (Romans 5:18–19). The blank boxes reveal the obvious—I'm not true God, and Jesus never sinned.

As true as this is, there were still some things about the diagram with which I wasn't comfortable. Finally, I realized what the problem is with this diagram. If I think of myself and my relationship to Jesus as the diagram outlines, two important components of the relationship are excluded. I have no relationship to the divinity of Jesus, and Jesus has no connection to who I am as a sinner. Do you see the dangerous position in which I'm placed if this is my relationship to Jesus? I might, if I follow this diagram as the pattern that links me to Jesus, think that my holiness is entirely utilitarian. What I mean is that I must use the holiness that I've been given as the power by which *I will now attend to, correct, and make up for my sin*; I must use my good side in order to make up for my bad side. The diagram leaves the ugly side of me up to me.

I've either got to be perfect as Christ is perfect, or be very skilled at hiding my dark side.

Do you suppose that one of the reasons so much of the culture thinks Christians are hypocrites and judgmental is that we expend so much energy on pretending to be perfect, working tirelessly to hide our imperfections and sins? Could youth, and adults for that matter, live their spiritual lives thinking that God's grace through Jesus Christ that has made us saints must now be used by us to work out our salvation?

God doesn't call us to hide our dark side, however. He calls us to confess and to be forgiven. Our connection to Jesus Christ is not only through the holiness we receive. Our connection is also through art notes the sin of which we are relieved. The diagram needs some serious alteration.

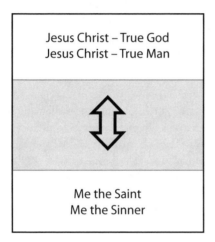

It is not just one of Jesus' natures that saves; it is the whole Jesus Christ. It isn't just one of my natures that is connected to Jesus Christ; it is both. I'm not called to hide my sinner side from God, but to receive the daily drowning of the old Adam by the Holy Spirit. Why? I don't hide because Christ's death on the cross has made atonement for my sin. Righteousness is not demanded from me to reconcile me with God, but instead is given to me. Thus the entire "me," sinner and saint, receives. It is the whole Jesus, God and man, who gives. If there is a sacrifice on my part through the righteousness I've received, and there is, it is the sacrifice of thanksgiving—living a life to the glory and honor of Jesus Christ, who has saved all of me.

Lutheran theology adds to our practice of youth ministry by highlighting the miracle that adolescent believers really are. They are miraculous beings perfectly holy before God dressed in the righteousness of Jesus Christ, who nevertheless struggle with new temptations every day. Much to their dismay, too often they fall to those temptations. They need not be discouraged by their conflicted natures, however, because they are connected to another miraculous being whose two natures daily provide their restored and forgiven relationship to God.

This leads us to the next point. Because Lutheran theology helps youth understand their relationship to Jesus Christ in its fullness, it helps youth to learn to know themselves in ever more meaningful depth. Self-knowledge isn't an easy lesson to learn, however, even for those youth with the best of intentions, as the following recollection illustrates.

## We Understand Ourselves

"This is so unfair, so \*\*\*\*\*\*\* wrong!" I say under my breath as I grab hold of another handful of stalks from the wagon and fling them on the frozen, snow-covered field glistening in the early morning winter light. My adolescent mind is racing, and my adolescent heart is pounding. My face is red, but not from the frigid temperatures. I'm angry.

"Ed and Dale don't go home on the weekends and work. Nooooo. They go home and have fun. They go out." I grab another handful of stalks. I hate the farm. I hate the chewing tobacco crop that requires us to work nearly year round. I hate coming home for weekends in December from Concordia High School—Milwaukee to strip the leaves from the stalks for bundling. Hidden by my gloves are my stained hands. The skin around my nails is cracked, and my knuckles are wrapped in tape. "They go to movies, go on dates; they sleep." I pitch another bunch of stalks. They hit the ground with more force than gravity requires.

Yesterday's load of stripped stalks is nearly unloaded, and Dad's gotten back on the tractor driving it forward. He stops, and I grab another armful of stalks and hurl them to the ground. "Stupid tobacco." I glare at my dad. He doesn't notice. He has no clue. He doesn't understand that when I get back to school Sunday night, Dale, Larry, Tom, and Ed will tell their stories—their exploits—and I'll just shut up. I think of the day ahead, stripping leaves and bundling, in the shed, heated only by a wood-burning stove in the corner. "Boring. ★★★★★★★ boring." Dad will talk. I'll have to listen. At least the radio will be on. I stop for a moment and stare at my dad as he grabs the last of the stalks and lobs them into an empty corner of the field. "Let's go," he says. I sit on the edge of the wagon, and he drives back to the shed. "I hate this," I say to myself. "I hate this farm and everyone in it! Get me the ★★★★★★★★ out of here."

My take on that December morning experience has changed in the forty-four years since it happened, but it remains one of my links to negative, adolescent feelings of injustice, anger, and unfairness. Today, my reflection on that morning is one of appreciation of the sacrifices being made. Now I can understand how the whole family was exerting extra effort so that John could go to Concordia and become a pastor. There were multiple prices to be paid: money for tuition, time for travel, and emotional distance. In retrospect, I can even appreciate the formative way in which the work itself prepared me for ministry, in which the demands of the office pay no attention to fairness or schedules.

On that December morning, however, none of this mature reflection was available. It just wasn't there, and could not be drawn upon in a pinch or understood if it were to be explained. Instead there was anger and resentment, quietly being stored up for the future, with no place to go. On one level of awareness the negative feelings seemed thoroughly justified, but on another there was guilt—a lot of guilt. How can someone who wants to be a pastor feel this way about his family, his roots? How can he let his feelings spill into expletives that need asterisks? How can he be so angry?

Do you ever encounter an angry teen in youth ministry? Do you ever counsel a teen deeply disappointed in himself or herself? What is the source of that anger? What has hurt them? Is the disappointment in their circumstances or in their behaviors, or both? When there is a relationship of trust that's been built over time, you may actually learn the answers to those questions. When you do, you have been allowed into a rare and special level of intimacy with a troubled teen.

To use Chap Clark's terminology, you have been admitted to the world beneath.[15]

Lutheran theology understands each one of us who believe in Jesus Christ as both a redeemed child of God and a fallen human being struggling against sin, death, and the devil.[16] We teach that we are *simul justus et peccator* because it lets us know who we are, and it explains the tension we experience in our lives between who we are in Jesus Christ and who we are as struggling, confused persons in a very mixed-up and often untrustworthy world. It is how we understand the conflicted goals and aspirations that emerge within our hearts—some that we know please our Father above, others that please the father below.

This truth has particular significance for adolescents because without this awareness, this understanding, the probability of teens drawing damaging conclusions from their experiences or their feelings increases exponentially. Take the sophomore in high school described above, this very idealistic young man home for the weekend from the school where everyone is intending to become a pastor or teacher in the Church.[17] What conclusions might he reach if he doesn't understand himself to be both sinner and saint?

- Feeling guilty over his anger toward his father, he might conclude he's not worthy to pursue something as lofty as the pastoral office. He quits.

- Noticing that it doesn't seem to make any difference at home or at school that he is so angry and feels so unappreciated, he might conclude that his behavior is inconsequential; God doesn't care, so why should he? He becomes cynical.

- Hiding who he really is, he separates his school life from his home life. Back at school, he talks about his wonderful weekend at home. He lies.

---

15 According to Clark, it isn't a rare teen who's hurt or angry—it's the generalized experience of a generation.

16 Another way we often describe the unholy trinity is "the devil, the world, and our own sinful flesh." You can take your pick—each triumvirate is equally effective and descriptive of the problem.

17 If you are wondering why our church body no longer has a twelve-year plan to enter the ordained ministry beginning at the freshman year of high school, consider that very few today make their lifelong career decision at age 13 or 14.

As a matter of fact, in this particular, case my choice of response was to take the anger and use it as a motivator to overcompensate, overachieve at school. I left no opportunity to excel unattempted as I strove to atone for myself as sinner by making myself the saint. The results were great—straight As, election as student body president, "A" ranking at the state speaking contest—but the spiritual costs were high.

I fear I'm being too open, engaging in too much self disclosure, but I believe the theological point behind the illustration, so important that I'm willing to risk it. While my illustration deals with a situation of confused family dynamics originating out of adolescent angst, the principles involved carry over into the more complex and potentially tragic circumstances of major adolescent missteps and sins. What does the Lutheran boy whose parents discover his stash[18] of drugs do? How will he respond? What does the Lutheran girl whose self-pregnancy test turns out positive do? How will she respond? What's going on in the mind of the Lutheran boy who can't pry himself away from the tantalizing, titillating pornography on the Internet that takes his dreams and puts them on the screen?

Will these youth feel so worthless they quit believing God can love them? Will their view of the world turn dark as they cynically conclude that nothing is genuine, nothing is true? Will they begin to live lives dependent on falsehood? Or will they overcompensate, overachieve, create a life course of self justification and personal achievement that is just as damaging in the long run to their spiritual lives as any of the negative options because it, too, has no room for the cross of Jesus Christ?

Do you see the theological implication of knowing oneself to be both a sinner and a saint? The Holy Spirit working through the Word can bring adolescents to know this, understand this, and take it to heart. "Everyone who commits sin is a slave to sin" (John 8:34). The overachiever and the runaway are both slaves to sin; as is the unheard, unnoticed teen in the middle. What sets them free? "If the Son sets you free, you will be free indeed" (John 8:36). The Son has set us free. The truth is that we are sinners who have been liberated from our slavery by a savior, Jesus Christ, who has through the gift of His Spirit made us new creatures (2 Corinthians 5:17).

---

18 Please accept any archaic terminology as illustrative of the challenge to keep up with language on the street. This is what it would have been called when I was a teen.

Let me see if I can make the application of this truth as direct as possible. Teens who have learned they are both sinners and saints not only believe the message of God's forgiveness for them through the cross of Christ, but also succeed in *forgiving themselves*; and that can be the more difficult task. Teens who have learned that they are both sinners and saints believe that their status as saint is a gift they did not earn and are liberated from the slavery of self-worth determined by personal achievement.

So what? So adolescents who understand themselves as believers before God who are saints and sinners don't despair over their sin, nor do they depend on their own righteousness. They live in the twin gifts of forgiveness and righteousness. With those gifts, patience with themselves and with others is not only possible, it becomes probable—with the help of the Holy Spirit. With patience comes even more gifts from above, the fruit of the Holy Spirit: love, joy, peace, kindness, goodness, and faithfulness (Galatians 5:22). Enveloped in the love of God in Jesus Christ, unbelief, cynicism, deception, and self righteousness lose their appeal. Christian love for those who reject or persecute becomes a real possibility. And isn't that really the proper approach by Christians to those who view us with suspicion?

I'm back in that cold December day. The sun sets early, and it is dark when we quit for the day and head for the house. I'm tired, yet filled with the pleasurable feeling of tangible accomplishment. We got a lot done, my dad, me and my younger brother. He smiles at us. I know he's pleased that I was there. So am I. I'm part of something really neat, a family. I'm not the person I was in the morning. As a teen, I'm allowed rapid transformations. The anger from the morning is long gone. In its place is deep affection. "It's been a good day," I tell myself. "This is a good place to be. This is where I belong." Am I aware of the contrast between a.m. and p.m.? A little, but I'm a teenager. There's a lot more to understand, a lot more to grasp about my two natures and my faith. Little by little, I'm learning who I am—a forgiven sinner and glorious saint.

## We Understand the Church

There are two conflicted arenas in our two nature existence—the personal and the public—my struggle as a saint/sinner and the struggle of the congregation of which I am a part as a group of saints/sinners.

Adolescents are involved in both conflicts. If my personal struggle to understand the two fails, there is damage. I discover I'm a hypocrite. If my public understanding of the struggle fails, there is another kind of damage. I see my church as nothing but a bunch of hypocrites.

Teens can be deadly accurate in their assessment of the congregation's flaws and heartlessly sharp in their critique of its shortcomings. They want something that is true, authentic, genuine, and trustworthy. The exuberance and optimism of youth raises their expectations. They believe the world can be changed, and they are the generation to do it. They have grown up reciting the creed, believing in "the holy Christian church, the communion of saints." They want a *holy* Christian church. They don't find it. Instead, they find us—the adult Christian world—and we don't look very holy.

Of course, the Church is holy. It's been redeemed by Jesus Christ, washed clean of sin and ugliness by His precious and innocent blood. Yet we know this vision of the Church is visible only by faith; which is why we confess that we *believe* in the holy Christian church. But in this world, it is made up of sinners and saints.

If there is a problem for young people today in accepting the congregations in which they have grown up because they don't measure up to their message, if there is an aversion to "organized religion" as researchers indicate, then certainly a key instrument at our disposal to restore a biblical understanding of Church is to teach what it means to be both saints and sinners; not just as individuals, but as a body of believers.

To be sure, this doesn't relieve Christian adults from putting forth every effort to measure up to the message we have received, personally and corporately. What a misuse of this teaching it would be if we use the saint/sinner dichotomy as an excuse to maintain the status quo, to inhibit a growing life of sanctification and good works, or to justify our inaction when we ought to be acting in the name of Jesus Christ. Teaching this doctrine in such a way that it becomes an excuse no better than "the devil made me do it" would only validate the most ugly beliefs about the Church, driving the next generation further away.

But if we begin with the personal struggle that all of us face in living up to the calling to which we have been called (Ephesians 4:1), we are better equipped to share the corporate struggle that we share together in representing Christ to the world. Since we receive the spiritual gift of patience for ourselves, relying on the Holy Spirit, in our personal struggle, we may expect the Spirit to grant the same gift to us together in our church.

# The Theology of the Cross

I happen to be writing this chapter while at a national Lutheran youth-worker conference in New Orleans. I'm sitting in the exhibitors' room during a break. No one else is in the room, no one that is except a sound technician by the name of Gary, a man in his mid-twenties.[19] He's on a short break before the next general session, and he wants to talk. I appear to be suitably nonthreatening, so he looks at the brochures on my table, finds an empty chair, and then asks me, "What are Lutherans?"

He's got a lot of questions. "Isn't the Old Testament God a bloodthirsty God different from the New Testament God?" He's interested, but most of his knowledge comes from the Easter specials on the History Channel or revelations coming through the National Geographic Channel (remember the Book of Judas?). He's surprised to learn that the Old Testament was written before Jesus came. He's confused about the idea of sacrifice. He tells me that he's not a Christian, but he's exploring. He's interested in Buddhism. I ask him what he thinks Christians are like; as if on cue, his response validates the argument presented by Kimball and Kinnaman. "Christians are so judgmental. They protest all the time."

I wonder why he's talking to me, but before I ask he answers the question. He's been listening to the presentations in the general sessions, and he's conflicted. This bunch of "Lutherans" doesn't fit his mental image of what Christians are like. I tell him some things about Lutherans. We like Jesus. We know the world is messed up. We call that sin. Some is the world's fault. A lot is our own fault. That's why Jesus came, to rescue us from sin. Gary counters with suffering in the world. If there is a good God, why would He let people suffer, he wants to know. Why is there evil? I tell him that we don't have an answer to personal tragedies and suffering, but when something bad happens, we weep with those who weep. He likes that. He shares his grief at

---

19 Not his real name.

the loss of a friend killed in an accident. He struggles with the loss. "He didn't deserve to die." I can tell the loss of his friend has hit him hard. He doesn't know how to handle it, and he wants answers. I tell him I don't have an answer. We can guess answers to "why?" but we don't really know. What we do know is that God understands our pain, because His Son was on the cross for us. This is what Jesus is all about, I explain. His facial expression gives hints of surprise and confusion. He hasn't thought of it this way before. He nods. Then he gets a call on his cell phone. He's got to get back to work. We shake hands, and I give him my card and invite him to contact me if he has more questions. I'd love to listen to him, I tell him.

Will I ever hear from Gary? Who knows? In this day and age we might be friends on Facebook before the week is out. The conversation we have certainly falls far short of a full presentation of the Gospel message, the kind I learned to share back in the 1980s. Nevertheless, I sense there is movement, more openness on Gary's part to hear the Gospel. He responds because someone is listening and seems to understand. I don't think he will respond to pat answers or a prepared speech. Few of his generation do. If I come on strong, Gary will think me just another "judgmental" Christian who thinks he knows it all, looking to notch another conversion on my evangelism belt. Apparently Gary has been a target before. But these "Lutheran" Christians who Gary's working with on stage aren't like that. Here he is listened to and understood. "Yes, your friend's death is tragic. I don't know why he had to die. All I know is that God is with us in our grief and suffering. Let me tell you about the cross."

My conversation with Gary illustrates the profound insight into our relationship to God Martin Luther provides in the Heidelberg Disputation.[20] Luther makes a distinction between two approaches to knowing God. One he calls a theology of glory, the other a theology of the cross. Gary is struggling with the loss of his friend from the perspective of a theology of glory, and in a theology of glory loss and tragedy is inexplicable. If there is a God, these things shouldn't happen. Pointing Gary to the cross as the starting point of understanding comes out of a theology of the cross. A theology of the cross assumes that in a fallen world fallen creatures suffer, but that God has chosen to suffer with us and for us. As long as Gary relates to God through a theology

---

20 See Luther's Works, vol. 31, *Career of the Reformer I*, ed. Harold J. Grimm (Philadelphia: Muhlenberg Press, 1957), 39–70.

of glory, God will be distant, an enemy, or nonexistent. Should Gary be led to see God through a theology of the cross, he'll know that God has been with him always, even through his darkest moments.

The problem of evil in the world troubles teens. Global warming, nuclear proliferation, collapsing economies, threats of pandemic diseases, geophysical disasters, and radical religion-driven terrorism form the outer atmospheric cloud of worry, while the daily distresses of adolescent life—family breakups, school pressures, enticements to drugs and sex, personal inadequacies and failures (or the pressure to sustain success?)—shape the air going in and out of adolescent lungs. Earlier I labeled these same anxiety-causing elements the magnifying glass of God's Law bearing down on us—the effects of living in a fallen world. In this chapter, we find the same elements being used as evidence in the case against God; why He is either uncaring, absent, malevolent, or the creation of human imagination.

In this environment, we need to teach our youth the difference between a theology of glory and a theology of the cross. Knowing this distinction prepares youth for today's world in three ways.

- First, the theology of the cross provides youth with a biblical response to the joys and sorrows that come with living in this world.

- Second, the theology of the cross establishes ground rules for understanding how and why God answers prayers.

- Third, the theology of the cross provides an antidote for the incessant media program that claims human atrocity and sin are proof that God doesn't exist.

## Understanding Our Joys and Sorrows

According to a theology of glory, the evidence of God in our lives is to be found in the blessings we receive, be they blessings of health, wealth, or whatever other benefit of this world we might desire. Gene Veith describes how attractive the theology of glory is. "Naturally, we want success, victories, and happiness. We will be attracted to any religion that can promise us such things. We want complete and understandable answers, evidence of tangible spiritual power, all conveyed by an impressive, well-run, and effective institution."[21] A glory theology places each of us in the center; God's purpose is to serve us and fulfill our needs, and a consumer culture not only promotes such a view, but it requires such a view. Eugene Peterson calls this attitude "the new Holy Trinity. The sovereign self expresses itself in Holy Needs, Holy Wants, and Holy Feelings."[22] In a glory theology, I know I have God's blessings, and I know that there really is a god when my needs, wants, and feelings have been satisfied.

Do you see the application to youth ministry? Teens have a lot of needs, wants, and feelings. A theology that is dependent on one's own degree of happiness is very much at risk, and you know why. Jesus said, "In the world you will have tribulation. But take heart; I have overcome the world" (John 16:33). Jesus is simply saying that in this fallen world, we are going to have trouble, all kinds of trouble, and we should not measure God's love toward us on the basis of how trouble free our lives might be. Our joys are gifts from a loving God, but they aren't the evidence of His love. Our tribulations have been permitted in our lives by a loving God, and our suffering is never evidence that God is rejecting us. The evidence of God's love for us is the cross of Christ, and the proof that God has not abandoned us in our suffering is the cross of Christ.

Because of the frequent turmoil that adolescent life entails, teens need to be reassured that their relationship to God has been established through the cross of Jesus Christ and His empty tomb and is not dependent on their life circumstance. The theology of the cross does this very thing.

## God Answers Prayer

People often do not take prayer seriously until they are in some kind of need, perhaps a life-threatening illness. A theology of glory expects God to answer our prayers the way we want them answered. After all, what good is a god if he doesn't do for you want you want? Richard Eyer tells the story of a man by the name of Mr. Witti who is dying. His daughter believes that God answers prayers, so she and her

21 Veith, 58.

22 Eugene H. Peterson, *Eat This Book: A Conversation in the Art of Spiritual Reading* (Grand Rapids: Eerdmans, 2006), 32.

prayer circle faithfully pray every day for his recovery. Nevertheless, his condition grows worse. In spite of the obvious direction her father is taking, the daughter believes that the fervency of their prayers will reverse his condition. The prayers have become a battle of wills, as Eyer points out. "Mr. Witti has surrendered to the will of God in confidence that God is still on his side. Mr. Witti's daughter, meanwhile, is still trying to get God to surrender to her will for her father."[23]

When Mr. Witti dies, his daughter is frustrated and feels defeated because she expects God's presence only in healing. She doesn't recognize God's presence in suffering and loss. A theology of the cross knows God's presence in weakness and suffering because God's greatest work on our behalf is the unfathomable weakness and suffering of Jesus on our behalf.

Christian teens have been taught how to pray. Most from little on have folded their hands, bowed their heads, and joined in table prayers, corporate prayers, and the Lord's Prayer. They more than likely have lifted their hearts to God as children praying for the recovery of a pet, as students praying for a better grade than on the last test, and maybe even as romantics asking God to help them find a boyfriend or girlfriend who will become a suitable mate. We teach Christian teens how to pray, but do we teach them how to receive God's answers?

This is not an easy lesson to learn. Paul is our instructor as he prays for his thorn in the flesh to be removed (2 Corinthians 12:7–10). He prays three times, and you can tell how much he believes that his ministry will be improved if God would grant this simple request. But that is not God's will. God does answer the prayer, but He answers it in a way that brings glory to God through the suffering of Paul. "My grace is sufficient for you, for My power is made perfect in weakness" (v. 9).

We teach a theology of the cross to teens so that they realize that God's answer of "No" or "Wait" to their prayers is not a rejection, but an affirmation of God's love and God's design for their lives. Early on, they need to hear that faith believes God's denial of their prayer is still God's love for them. Do we know the details of how this is so? No, we do not, but we do know that it's the truth. Eyer puts it this way. "How then shall we pray? Pray, not as a technique to get what we want from

23 Richard C. Eyer, *Pastoral Care under the Cross: God in the Midst of Suffering* (St. Louis: Concordia, 1994), 26.

God but as a way of entrusting our lives to his care whatever that may encompass."[24] A theology of the cross understands that prayer is not our attempt to force God to surrender to our will, but is really our request that God would help us surrender to His will. When the enemies of faith attack our youth with powerful arguments about God's failure to answer their prayers, teens trained in a theology of the cross have a defense that heals their hurting psyches—God's grace is sufficient for them too, and in their weakness God is showing His strength.

## God Really Exists

When our teens learn the meaning of the theology of the cross and apply it to their own lives, it not only strengthens them when they experience joys and sorrows and undergirds their confidence in prayer, but it also introduces them to the field of apologetics—the reasoned defense of the Christian faith.

Over and over again, opponents of Christianity will build their case against the existence of God on the basis of evolution. There really is no need for a god because all known processes can be explained, or soon will be explained, by means of scientific exploration. Everything has a natural cause. This, however, is their weakest argument and they know it. It simply runs counter to human intuition to imagine complexities like the human brain or the DNA molecule have happened by accident, no matter how much time is allowed. The evidence for a designer of some kind is too strong.

A more effective rationale for atheism finds its roots in the destructiveness of nature and the perversity of humanity. If there is a God, how could He allow the Indonesian tsunami? If there is a God, how could he have allowed the Holocaust? These are the kinds of questions posed to Christian youth at younger and younger ages, challenging their growing faith. Social studies and English classes are a greater threat than biology or earth science. That God can't be measured in the laboratory is easily understood; that God is absent in great tragedy is not.

Youth need to know how God has chosen to intervene in human affairs, and there is no better place to begin than the theology of the cross. Veith points out that "The hiddenness of God is one of the most

---

24 Eyer, 59.

profound themes in Lutheran spirituality."[25] Miracles do occur, of course. Upon occasion, God does display His omnipotence through acts of direct intervention—the exodus from Egypt, for example—but most often God works behind the scenes.

How should we inform our youth? Take youth through the Old Testament and explain how routinely God chooses the least likely candidates to play major roles in the history of salvation. Moses makes excuses, Gideon hides in the winepress, and David isn't even invited to the anointing ceremony when Samuel arrives to name Israel's next king. We can introduce youth to the *modus operandi* of God in the New Testament. Jesus isn't born in a palace but in a stable. Mary isn't a queen but a humble village girl. Nazareth isn't the capital; it's a backwater hamlet with a bad reputation. The disciples aren't learned professionals; they are tanned day laborers or worse—tax collectors and zealots. More examples are available, but these are sufficient to get us to Golgotha, to the cross. God's intent is to save humankind, not by military might, wise political guidance, full economic inclusion, gross national product, or anything else that we could have surmised. God saves humankind by the death of Jesus Christ on the cross. Paul's thorn in the flesh is not an aberration from God's normal procedures. For those in tune with God's methods—like Isaiah in his fifty-third chapter—the cross is no surprise. God once again shows His power through weakness.

That God works through weakness—that He is so often hidden—troubles adults and troubles youth too. This isn't how we would do things. But what would happen if God did act as we wanted in every circumstance? What then? Think of it this way. *If* God intervened to rescue us from every possible harmful event, would we honor Him? *If* every disappointment was avoided, would we worship Him? *If* every consequence of our own foolishness was averted, would we pray to Him?

A thoughtful analysis of these questions reveals that *if* all those *ifs* did occur, we would have no awareness of it, for we would never know what had been avoided. No, the response of sinful human beings would be to continue on our merry way honoring, worshiping, and depending ourselves, all the while freely sinning against one another in

---

25 Gene Edward Veith Jr., *The Spirituality of the Cross*, 2nd ed. (St. Louis: Concordia, 2010), 56.

ever more perverse ways. Somewhere in this paragraph lurks the reason why God drove Adam and Eve out of the garden and placed the angel with a flaming sword in front of the tree of life (Genesis 3:24). Driving us from the garden was a blessing because it freed us from living in a fallen world forever. Nevertheless, it does mean that we live in a fallen world. Intuitively, we know that something about suffering is essential to salvation. Our weaknesses must be made obvious to us or we risk thinking Satan's promise has been fulfilled and we are like God. In His mercy, God permits us to learn how weak we really are. Lutheran Christians understand that the hiddenness of God is very much related to the fallenness of man. The theology of the cross expresses that God chooses a way of salvation that changes our hearts without violating our wills. When Paul tells the Corinthians in his First Epistle that God makes foolish the wisdom of the world (1:18–31), this is what he's writing about. "For the word of the cross is folly to those who are perishing, but to us who are being saved it is the power of God" (v. 18).

Okay, that last paragraph is getting pretty deep. Let's take a breath and think about what this means for a moment. Can I be more precise? What the Bible is teaching us here is that God's ways are far beyond our own, that what we don't know about God won't hurt us, and that we know it won't hurt us because God has shown us His love through the salvation won for us by Jesus on the cross. Lutheran Christians do not fear the hiddenness of God, but by the Spirit's power, we trust it.

The theology of the cross is essential in a Lutheran understanding of theodicy—a technical term meaning the attempt to give an answer for why God lets bad things happen. And theodicy is what leads us back to youth ministry. Youth ask why bad things happen in the world and why bad things happen to them. This is the question that haunts Gary, the sound technician from New Orleans. They need a clear answer: bad things don't tell us our faith is gone—bad things tell our faith to get going! Bad things aren't evidence that God's abandoned us—bad things are God's invitation to jump into His arms. Bad things aren't purposeless events in an empty, random universe—bad things are the proof of meanings deeper than we can fathom. Youth need to know that the cross is a very, very bad thing, but it leads to the resurrection, the best thing there is.

# The Doctrine of Vocation

I've often contemplated just what it was that convinced me professional sports was not to be my vocation:

- Could it have been my Little League career as a second string right fielder, inserted to pinch-hit regularly because I was too slow to get out of the way of wayward pitches, managing to reach base only seven times one season—five times because of the bruises on my arms and legs?

- Could it have been my intramural basketball career in high school when my teammates realized that, though I was the tallest in my class, throwing the ball to Oberdeck was the same as throwing it out of bounds? I recall with fondness the looks from the opposition my sophomore year as I was getting off the team bus at away games, the home team wondering just how good the tall kid was (then watching as they assumed I was injured, since I was seated behind the team, keeping stats).

- Did I realize that golf wasn't my game when I crushed my older brother's cheekbone when he was trying to teach me how to follow through on my golf swing? I did follow through just as he told me; unfortunately, he was standing right behind me at the very moment I mastered the technique.

- Did knowing I hold the wrestling record for being pinned in the least amount of time (15 seconds) at my hometown junior high at all inhibit me from approaching other full-contact sports?

- And what about my cross-country running career? Did I take the hint when I found myself still running on the JV squad as a senior? Or was it at the conference meet when the JV heat was delayed because they discovered seniors weren't permitted to run JV? My coach, God bless him, took up my defense before the other coaches. "Let the boy run," he said with confidence. "It won't may any difference." They did, and it didn't.

Now, I'm not really a very good example of my point here, because I already knew from early on that God had not called me to be a professional athlete. I believed that God wanted me to be a pastor. That was my calling, my vocation, and I had believed it from about second grade on—with a brief hiatus during fifth grade when I thought architecture might be fun. I've since discovered that most people make career decisions much later in life. With some frequency, I've found myself counseling college students who are all muddled up, not knowing what their major ought to be or what God might want of them in their lives. And if this happens at the college level, all the more so in high school as graduating seniors look at the job market, consider technical schools, or examine the route of higher education.

"What does God want me to do?" isn't necessarily the way most young people ask the question of vocation. They probably aren't familiar with the term and would phrase their search more in terms of "What do I want to do?" or "What do I seem talented enough to do?" Nevertheless, vocation is what this is all about, and vocation is the third doctrine that I feel has a special role in helping youth understand the nature of the Church in the world and their place in the Church.

## Luther on Vocation

There are three ways in which the term vocation is understood, all finding their beginnings in the Latin verb voco, which means "to call or summon." First, there is the call of the Holy Spirit through the Gospel to faith in Jesus Christ—a call every Christian has received. A second and more common meaning has to do with an occupation—a career that a person chooses. Sometimes it is used in contrast to higher education, as when a teen decides to take vocational education courses. The third meaning is an ecclesiastical term, a call to full-time ministry in the Church. Roman Catholics most commonly use the term in this way, as when a young man has a vocation for the priesthood. Luther wrote extensively about vocation, pointing out that every person has a "station," or as it would be in German, a "stand." Stations are naturally helpful in providing for others. Stations are both occupational and biological—that is, my occupation may be that of coal miner, while at the same time I have the vocation of son, husband, and father; so that at any given time I might occupy several stations.[26]

---

26 Gustaf Wingren, *Luther on Vocation*, trans. Carl C. Rasmussen (Philadelphia:

Luther's understanding of vocation, however, differs from the medieval perspective in a profound way. Medieval Christianity views stations as the realm in which Christians perform the works necessary for the grace they have already received in Christ to be effective in their lives. Or put another way, by doing good deeds for their family and neighbors, and by faithfully performing the tasks of their occupation, they are gaining the credit they need for heaven. Vocation, according to this view, is our work done for the benefit of God and in order to earn salvation.

Luther turns vocation completely around. Rather than our work done for the benefit of God and to earn salvation, vocation is God's work in us, providing for the needs of family and neighbor. As you can see, Luther's perspective flows directly out of the doctrine of justification by grace through faith. Good deeds done in one's vocation cannot earn salvation, because believers are already justified by grace without the works of the Law. And God does not need our good works either.

Luther's keen insight is this. While God doesn't need our good works done according to our station in life, our neighbor does. In fact, this is how God providentially cares for His creation. Farmers plant and harvest their crops; babies are fed and changed by their mothers; fuel is delivered to gas stations by tanker drivers; electricians wire houses according to code; and police officers patrol neighborhoods— each one fulfilling one of the many stations they have in life, and in so doing providing God's care for everyone else by providing food, child care, transportation, safe houses, and safe neighborhoods. As Wingren explains, vocation is not restricted to Christians; everybody is in on it. "Even persons who have not taken the gospel to their hearts serve God's mission, though they be unaware thereof, by the very fact that they perform the outer functions of their respective stations."[27]

Rather than me using my neighbor to please God with my life, God uses me in order to care for my neighbor. If I should happen to wonder who will take care of me while I am busy fulfilling my station, the answer is obvious. God has the same relationship to my neighbor as He has with me. My neighbor's vocation is to care for me through his own station in life. Luther has a term to describe this mutually

Muhlenberg Press, 1957), 7.

27 Wingren, 7.

interwoven relationship: "In the exercise of his vocation man becomes a mask for God."[28] Behind each of us, God is at work, and we are His masks.

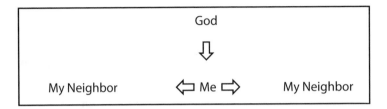

The Lutheran doctrine of vocation helps define our understanding of how God works in the world and how each of us participates in that work. But how does vocation apply to youth ministry? I suggest three specific ways in which adolescents are benefited by an understanding of this doctrine.

- First, the doctrine of vocation assures youth that they have a purpose, not only in a future career, but also in service to God right now.

- Second, the doctrine of vocation affirms youth in their biological station of son or daughter and sheds new light on family relationships.

- Third, the doctrine of vocation connects youth to the mission of God in the world.

Each of these statements deals with questions adolescents ask. "Why am I here? Why am I here with these people? Is there something that God wants me to do?"

## Purpose

I'm sitting in the back of a rental van as several colleagues and I are leaving Indianapolis on our way back to Concordia University Wisconsin after participating in a conference of over one hundred independent colleges and universities on the subject of vocation—not the vocation of teaching in higher education, but the teaching of

---

28 Wingren, 180.

vocation in higher education: "Vocation in Undergraduate Education: Extending the Theological Exploration of Vocation." At the moment, however, my mind is not on how we go about emphasizing one's life work as something more than just a career among our students. The conference has been intellectually stimulating, and my brain is tired. Often I'm the one driving when attending similar conferences, and since this time I don't have to keep my eyes on the road, I'm content to sit in the back and look at the scenery as we leave the fair city of Indianapolis.

We haven't gone very far when I notice something curious. On the right side of I-65, I see a large hospital complex. On the building nearest the interstate is a sign that reads "Clarian Cardiovascular"—a hospital specializing in heart care. I glance to my left, and there on the west side of I-65 is another large sign on a factory building proclaiming "Peerless Pump Company." Maybe it's just me, but I find something strangely humorous in these two corporations being to my right and my left. On the surface they seem very different places. One is a sanitary healing environment; the other is a working factory floor. One is occupied by highly trained and well-compensated experts in their field; the other is taken up by skilled factory workers and engineers less well remunerated. One focuses on the intricate biological and physiological functions of the human body; the other deals with carefully engineered pieces of metal, rubber, and plastic connected to motors, electric and otherwise.

There are, no doubt, working conditions even more vastly different from each other; but as I muse in the rear seat, these two seem quite the opposite. Yet at a fundamental level, Clarian Cardiovascular and Peerless Pump have the same goal—efficient movement of fluids through a system. The basic engineering behind both, I reason, must be similar: keep the fluids flowing. Clean out whatever might obstruct, make sure the proper pressure is maintained, and keep up the beat. Yes, I surmise, they are both really in the same business working with the same principles to accomplish the same goals.

Can this be a paradigm for understanding the value and purpose, nobility and honor, admiration and esteem that is due every calling that serves for the benefit of our neighbor? Within the Lutheran doctrine of vocation, I believe it fits quite well in this respect. It affirms meaning and purpose—theological meaning and purpose—behind every God-pleasing occupation, because each is really in the same business, working with the same principles to accomplish the same goals. Every worker is a mask for God working through that occupation to care for God's creation and work God's will in the world.

"Why am I here? What am I supposed to do?" the teen asks; the guidance counselor helps as much as she can, using a variety of inventories to assist. More than likely, Christian youth have heard that they are to "do good to everyone" (Galatians 6:9–10) and that one ought to "rejoice in his work" (Ecclesiastes 3:22). Nevertheless, at an age in which identity and meaning are so very important, adolescents need to know there is a point to what they find themselves doing—that it is meaningful.

The doctrine of vocation teaches youth that there is purpose and meaning in their lives that goes far beyond the minimum wage earned by flipping burgers and asking if the patrons want to supersize. Think of all the jobs that seem boring and pointless, work that seems meaningless other than to get to the next level. But those jobs are not pointless. The young woman taking my money at the first window might be bored out of her mind, but what she has just done by making change has been God working through her to attend to my hunger. Is it a humble task? No doubt, but it is not a meaningless task. Ought not youth to know this?

Perhaps you have noticed that some people seem to intuitively understand the meaning behind their work. I've begun to study airline attendants, and I've observed that some of them long ago tired of being ignored while explaining how to buckle a seat belt and place the oxygen mask over one's head while pulling the strap to tighten in case of a sudden loss of cabin pressure. I can understand why some might have lost their enthusiasm for reaching over two people to hand me my cranapple drink as I sit in the window seat. But then occasionally, there are the airline attendants whose cheerful service and genuine smile as they point out the exit lighting scheme indicates something else is going on. Maybe they are new on the job or are simply happy to have employment. But then again, maybe they believe they have a vocation—and while they might not describe it this way—they have a calling to be God's servant to me while I travel.

There is a vocation of student, and most in our youth groups have that vocation. Our teens need to know their education is for a purpose.

When the drop off in involvement in youth group begins, say around junior/senior year as the teens find their part-time employment and schedules get really difficult, they need to hear us supporting them in their *vocation*, whatever that humble employment might be. Of course, we will want to make sure we haven't confused justification with sanctification—their work done for others isn't establishing their relationship to God. That task was completed by Jesus Christ. But we do want them to sense the significance of what they do, even to go so far as to call it "cooperating" with God. That's how Luther describes it.[29] At an early age, they need to hear that God is working through them to benefit their neighbor.

## Family Relationships

"How long does it take to drive a quarter mile?" my wife asks, her voice masking fear by taking an angry tone. "She's usually out of there by 11:30." Her irritation is barely under control while mine is still at the sub-fury stage. Our older daughter, a senior in high school, isn't home yet from her twice-a-week evening shift at St. Louis Bread Company. Though it's at most a fifteen-minute walk from where we live, we let her drive so that we don't worry about late night walks. It's already 12:30 a.m. and she's not back yet. We are worried. We call the store to see if she's still there. A guy answers—he's mopping floors—who tells us she left over an hour ago. Our fretting escalates to heights previously unreached. We decide to wait; fifteen minutes, thirty minutes, finally we can wait no longer. "I'm calling the police," my wife says. "Yeah," I respond.

At 1:30, my wife and I are both standing at our front door waiting for the police when down the street we see headlights. The car is followed by a second vehicle, and we can tell from the roof attachments on that car that the police are arriving. The first vehicle is approaching very slowly, and with relief we recognize our car. Our daughter parks the car; as she gets out, she notices the squad car pulled up directly behind her and her parents standing under the light at the front door. In a second, her face takes on a startled, surprised expression. She looks at us quizzically. The officer steps out of the squad car. "Is this the missing girl?" he calls across our lawn. We wave back, nodding. "It's her." He gets back in the squad car and drives

---

29 Wingren, 17.

away. In the meantime, our daughter's expression has moved on from startled surprise to her own version of angry. "What's this? You called the police?" "Well what did you expect? It's 1:30 a.m. You should have been home two hours ago." Not wishing to wake the neighbors, the conversation takes place with sharp, hissing whispers. Now back in the kitchen, the conversation is calmer than one might expect. Our relief softens our hurt. The missing child had left work with another sandwich/soup maker, and they had sat in her car talking. Time got away—she didn't realize it was so late. That was all. We explain our fears, telling her how scared we were. She understands. "Don't do that again," we plead. "Just give us a call."

This event occurred before everybody had a cell phone; so if it were to happen today, it would be even harder to forgive. Sometimes adolescents can be maddeningly unaware and forgetful. Events like these, however, are some of the reasons we don't often think of adolescence itself as a vocation. Nevertheless, Lutheran theology does. Adolescents have neighbors.

Some of the neighbors whom adolescents benefit live in the same house with them: their parents and siblings. Too often our family relationships aren't considered when we think about vocation. Nevertheless, they should be.

Let me frame the question this way. What is the vocation in the home for an adolescent son or daughter? How is God caring for the parents in a family by providing them with teens under their roof? Granted, it is not the usual way we talk about family relationships. More often, the discussion is driven by adults who describe youth as hormone driven monsters, aliens from some other planet, or somewhat dangerous beings. It's as if there is no relationship between teens and the adults who were once teenagers themselves.[30]

This approach to adolescence is not helpful, and frankly, when we speak about teenagers in this way, we are engaging in a denial of the doctrine of vocation. Rather than emphasizing the distance between parent and child, or fearing adolescence as some kind of curse, Lutheran theology, through the doctrine of vocation, can emphasize the similarities shared by parent and child and affirm the blessing that is adolescence.

---

30 Smith and Denton, 264.

We might think of the vocation of adolescence solely in terms of preparation: through obedient cooperation with parents, teens learn what it means to be an adult; through persistent application of intellectual abilities at school, teens prepare for a career in the adult work world; through cultivation of genuine friendships, teens learn the social competencies necessary to survive in our culture. This is all true. But to think of the vocation of adolescence only as preparatory to a future in which teens will be the masks of God in their various vocations is to lose sight of the vocation of adolescence in the present. The Lutheran question is this: In what ways are teens serving as masks for God's providential care for their neighbors now?

When we approach adolescence with this question in mind, we no longer can accept the negative images of teens held by so many among the older generations. Instead, we must ask ourselves what blessings are brought to the household by the teens living among us.

Now I've set myself up for a severe challenge. In her vocation as a teen, how did my older daughter bless my wife and me by coming in two hours late from her evening part-time job? How did her behavior demonstrate God's care for us? Of course, in a direct manner, it didn't any more than adult carelessness or sinfulness within any other vocation is God at work. No, we would have to say such cases illustrate the failure of vocation rather than its fulfillment.

But let's think about it a little harder. Didn't my daughter's action that evening result in heightened awareness on our part of our love for her? Didn't it provide us the opportunity to fulfill our vocations as caring parents in ways that we hadn't before? Weren't we compelled by the circumstance to rely on one another more deeply as we shared our parental concern with each other (and with the local police department, who were enabled to fulfill their vocation)? And didn't it allow us to practice confession and absolution when she got home?

Now that I've made a case for adolescent vocation out of family problems, stretched as the argument is, arguing the case for adolescent vocation as an influence for family joy is much easier. Teens bring life, hope, and energy to the household. They lift spirits and tell jokes. They remind parents that they were once immature too, but lived through it. They make us laugh.

Without using the word *vocation*, Luther in the Table of Duties from the Small Catechism describes the vocations housed within the home. Each vocation is supported by a Bible passage. To parents, he quotes Ephesians 6:4: "Fathers, do not provoke your children to anger, but bring them up in the discipline and instruction of the Lord." To children, he cites the words just prior to those above. "Children, obey your parents in the Lord, for this is right. 'Honor your father and mother' (this is the first commandment with a promise), that it may go well with you and that you may live long in the land'" (vv. 1–3). But to those under the heading "Young Persons in General," he draws on 1 Peter 5:5–6.

> Likewise, you who are younger, be subject to the elders.
> Clothe yourselves, all of you, with humility toward one
> another, for "God opposes the proud but gives grace to the
> humble." Humble yourselves, therefore, under the mighty
> hand of God so that at the proper time He may exalt you.

God's wisdom is here for the taking. Teens who learn that they are masks of God within their homes for the benefit of parents and siblings don't become proud. They become humble—surprised by the depth of meaning and purpose they have in their own home.

Couldn't this be a way of understanding the good relationships that parents and teens enjoy? Couldn't it also be a way of restoring relationships that have deteriorated? Vocation certainly doesn't allow for God to remain on the outside of family relationships. No, He's right there in the middle, working within each of the members for the benefit of the others. When we recognize and admit that presence, we are all humbled; we stop accusing the others of not cooperating and start asking ourselves how we might "cooperate" with God. It's a start!

## The Mission of God

Emily has taken over complete control as we walk down the sidewalk in Stevens Point, Wisconsin, on a gorgeous summer evening. Unphased by the fact that she's a sophomore in high school who is teamed up with a pastor—a professor, no less—she gives me the pencil and clipboard that Ongoing Ambassadors For Christ (OAFC) uses on calls so I can record while she makes the visits.

On such a beautiful evening, many people aren't home, but those who are cautiously open their doors when Emily knocks. She introduces us and asks permission to take the survey. Her winsome personality soon disarms the hosts, and soon they are freely chatting with her. By the end, she asks the eternity questions and shares her hope in Christ. While we walk along the sidewalk, a woman comes up from behind and asks who we are. She tells us we knocked on her door three houses back, but she couldn't get there in time to answer. Emily tells her who we are and what we are doing. She explains that we are from the Lutheran church and are canvassing the area. "Oh, I belong to that church," the woman tells us. "I'm so glad you are here. I heard that we are hosting a group of youth. How many of you are there?" "About a hundred and seventy-five," Emily answers. "Is this gentleman training you?" the woman asks, nodding toward me. "No, she's training me," I respond, and we continue with the visit leading up to mutual confessions of faith in Jesus Christ.

Though I had been on many OAFC weekends and had led many visits, Emily was training me. She was training me to appreciate the vocation God has given youth to share their faith, which they do in both formal and informal ways. Youth are not excluded from the calling to witness their faith by word and deed in the world. Youth participate in the mission of God, and it is part of the vocation of being a teen. Many, many times I have been blessed by the testimony of faith given by an adolescent who, just like Emily, has not only confidence but also boldness in sharing what is most important to her.

The connection to mission established by the doctrine of vocation for adolescents brings to the forefront the special gifts teens have. When Paul wrote to Timothy, "Let no one despise you for your youth, but set the believers an example in speech, in conduct, in love, in faith, in purity" (1 Timothy 4:12), he wasn't communicating with an adolescent. Timothy would have had a few more years of maturity by the time he was leading a congregation. Nevertheless, the comment still holds true. We do a disservice to teens if we fail to recognize their role in taking the Gospel to our culture and into the future. We should not despise their efforts nor hide from them their opportunities.

In youth ministry, therefore, we need to impress on the youth in our care the challenge that belongs to them. Since youth have a vocation as teens within the family, it comes as no surprise to us that youth have a vocation within the family of God. We need to let youth know that they matter to the Church. They need to know that their participation in worship is inspirational for the rest of the congregation who witness the faith being passed on to the next generation. They need to know they can make a difference in their church and in the world. They need to be taught to ask themselves not "What would Jesus do?" as if we can match the work of Christ, but "What would Jesus have me be?"

While they mull that question over in their minds and search for their place in the Church and in the world, we as the older generation can help them to see themselves as masks of God not only for physical needs of people, but also for spiritual needs. But teens will need our assistance. Our ministry to teens is one of guidance, to be sure, but guidance seasoned by encouragement.

The Gospel is an amazing, miraculous belief. There is wonder in our hearts and minds when we realize the sheer audacity of believing that the Creator of the universe and everything in it pays any attention to us at all! There is delight that we share in knowing that God has determined our significance to be so great that His love gives us His own Son to be our Savior. We can prompt our youth, encouraging them to brainstorm the possibilities of what God could do through them. Perhaps the best descriptor for joining wonder and delight with the love of God is the word *vision*. Teens can gain a vision for how privileged they really are, which leads them to wonder what God might want to accomplish through them.

Do you recall the issue with which this chapter began? Will the next generation want to be called "Christian"? Teens that have been taught the truth about vocation will recognize the significant role they have to play and will mature with a sense, not of foreboding, but of anticipation, looking forward to the challenges of faith and the victories of faith that lie before them.

## To Be Christian Youth

Who, what, and why are the interrogative pronouns that are driving this chapter because the answers to those questions reveal our personal beliefs at the most basic level. *Who* are we, after all? God reveals in His Word that we are His creation, but fallen in sin—yet by His action of reclaiming us we are once again His children, embroiled in a bifurcated existence as saints and sinners, surprised by how good we are and by how bad we can be to ourselves and to each other. Teens understand this mystery better than we might expect. Let's talk with them about it.

*What* is God? What is God like, and in what ways can we depend on Him? God takes care in His Word not to reveal too much about Himself other than to assure us over and over again that we need not fear; He is beside us—no matter how empty that space may seem to our rational senses. We learn that God is all powerful yet restrained, a God whose love is jealous yet gentle—He will not against our will force His affection on us. And so He is a hidden God, full of surprise, because we find Him in the places where we least expect: in our pain, in our disappointments, in our crosses. Adolescents comprehend this mystery better than we give them credit for. Let's talk with them about it.

*Why* are we here? Is there purpose and reason that we should be? Or is everything pointless? We learn from God's Word that we have been created for relationships, and those relationships have a purpose. There is a calling toward which we are drawn, and through that calling we will be the hands of God for family, neighbor, and stranger, providing for them the blessings that God intends. Adolescents are looking for their purpose, their calling. There are so many possibilities to consider, so many means of service to discover. Let's talk about it with them.

To assist us in talking about it, I am suggesting a new term to describe how Lutheran theology informs youth ministry through these three doctrines. I am calling it "vocational catechesis."[31] What would the effect of vocational catechesis be in lives of Christian teens? To describe it, I'm going to borrow an image used by N. T. Wright that draws on Shakespeare.

> Suppose there exists a Shakespeare play, most of whose
> fifth act has been lost. The first four acts provide, let us
> suppose, such a remarkable wealth of characterization, such a

---

31 A quick Internet search reveals that "vocational catechesis" is a term used in the Roman Catholic Church to refer to a program guiding members toward holy orders. Though the term is used in this other context, I don't think that ought to prevent its application here. See "Awakening Vocations," http://www.awakeningvocations.com/awakeningvocations.html (accessed July 29, 2009).

crescendo of excitement within the plot, that it is generally
agreed that the play ought to be staged. Nevertheless, it is
felt inappropriate actually to write a fifth act once and for
all: it would freeze the play into one form, and commit
Shakespeare as it were to being prospectively responsible for
a work not in fact his own. Better, it might be felt, to give
the key parts to highly trained, sensitive and experienced
Shakespearian actors, who would immerse themselves in the
first four acts, and in the language and culture of Shakespeare
and his time, *and who would then be told to work out a fifth act for
themselves* [italics in original].[32]

Our youth are like the Shakespearean actors. They need to learn
the play and learn it well. So much of it has already been written;
the first act involves a fall; the second a chosen people; the third, a
promised Savior; and the fourth, the Savior's Bride. But the fifth act
hasn't been written. The fifth act is their lives in Jesus Christ, which
are being lived now and into the future. There is a definite trajectory
to this play. All the previous acts lead up to the present. Vocational
catechesis emphasizes that although the fifth act has already begun,
drama coaches are in the wings ready to help young actors live out
Paul's advice.

Therefore, my beloved, as you have always obeyed, so now,
not only as in my presence but much more in my absence,
work out your own salvation with fear and trembling, for it
is God who works in you, both to will and to work for His
good pleasure. (Philippians 2:12–13)

The effect of vocational catechesis is to know oneself well; and
though the journey toward self-knowledge lasts throughout one's life,
self-knowledge has a beginning. That starting point is the interaction
of First Article gifts of social, cognitive, intellectual, and physical
development creating the self-aware individual—usually demonstrated
by sudden and embarrassing self-consciousness. In the awkwardness of
those years, the Third Article gift of God's Word begins to train us in
managing our dual nature of saint and sinner.

---

32 N. T. Wright, *The New Testament and the People of God* (Minneapolis: Fortress, 1992),
140.

The effect of vocational catechesis is also to know God well, to know God's purpose and intention through the working of Law and Gospel, and to trust God's silence when He seems distant, knowing that the only time God was silent was at the cross. First Article circumstances surround the teen with possibilities and temptations; but to know God well results in being in God's presence, receiving frequently and relying heavily on the Third Article Means of Grace.

The effect of vocational catechesis is to hear God's call in one's life. This doesn't mean knowing with precision the plans God has for us— no one can know that, though we do know the plans are nothing to fear (Jeremiah 29:11). No, the effect is confidence that there is purpose and meaning in the most ordinary and mundane. Jesus was a king, but He lived as a carpenter. Teens are daughters and sons of God through faith in Christ Jesus, though their vocation at present may involve cutting a lot of grass. God already is working through His will in the world through them at school, in the part-time job, in the family, and in His mission of reconciling the world to Himself through Jesus Christ.

The next generation of Christians will need to be more fully equipped with an understanding of who they are as sinners and saints, what God is like as He works in the world using the theology of the cross as His weapon of choice, and why they are here—their vocation as salt and light in the world. If our youth don't know who they are, won't they be at risk for the false personas of the world? If our youth don't know what God is like, won't they be in danger of thinking that the hidden God has abandoned them? If our youth don't know that they have a vocation—a calling filled with meaning and purpose— won't they be in jeopardy of offering up the one true faith as a sacrifice to the gods of mammon that surround them?

Eutychus identified himself with the followers of Jesus Christ. Whether or not he ever called himself a Christian we can't know, nor do we have a clue into what vocation Eutychus was led. One thing seems certain from our discussion of our culture and these three doctrines, however. The pagan world into which Eutychus was growing up isn't all that distant from the world in which our teens live.

# PART III

# Noticing Eutychus in Our Practice

We are all in our academic robes, as we ordinarily are for the end of the year commencement ceremony, but this is a graduation like none other Concordia University Wisconsin has ever held. The entire faculty is in a narrow hallway on folding chairs facing each other. We have been here for nearly two hours after passing through the metal detectors, where I lost my nail clippers. The signal is finally given, and we stand and march into the packed field house, recently air-conditioned for this event. As we process, they watch us closely while we take our seats to the right of the stage.

Never have I seen such intensity on human faces. They are stationed at the four corners of the stage with one standing front and center. They are positioned at the top of the bleachers. Less noticeable are the ones seated in the crowd. They watch everything.

Anticipation mounts. Parents and graduates are already tiring, having sat for well over an hour on bleachers and folding chairs. We all wait, and then it happens. The strains of "Hail to the Chief" are heard, and the platform party emerges from the door behind us, passing through the narrow aisle that divides the faculty, and then I see him— the president of the United States. I am only five feet away as he passes by, the most powerful and the most criticized man on earth. I stare at him.

All eyes are on him—except their eyes. They don't look at the president. They look at everybody else. Nothing escapes their scrutiny. No raised eyebrow, no tilt of a head, no sudden movement of an arm is missed. If they were intense before his entrance, their concentration has now become hair-trigger sharp. Eyes always moving, they are constantly in communication with one another through the hidden mikes and spiraling corded earpieces emerging from the back of their collars. They are in full readiness mode, prepared at any moment to take a bullet to save the life of the man at the podium. Nothing escapes their notice.

The speech is delivered, the audience applauds, and the president leaves the stage. He passes down the narrow aisle once more, shaking a few hands, and is gone. I look back at the stage. They've disappeared! Every last one of them is gone.

Have you ever wondered what kind of training regimen is required for Secret Service agents? Whatever education is mandated, its effect prepares persons whose ability to be aware, attentive, and alert is unsurpassed. Nothing escapes their notice. They see everything.

We aren't going to see everything in youth ministry; frankly, we probably don't want to. But this question ought to be asked: "What kind of training regimen do we need so that we are aware, attentive, and alert to the circumstances, opportunities, and ministry moments we will encounter in youth ministry?" How shall we notice Eutychus in our practice? And how will our Lutheran theology help us in the process?

First, we can use our trinitarian framework in order to fix in our minds the multiple factors involved in youth ministry. As we serve, we can understand what we observe in terms of gifts from above and gifts from below and then identify what kind of gift from above or below we are working with. Following this route leads us to ask a series of theologically derived questions about the event, lesson, or situation in which we are involved. In this way, we equip ourselves for the ministry moment. We will study these questions in our next chapter.

Second, and no less important, we can grow in our observational skills. Let's think of ourselves as God's secret service, keeping our eyes open to anything threatening the spiritual or physical well-being of our youth. Remember the threats to Eutychus? He's young, bored, at risk, and nobody notices. So let's take a deeper look at what it means to be young in our culture today. Let's explore boredom—not just any boredom, but boredom with the Church. And then let's investigate the ways in which young people place ... themselves at risk.

We do this so that we notice.

# CHAPTER 9

# The Ministry Moment

A re we ever really ready for the ministry moment, that place and time when the First Article gifts and the Third Article gifts meet in a situation of real life that applies to a difficult situation the accomplishments of Jesus Christ as described in the Second Article?

I am reading about the tragedy in the paper as I eat breakfast on a humid summer morning. A teenage girl out with a church youth group at a Christian music festival was on a carnival ride. She wasn't strapped in properly as the swinging chairs rose into the air and spread out as centrifugal force took hold. She fell from the chair, crashed to the earth, and died within minutes. I hate reading articles like this, and though I know I'll be thinking about the event the whole day, I nevertheless read on. The article shares more details such as the church of the youth group, and I realize I know the church. The story is told of how the girl had texted her youth leader, asking her to come over and watch her on the ride. The youth leader was on her way to the ride when the accident happened. She didn't see the fall, but she saw the commotion immediately after. I look more closely at the name of the youth leader. I know that name. Why do I know that name? After a moment, I remember. She's registered for REL 227 Youth Ministry I in the fall semester. She will be in my class.

Now the article really has my attention. This young woman, serving her congregation as a youth leader, is where none of us ever want to be. She's in the middle of a crisis, a real crisis: requiring quick action, personal ministry, and service to multiple persons all at once, while at the same time holding her own emotions of shock and grief at bay—at least for the moment.

Before the semester begins, the youth leader asks to meet with me and another one of her professors. She wants to tell us what happened and what continues to happen for the family, for the church, and for herself. Showing maturity far beyond her years, she tells us about the prayer gathering immediately after the accident, the response of the family who weren't members of the church but had allowed their daughter to participate, the care provided to the family, the spontaneous gathering of youth and adults at the church, the service held at the church, the counselors who came to spend time with the youth and who would continue to do so for several more months, the surge in attendance at youth meetings, and the counselor to whom she goes for help in her grief and loss.

The other professor and I are humbled by her story. We hurt for her, but at the same time we see something of the strength that she has. She's been where none of us ever want to be, yet those in service to the Lord Jesus will find themselves called to be present at just such times and places. To our amazement in ministry moments, we find ourselves equipped to serve. So much that she did at the scene, in the days that followed, and in the months since have been the right things to do, including finding ways to help the youth group honor the memory of their friend.

When Jesus promises the disciples that they need not worry about what to say when brought before the rulers and authorities because the Holy Spirit would give them the words to speak (Matthew 10:19–20; Mark 13:11; Luke 12:11–12), the situation is considerably different from the circumstances of the youth leader. Yet at a deeper level, they are the same; under conditions of great stress and pressure, a confession of faith must be made, and the Holy Spirit provides the words. Inevitably there comes a time when volunteers and professional church workers experience the Holy Spirit at work in just this way.

Does that mean we don't need to learn Scripture passages, study issues of human development, or learn counseling skills as we have opportunity? Won't we just automatically have the words to speak? The answer to that question is a resounding no! The promise of the Holy Spirit's presence with us at our time of need does not in the least relieve us of the responsibility to be well trained and well prepared. We abuse this promise if we use it to defend any tendencies toward laziness on our part.

If training on our part was unnecessary, then the three years Jesus spent with His disciples was a waste of time. He could just as well have zapped them with the Spirit and let them loose on the world. But He did not. He spent time with them alone, in small groups, and in large crowds. He taught them by word with moving parables, aphorisms, and sermons; He also taught them by example. He let them experience success (Luke 10:17–18) as well as failure (Mark 9:28–29). Though the disciples were often in the habit of missing the point (Matthew 17:4), they learned well enough so that at the right time the Holy Spirit could draw on their own memories in order to give them the very words of Jesus (John 14:26). Likewise, when the Holy Spirit came upon them in the upper room at Pentecost, miraculous ability with languages and courage never before witnessed were received by the disciples. Using those extra-special gifts, they drew on the training they had received at the feet of Jesus in order to give testimony to the life, death, and resurrection of Jesus Christ.

The point I'm making is simple. The youth leader dealing with a tragic death was given actions and words, but they didn't come out of thin air. The Holy Spirit was making use of the rich resources already present in her life of learning and love for the Lord Jesus. She already had the comforting message of Jesus. What she received from the Holy Spirit was the wisdom to know when and how to share it.

The answer, therefore, to the question with which this chapter began is a qualified yes! If we believe that out of our own resources we can be ready for the ministry moment, we will no doubt find ourselves sadly disappointed. On the other hand, we are most certainly ready for the ministry moment. We are ready on two fronts: we are prepared through the training we have received for ministry, and we are made ready through the guidance we are given through the Means of Grace. It is to our own preparation for ministry that we now turn our attention, and to do so we will recall the component parts of the gifts from above and the gifts from below.

# Matching the Triangles

The ministry moment brings together all of our training and gifted ability with the life experience of the person to whom we minister. The ministry moment connects the two triangles we observed in chapter 5, thereby initiating a potentially powerful interaction. Let's examine the relationship between the gifts from above and the gifts from below as they meet in the ministry moment, the place where practical theology happens.

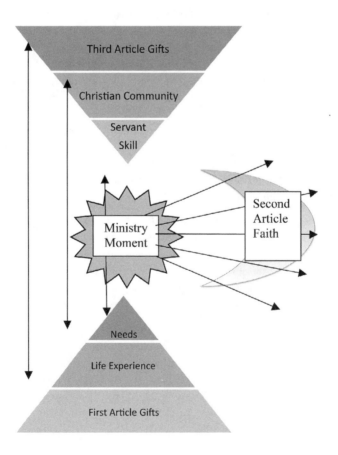

First, notice that each component part of the two triangles has a special connection to its counterpart. As was mentioned earlier, God is the giver of the First Article gifts through creation and the giver of the Third Article gifts through the work of the Holy Spirit. There is nothing we have that we have not received (1 Corinthians 4:7). The connection is the giver, the Trinity. When we receive these gifts, we comprehend the Third Article gifts through our First Article gifts. Our "reason and all our senses" allow us to recognize the spiritual gifts that we receive, without which we would be unaware of God's work on our behalf.

The second layer of our triangles is also not without connectivity. Christian communities of which teens are a part are all different, a fact hinted at by the differences in the letters Paul wrote to congregations and by the unique circumstances of each of the seven churches to which John wrote in Revelation. In my experience, I have yet to come across two identical congregations. They are as unique as the fingerprints on your hand. If the subject under discussion is youth ministry, the unique qualities of each congregation become even more pronounced. How many youth does the congregation have? To what degree is the congregation committed to youth ministry? What resources of time, staff, money, and space are dedicated to youth ministry? What is the history of youth ministry within this fellowship, and to what degree has that background enhanced or inhibited the spiritual growth of the teens now in the church? The gift of the congregation to teens is the gift of a community faith environment in which to grow. The characteristics of the environment will fall anywhere along a broad spectrum of possibilities.

If the environment provided by the congregation was the only variable involved in the spiritual growth and development of teens, then the responsibility for the teen outcomes would rest squarely on the congregation and its leaders. Of course, the influence of the congregation on the lives of teens compared to the teens' life experiences is not balanced, but is heavily weighted on the side of adolescent life experiences. Those life experiences include the influences for good or ill from family, community, school, media, and culture—the gifts of God from below. We might be tempted to assume that time is the key variable, with the teens most involved in our youth ministry receiving the greater influence. We must resist that assumption, for although this might be true in many cases, the glimpse into an alternative life of faith witnessed by the casual participant from an uncommitted family may prove in the long run to be just as formational as the consistent participation by the youth group's inner core.

The points of our equilateral triangles meet through the interaction of the servant's skill and the teens' needs. We might say this interface is the moment of truth for youth leaders as their gifts, knowledge, and preparation come into direct alignment with the felt, expressed, comparative, and normative needs of adolescents. But care needs to be taken to sort out which needs the youth leader is gifted to fulfill. We study adolescent psychology and adolescent culture in order to be prepared, but we are not psychologists or sociologists. Our vocation is to be the Gospel presence, and not just presence but also articulation of the love of God in Jesus Christ for teens in the ministry moment. Therefore, as significant and important as teens' felt, expressed and comparative needs are, the needs don't control the moment. We will be aware of those needs, identify the implications for the individual and for the group created by those needs, and assess our own capacity to meet those needs, but we will remember that our calling in ministry has more to do with the normative needs. What do the teens need to know, understand, and believe as a result of this lesson, event, or life experience that they may not have known, understood, and believed beforehand? Normative needs aren't always comfortable, but they are always necessary or they wouldn't be normative.

Notice already that even before I get to where I'm planning to apply our Lutheran theological distinctiveness into the ministry moment, I already have started doing so. That's the power of our theological underpinnings and commitments when we are aware of them. In the previous paragraph, I've assumed that when I suggest we are the Gospel presence in the ministry moment, as Lutherans we realize that Gospel presence may actually include a rather sharp rebuke from the Law.[1]

Ministry moments may require that teens feel the sharp accusations of the Law that will awaken the conscience and lead to repentance and forgiveness. We can't avoid involvement in rightly dividing the Word of

---

1 The term "Gospel" is being used in the "broad sense" here, that of God's entire message in the Bible. By contrast, there is a "narrow sense" of the Gospel when it refers only to the Good News of salvation through the life, death, and resurrection of Jesus Christ. It is the narrow sense of the Gospel that finds its opposite in the demands of the Law.

God and assisting teens to address their dual natures of saint and sinner in a manner consistent with their Christian faith. Likewise, being the Gospel presence and the persons to articulate that Gospel allows us to help hurting teens through difficult situations by reminding them of God's presence, even when teens feel His absence most keenly. Do you see where this places us in our practice of theology? We are bringing teens out of a theology of glory and into the theology of the cross. The next step is to ask teens to consider not only how others are serving them in the situation, but also how God might use them to help and serve others. Situations that previously seemed meaningless take on genuine significance when viewed through the doctrine of vocation.

## Ministry Moment Foci

Bringing the triangles of gifts from above and gifts from below into relationship for ministry leads inevitably into the development of a comprehensive approach to youth ministry and does so in a threefold manner.

When we consider the work of God in creation (including information from developmental adolescent psychology, sociology, and even the most recent research into neurological brain development) and connect this information with a confessional commitment to the work of God in salvation as the Holy Spirit works through the Means of Grace to bring, nurture, and sustain faith in the heart and mind, we have the makings of a holistic approach within a trinitarian framework.

When we consider the Christian community—the Bride of Christ—having all its glory through worship and the preaching of the Gospel as well as all its flaws through the everyday interaction of saints/sinners in the administering and receiving of Christian education and pastoral care and connect this community with the formative experiences adolescents bring to the community by virtue of their family life, school environment, peer influences, and media-formed worldview, we have the foundation from which a comprehensive understanding of adolescence emerges.

And finally, as I continue to construct incredibly long sentences, when we evaluate our own roles as servants called to bring the gifts from above as they have been mediated to us through our own training, life experience, and spiritual maturity and connect those gifts to real flesh-and-blood teens who have tremendous needs—some of which they are aware and many of which they are not—and who also have gifts to offer the community, we have the core components of a mentoring relationship.

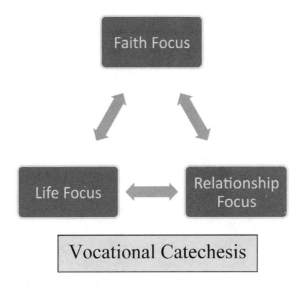

These three foci—faith, life, and relationship—taken together form what I consider a theoretical foundation for vocational catechesis. The gifts from above and the gifts from below are accounted for. When we put them all together, we have a way to describe the variables of a growing commitment in faith to Jesus Christ. We have a way of looking at youth ministry that prepares us for the ministry moments we encounter.

## Servant Limits

Our actions as leaders in the ministry moment are informed, guided, and driven by our theological presuppositions. Lutheran theological presuppositions provide a clear framework from which to serve faithfully, knowledgeably, and effectively. But there are limits, and we had better take them into account from the beginning.

What do I mean by limits? We are limited by *not being the Holy Spirit*. We can't force; we can only exercise the calling to which we are called and then pray that the Lord's will be done. I point this out because many of us who are volunteers or full-time church workers are the type of people who take responsibility; and that is a good thing. But it is not a good thing if we take responsibility, for outcomes outside of our control. We present the Gospel; the Holy Spirit leads to faith. We suggest appropriate Christian behaviors; the saint/sinners in front of us choose to do with our suggestions as they will.

We are responsible for a lot. If we lead a mission trip, then we take care that all the liability issues have been accounted for and the covenants signed by youth and parents are all clearly understood. If we are engaged in fund-raising, we work with our youth treasurer and the church treasurer to monitor how the funds are gathered and disbursed. If we lead the evening Bible study, we prepare the study or review the prepared curriculum and send it through our Lutheran filters to make sure we aren't somehow misrepresenting the faith we confess.

There is also a whole lot for which we are not responsible. For our own health and well-being in service to Jesus Christ, we need to be able to distinguish the one from the other. Let's say a youth leader has been very faithful in sharing what a precious gift life is, whether talking about beginning of life or end of life scenarios. The leader's teens have studied both Jeremiah 1:5 ("Before I formed you in the womb I knew you, and before you were born I consecrated you; I appointed you a prophet to the nations") and Isaiah 46:4 ("Even to your old age I am He, and to gray hairs I will carry you. I have made, and I will bear; I will carry and will save"). Because the youth leader is theologically astute, the leader isn't surprised to find herself guiding a pregnant teen away from an abortion, nor will she be shocked when she finds herself counseling a teen who already made the trip to the reproductive "health" clinic. Both ministry moments involve beliefs about us, about God, and about how Christians live as saints and sinners. Because the youth leader is grounded in her theology, she recognizes that the life-affirming choice made by the one teen isn't to the leader's credit, nor is the life-denying choice made by the other teen the leader's fault.

The point I'm making is pretty obvious, but since I've failed to account for it so often in my own ministry, I feel compelled to point it out. Our concern as the skilled servants in the ministry moment is that we are doing what we have been called to do faithfully (not perfectly, which is beyond us, but faithfully!) and then leave the outcome to God. To some degree, you can see, this tests our own faith in God's presence, because the times when the outcome isn't to our liking are much too frequent, at least to my liking.

What outcomes do we want? In our vocation—God working through us for the benefit of teens—we want to see faith grow and trust solidify. We want to see a growing recognition in teens of the joy of being a child of God. We look for ways in which they reflect the freedom of the Gospel in their lives, knowing they have been saved by grace. And we want them to know that when they sin,[2] no matter what it might be, Jesus will not abandon them. We want them to know and trust the Bible when John writes, "My little children, I am writing these things to you so that you may not sin. But if anyone does sin, we have an advocate with the Father, Jesus Christ the righteous" (1 John 2:1).

## Practical Theology

Thinking even more deeply about the ministry moments that we encounter in service to the Lord Jesus Christ, I realize that we can divide them into two types: planned ministry moments and spontaneous ministry moments, the ones we are ready for and the ones that we are not.

## Planned Ministry Moments

It takes no time at all for us to learn in ministry that even the ministry moments for which we plan will contain spontaneous, serendipitous, and downright surprising elements. Nevertheless, we are not thereby absolved from preparation and planning. Planned ministry moments include Sunday morning Bible classes, activity nights, recurring athletic competition, yearly events that the congregation expects of the youth (e.g., Easter breakfast), fun trips, mission trips, servant event trips, and so forth. I guess you can say it includes

---

2 Notice I didn't write "if they sin." We all remain saints and sinners in this life. As soon as I stop having a problem with sin, I'll let you know. No, come to think of it, you'll find out by reading my obituary in *The Lutheran Witness*.

anything for which you, along with the youth leadership team, have to prepare.

Planned ministry moments involving instruction are natural settings for vocational catechesis—teaching that brings Lutheran theology into play in students' lives through an emphasis on who we are, who God is, and what God is calling us do. I suggest that in our preparation, we raise up a series of questions to ask ourselves about the Bible accounts we are using, the curriculum pieces we are appropriating, and the experiential activities we are incorporating. We have a theological framework that is sound. Let's use it and make sure that in our vocational catechesis we leave by the wayside no opportunity to emphasize our theology. Regarding any lesson or activity we are planning, we can ask the following questions:

- Are any gifts from below highlighted?
  - ❏ Adolescent development
  - ❏ Cultural awareness
  - ❏ Family issues

- Are any gifts from above highlighted?
  - ❏ Means of Grace
  - ❏ Community of faith
  - ❏ Leader skills

- How is the Law expressed?
  - ❏ As hammer
  - ❏ As magnifying glass

- How is the Gospel delivered?[3]
  - ❏ As Christ our substitute
  - ❏ As Christ the victor

- Are youth lifted up by God's grace?
  - ❏ Guided by the authoritative Word
  - ❏ The Sacraments, where Christ and forgiveness are promised

- Are youth directed to their true condition?
  - ❏ As sinners struggling against spiritual enemies
  - ❏ As saints washed in the blood of the Lamb

---

3 In this framework, the Gospel in the narrow sense is the avenue through which the central doctrine of the Christian faith, justification by grace through faith, is addressed.

- Is the hiddenness of God acknowledged?
    - ❏ Through power made known in weakness
    - ❏ By relying on the centrality of the cross

- Are youth challenged in their vocation?
    - ❏ As masks of God serving the neighbor
    - ❏ As participants in the mission of God

These eight questions may seem an overwhelming burden to be carrying around. How can I keep track of all this theological baggage, while at the same time being present with something meaningful for my youth group? And besides, one might say, I'm just leading a Sunday morning Bible class. Isn't this overkill?

Let me respond in two ways. First, using these questions as a theological filter will help you gain confidence that your youth ministry is genuinely Lutheran. The questions are well worth the effort on that account alone. Even if the event is a Sunday morning Bible class, the Sunday morning Bible class is a significant teaching moment. Given the frequency with which curricula from non-Lutheran sources are used, the need for careful review is all the greater.

Second, keep in mind that no single event or activity is going to touch all of these questions! Running through the checklist may reveal only one or two that seem to have a direct application. But now, having taken the time to think in a theological manner about the event, your own role in leading or monitoring a discussion, giving direct instruction, or guiding an experiential activity is more focused. You are less likely to be distracted or drawn away from your objectives. In addition, you will be able to ask if the activity has any underlying message, a hidden curriculum that in the long run undermines a full understanding of God's grace in Jesus Christ. For example, a lesson on faith may lead the youth to trust in their faith as the object on which they are focused, rather than seeing their faith as the connection to the promises of God that cannot fail. The former turns our eyes inward to ourselves, while the latter focuses our eyes on the cross of Christ.[4]

---

4 See chapter 7's discussion on Baptism and how Lutherans answer the question "How do I know that I'm saved?"

# Spontaneous Ministry Moments

Spontaneous ministry moments by definition happen anytime and anywhere. Frequently, they happen within the planned ministry moment, sometimes because the planning has failed, but sometimes because the planning has succeeded beyond our expectations—as when the discussion goes deeper than we expected. Spontaneous ministry moments create a third reason for engraving our template set of questions into our minds. Familiarity with viewing our experiences through the filter of these doctrinal questions creates over time a Lutheran approach not just to lessons or events, but to ministry in all its many manifestations. We then have a Lutheran perspective, a Lutheran worldview if you will, that is not only accessible when we are preparing lessons or planning events, but is our default response when the unexpected, be it serendipitous or tragic, happens.

Therefore, in order to take this discussion out of abstract speculation and place it firmly into concrete experience, let's ask some practical theological questions. What are the spiritual needs of a youth group that's just been hit with a tragedy? What servant skills are required to meet those needs? What resources do the youth themselves bring to serve each other?

I return to my youth ministry student who was the leader of the group that experienced the death of a member while on an outing. If I were in that situation, what would I be feeling, thinking, and doing? How would I respond as a Lutheran Christian youth leader?

First, I am feeling shock; I am numb. But I soon let that pass as I realize the moment that I'm in and my responsibility to minister to my group. My template kicks in, and I realize that the magnifying glass of the Law is frying us all because death has raised its terrifying visage in shocking display against our friend. We have just had our faces shoved into our true condition as saint/sinners struggling against sin, death, and the devil, and at this moment the devil wants us to despair. God, it seems, has turned His face away from us and allowed this terrible thing to happen. Yet I know that though He seems hidden, He's still present, and rather than blame God, faith asserts that now is the time to call on God and remember the cross of Jesus Christ. I must rely on the gifts from above, the Holy Spirit's promise to give words to speak, because my own gifts from below will be inadequate to deal with the grief and pain that my youth group and I feel. While all this is racing in my mind, my emotions begin to serve in their own way, because gathered in pairs and small groups, we are crying, weeping with those who weep (Romans 12:15).

As the initial shock wears off, many begin to ask, "Why did this happen?" I know we don't have an answer to this question, and any answer we try to give will be hollow, heartless, and false. So I do my best to shift the question from "Why?" to "Who?" Who is with us now to comfort us? Of course the answer is Jesus, who has sent His Spirit among us to remind us of His presence with us and of His promises to our friend. My resource isn't my own shallow words, but words that have authority, words from the Bible. So I'm in the Psalms; John 14; and 1 Corinthians. But I'm also praying, and though the prayers sound repetitive because I continue to pray for the same things—peace, understanding, comfort, help with all the grief—I am also praying that God would bind us together in love and help us to hold on to one another.

While engaged in serving others, I realize I also will need to be served. So I ask others to pray for me and for the group. The adrenaline rush that has helped me serve effectively wears off, and I return to the shock and numb feelings. This will be a pattern for some time to come, but I'm not surprised by it. I will need a counselor to talk to; especially after listening to our youth tell their stories of where they were when it happened, what it felt like then, and how they feel now; especially after weeping with them; especially after sharing the hope in Christ— the Victor over death, over and over again.

This description omits so many details that happen in an emergency, such as contacting and speaking with rescue workers, EMTs, parents, park personnel, reporters, and other media. This description doesn't address the attacks of false guilt that Satan will marshal against me, as if somehow it was my fault: "If only we hadn't come to this event . . ." Neither is there an acknowledgment that the grieving will go on for months, that there will be a vocation for each member of the group to comfort and encourage one another, and that sooner or later the group will need to find a way to memorialize the event, honor their friend, and move on. But this internal dialogue does illustrate how our theology informs our interpretation of the event and the actions that follow. It is a ministry moment we had not planned and would never want, but for which we are nevertheless prepared.

When we pull back and consider the less emotionally draining, the less dramatic-planned ministry moments, we find ourselves almost in an academic environment in which we can identify objectives, work with a theme, and run our study past the vocational catechesis checklist as we determine the steps we will take. Then again, here I'm assuming that we have time for leisurely consideration of our educational objectives and our learning strategies. As you well know, that kind of time is rarely available. Because we so often function on the fly even in our planned ministry moments, having a Lutheran default mode by which to operate is even more significant. Nevertheless, should you have time, I've provided a vocational-catechetical-oriented planning template at the end of this chapter.

## Summary

Is Paul operating on a default mode when he descends the stairs to street level and kneels beside the crumpled body of Eutychus? I'm uncomfortable calling it a default mode for Paul because that implies that there are other modes that he could choose to deal with the tragedy. But for Paul, there is no other mode of operation. He recognizes the severity of the situation, realizes the trauma the crowd is experiencing, and he prays. *He prays!* He puts himself, the congregation, and Eutychus in the Lord's hands, and the Lord, whose resurrection is the message that had brought them all together that evening, raises the teen from death.

In this chapter I have, to some degree, taken what is simple and made it complex. Paul reminds us that the complex vocation to which we are called is actually quite simple. We prepare according to our gifts, we pray, and then we serve.

# MINISTRY MOMENT TEMPLATE

**Type of Activity**

**Theme**

**Objectives:** By the end of this activity the youth will be able to . . .

**Scripture**

## Vocational Catechesis Checklist

❏ Gifts from Below   ❏ Means of Grace   ❏ Gifts from Above
❏ Saint/Sinner      ❏ Law              ❏ Cross
❏ Gospel            ❏ Vocation

## Introductory Activity

## Main Points

1.

2.

3.

## Summary

## Worship Suggestions

Songs and Hymns

Prayers

**CHAPTER 10**

# Noticing the Young

The twelve-hundred-seat-capacity Chapel of St. Timothy and St. Titus on the campus of Concordia Seminary in St. Louis was packed on that spring day in 2000. Though I've attended the funerals of both a sitting and an emeritus president of The Lutheran Church—Missouri Synod in the same sanctuary, the service on this day was by far the largest funeral I have ever attended. The chorus of Lutheran High School South was seated in the south transept, while the school band was arranged in the north transept. Hundreds of teenagers filled the pews, along with parents of high school students, teachers, and not a few notable members of the larger community. The chorus sang magnificently, the band played with energy combined with solemnity, the readers held forth on the hope of the resurrection, and the preacher preached Christ crucified. The service was a life-in-Jesus-Christ-affirming celebration giving thanks to God for a life of meaningful service.

So whose funeral service was this? Was it for the principal of the school, suddenly taken by a heart attack; a beloved teacher, cut down in her prime by disease; or a student killed in a tragic auto accident? No, it was none of the above. This funeral was for a single man, a lawyer in his early sixties who happened to have contracted pancreatic cancer. What had he done to gain such attention at his passing? He noticed teens.

We have already commented on the incident with Eutychus and how the simple act of noticing the young person in the window could have prevented the whole traumatic episode. In what ways do we notice the young? The funeral was for a man, Mr. Emde, who had a gift for noticing teens. He was a supporter of the high school, attended as many events as he could, took students to professional sporting events, and got to know students well enough to give them guidance and advice.[1] His funeral was a testimony to the impact he had not only on the students but also on their families and on the entire school. Yet what he did was so very, very simple. He noticed teens.

## Culture Notices the Young

The way that our culture notices the young is not helpful. That is the thesis of a book written by Alex and Brett Harris, twin brothers from Oregon who were eighteen in 2008 when they wrote the book. Somewhere in their education, they discovered that the time of life classified as "adolescence" is a rather recent phenomenon, beginning really no more than one hundred years or so ago. The time between childhood and adulthood was rather short—nearly nonexistent—in earlier generations. As soon as one was physically able to assume adult responsibilities, one was given adult responsibilities. As examples, they cite the fact that George Washington was already in charge of a surveying team and David Farragut was already in command of a ship while they were still in their teens. The Harris brothers build a case that in prior generations, teens were both producers and consumers within society. But in the late nineteenth and early twentieth centuries, that changed. "By completely removing children from the workplace and mandating school attendance through high school, teens' once

---

1 In contemporary culture, an older man hanging around a high school and spending time with kids raises suspicion. Churches and schools have the responsibility to conduct background checks and take other measures to ensure the safety of children and adolescents. Adults who develop genuine mentoring relationships with teens will have no objections to background checks because they realize these precautions also protect them in their role in guiding teens.

established role as key producers and contributors came to an end. Suddenly their role was almost exclusively that of consumers."[2] With no pressing need to develop the skills necessary to enter the adult world, teens naturally put off preparing themselves for the adult world. Instead, expectations of teens by society and by themselves plummeted, with teen years becoming a wasted time of partying. Rather than a time of preparation for the adult world, adolescence became a time to avoid the adult world.

The Harris' analysis of teen life seems harsh, but it matches the attitudes of society toward teens. Alex and Brett tried an experiment to validate their conclusions. They did a Google search, using "teens" and "expectations" as the search terms. "Here are some of the suggestions it gave us as we tried to Google *teens* and *expectations*:

- *teens and drugs*

- *teens and alcohol*

- *teens and smoking*

- *teens and drinking*

- *teens and marijuana*

- *teens and cell phones*"[3]

I'm surprised they didn't find *teens and sex*, but maybe they did but thought better of including it. Their point is simply this: society has low expectations of teens today. Society doesn't expect or demand excellence, and most often, it rewards mediocrity. This has also become the expectations of teens for themselves. The rest of their book is a call for teens to demand more from themselves and show the impressive things of which they are capable.

## The Church Notices Teens

Society, when it does notice teens, tends to notice the negatives associated with adolescence. How well is the Church doing in

---

2 Alex Harris and Brett Harris, *Do Hard Things: A Teenage Rebellion against Low Expectations* (Colorado Springs: Multnomah, 2008), 34.

3 Harris and Harris, 37.

noticing teens? Every month, the Department of Youth Ministry of The Lutheran Church—Missouri Synod sends out an e-mail bulletin. The June 2009 bulletin contained some information that I found disturbing. Here are the thoughts shared by Rev. Terry Dittmer.

> Sometimes I get the feeling that a lot of folks in the church think "Oh, it's only youth ministry" kind of like Jeremiah said, "I am only a youth." It's like they think as long as we have a youth gathering every three years, we're always going to have teenagers. Reality is that's just not true. In 1980 for the first national youth gathering, our pool of eligible youth in the LCMS was about 220,000 15–19 year olds. Thirty years later, for the 2010 gathering, we are looking at a pool of about 100,000 14–19 year olds, fewer than half of what we had in 1980. We've always done a good job taking care of the kids born to us. But, like all denominations, we are an aging church.[4]

There are far fewer teens among us than there used to be. We can speculate as to the causes. My guess is that it has to do with three variables: smaller families, backdoor losses, and lack of mission outreach. It's cold comfort that most denominations are suffering from the same ailment. Nonetheless, the implications for us are startling. The number of children enrolled in our Lutheran elementary schools remains constant, while the number of our own member children declines. Likewise, in the Concordia University System, we see fewer freshmen from the LCMS matriculating—and yet at the same time, the percentage of LCMS students choosing to attend a Concordia continues to rise. Perhaps our first response to these statistics is to realize what a precious gift and resource we have in our young people and commit ourselves seriously to noticing them!

Unfortunately, sometimes the Church has chosen to notice youth by segregating them into their own enclaves. It is one thing to notice youth by providing them with their own building, their own program, and their own "youth" pastor. It is quite another thing to notice them by being with them on a mission trip or standing beside them while reciting the Apostles' Creed.

---

4 Terry Dittmer, *Department of Youth Ministry E-Bulletin*, June 2009.

Two authors in particular have sounded the alarm over the challenge presented by these two paths of "noticification." Ivy Beckwith explains in no uncertain terms what is lost when young children are shuffled off to their own "children's church" while the adults in the sanctuary engage in real worship. "By excluding children from corporate worship, churches have shortchanged them, denying them a weekly opportunity to express their faith and care for their souls."[5] Children who are given their own "fun" time are cut away from the enculturation provided by the worship service. They do not see adults—their parents—engaged in worship. They do not learn the ropes of worship as the pattern alternates between the Ordinary and the Propers for the day. Of course they will object when at some arbitrary age they no longer are given their own fun time. The adult worship will be boring.

Mark DeVries takes up were Ivy Beckwith leaves off: the youth group years. DeVries uses the image developed by Stuart Cummings-Bond of a one-eared Mickey Mouse to describe his analysis of youth ministry that notices youth by removing them from the worshiping body of believers. If you see a diagram of this concept, you will be surprised by its simplicity. It is simply a large circle and a smaller circle touching at one point.[6] The smaller circle is the youth group that is so well provided for by the congregation that it has everything on its own—everything that is, except what teens really desire: significant mentoring relationships with responsible adults who are willing to lead them into the adult world. No one should be surprised at the drop off when students begin to grow out of youth church. Adult church is a foreign environment. It wasn't part of their lives before, so why should it become a part of their lives now? This is why DeVries calls these arrangements "orphaning structures." They create orphans by failing to connect the coming generation of youth with the generations above them, who can be so helpful in assisting the spiritual growth and maturation of youth.

To be fair, congregations that are large enough and well-staffed enough to create a one-eared Mickey Mouse generally have done so with the best of intentions, feeling that by providing these resources,

---

5 Ivy Beckwith, *Postmodern Children's Ministry: Ministry to Children in the 21st Century* (Grand Rapids: Zondervan, 2004), 142.

6 Mark DeVries, *Family-Based Youth Ministry* (Downers Grove: InterVarsity Press, 2004), 42.

they have given their youth every advantage. Unfortunately, without connecting those advantages to the previous generation and to the worship life of the entire Christian community, the advantages rapidly deteriorate into disadvantages. No wonder that when Chap Clark describes the feelings of abandonment that so many youth have, the Church comes under criticism as much as any other institution.[7] It may be that the congregation, unknown even to itself, has segregated the youth so that the adults don't have to mix and mingle with those loud, boisterous, and obnoxious young people, all in the name of effective ministry.

Since I'm on the theme of effective ministry, this is an appropriate time to mention that even if a congregation has a large staff and responsibilities for youth ministry and confirmation class have been given over to a DCE or lay minister, the pastor's role remains significant. The larger the congregation, the more difficult this becomes, but pastors are key ingredients in the congregation's recipe for noticing youth. For a teen to say "Pastor knows my name" may seem inconsequential; nevertheless, it is the place to begin. And when a teen can say "Pastor knows I'm on the volleyball team" or "Pastor asked me about the high school drama production," the teen knows his or her life is worth a slice of the pastor's time and attention. If one simple action can have such influence, how much more when the pastor is there with other staff members and volunteers at the car wash fund-raiser or the mission trip? The upshot of such behavior on pastor's part is that the teen, knowing that the pastor has an interest in her or his life, may be willing to seek the pastor's guidance and help when the unexpected crisis arises or when the chronic situation becomes too trying to handle alone. And if the trust level of the relationship becomes very strong, Confession and Absolution may also become part of the agenda.

Moreover, while such attention is noteworthy for the teen's sake, it is also meaningful for the congregation, because their shepherd is modeling the very behaviors that will be so helpful for encouraging teens. I'm taking for granted, by the way, that this behavior is genuine, that the pastor really is interested in following the exploits of his flock, and he's not being manipulative in some devious way.

---

7 Clark, 186.

Now, having encouraged pastors in their role in "noticification," it's time to do the same for others, be they full time or part time. Your role consists of two parts: first, that you yourself notice the teens under your care and attend to them; and second, that you seek out and encourage other adults in the congregation who may not have the time or gift for lengthy commitments to youth ministry nonetheless to be involved in a ministry of taking notice.

According to Search Institute research, teens need relationships with adults who are not part of their own family. The reason for this becomes clear once we think about it. Parents are often too close, and relationships with parents too conflicted, to allow teens to accurately assess the guidance or rules the parents have established. The adult who is outside the family is the sounding board against which teens can blow off steam without repercussions. But once the steam has been exhaled, the adult outside the family can reinterpret the situation in ways the teens might never have considered. The trusted other adult can say, "No, I don't think your mother is being unreasonable or oppressive; I think she's trying to tell you she loves you and cares deeply about you."

How many outside adults does one teen need? Three or four would be great, but having one adult whom the teen knows is crazy about him or her makes a tremendous difference.

"Researchers found that young people who had the highest self-worth, most positive hopes for the future, and most cheerfulness were young people who had social support from "special adults." These special adults can include anyone, such as a neighbor, a teacher, or an interested adult in the congregation."[8]

Realize that as a youth leader or director, one of your less recognized but more significant tasks is securing those adults who can be encouragers for the teens with whom you work. The researchers found that only 43 percent of girls and 39 percent of boys have the support that's given by adult nurturing relationships. Sometimes there is hesitancy on the part of others to be involved because they feel they are encroaching on the parent's prerogatives. While in previous generations our culture not only allowed but expected adults in the entire community to assist in disciplining others' children when the

8 Jolene L. Roehlkepartain and Eugene C. Roehlkepartain, *Prescription for a Healthy Church: Ministry Ideas to Nurture Whole People* (Minneapolis: Search Institute, 2000), 30.

parents weren't around, that's no longer acceptable adult behavior. Your adults don't want to step on parents' toes, and, of course, neither do you. Therefore another level of instruction is to let parents know the blessings that other adults can be for their children, that they aren't a threat to their parental authority, and, in fact, they can become a main support in good parent/teen communication. Mr. Emde was that kind of influence for my son; my older daughter confided in Connie, her volunteer youth leader at church; and my younger daughter told me not long ago that she has three dads! My response as a parent is to repress feelings of jealousy and instead rejoice. Especially for my youngest—in today's world, a young woman can't have too many watchful fathers!

## What to Notice about Teens

Search Institute for some time has been in the forefront of noticing youth and drawing from their research the very things that youth need. If you have taken college level courses in youth ministry or adolescent psychology, you may have already studied the forty developmental assets that Search Institute found. These are assets that correlate in a significant manner with positive teen development outcomes.

> Surveys of thousands of sixth- to twelfth-grade youth across the United States have found that the more assets young people experience, the more they engage in positive behaviors, such as volunteering and succeeding in school. The fewer assets they have, the more likely they are to engage in risk-taking behaviors, such as alcohol and other drug use, antisocial behavior, and violence.[9]

Researchers are ready to point out that correlational research cannot prove cause and effect; it only measures the strength of variables moving in the same direction. Yet it makes sense that if these assets are present when there are positive outcomes, then we ought to pay attention to the assets and promote them as much as possible. But the fact that there are forty developmental assets should tip you off that this chapter will not present even a cursory overview of all of them. I will, however, give the basic outline.

9 Roehlkepartain and Roehlkepartain, *Prescription*, 13.

There are twenty assets that are internal and twenty that are external. Internal assets are those characteristics that come from within teens, aspects of character and personality coupled with self-awareness. The external assets are those coming from the environment surrounding teens.

The internal assets are divided into four categories: (a) commitment to learning, (b) positive values, (c) social competencies, and (d) positive identity. *Commitment to learning* includes achievement motivation, school engagement, homework, bonding to school, and reading for pleasure. *Positive values* include caring, equality and social justice, integrity, honesty, responsibility, and restraint. *Social competencies* include planning and decision making, interpersonal competence, cultural competence, resistance skills, and peaceful conflict resolution. *Positive identity* includes personal power, self-esteem, sense of purpose, and positive view of personal future. While each of these can be encouraged and supported by adults and peers, they are assets that require not only the impulse, but also the cooperation of teens.

The twenty external assets are also divided into four categories: (a) support, (b) empowerment, (c) boundaries and expectations, and (d) constructive use of time. These differ from the internal in that they can be provided to some degree by those who live around teens. For example, *support* includes such variables as family support, positive family communication, other adult relationships, caring neighborhood, caring school climate, and parental involvement in schooling. *Empowerment* includes community values youth, youth as resources, service to others, and safety. *Boundaries and Expectations* include family boundaries, school boundaries, neighborhood boundaries, adult role models, positive peer influence, and high expectations. *Constructive use of time* involves creative activities, youth programs, religious community, and time at home.[10] These can't be created or generated by the teen; they must be supplied.

Search Institute has given us a list of things to notice. I like to highlight the external developmental assets because we can more readily act to provide positive change through them. But we are able also, depending on our own life circumstance, to notice what internal assets seem to be operating in a given teenager's life. So, for example, we can observe teen behavior to see what level of commitment there

---

10 Roehlkepartain and Roehlkepartain, *Prescription*, 18–20.

is to learning, Asset 22, "Bonding to School." Or we can look at Asset 7, "Community Values Youth," and ask what evidence is there within our congregation community that we value youth. But the question cannot be asked or answered in a simple manner. We must probe deeper in order to ask how the teens might answer that question. As a matter of fact, Search Institute has done just that, and found that only 20 percent of teens feel that their community values them.[11] In any case, these lists provide us with a strong, research-based list of items to notice within and around teens. Search Institute summarized how the assets support ministry by appealing to the growing life of sanctification.

> From a Lutheran perspective, asset building can be considered consistent with the "third use of the Law" (Formula of Concord, Epitome, Article VI) that serves to encourage good works in believers. Asset building fosters discipleship on three levels:

> • The asset framework helps us understand the world young people live in, the challenges they face, and the strengths they need—as they seek to live a Christian life.

> • Asset building focuses on strengths—gifts to be nurtured for and with young people. The asset framework is a tool to help us influence young people's growth and discipleship.

> • Finally, the asset-building approach reminds us (regardless of our age) of the importance of being positive guides and role models for young people in our families, congregations, and communities.[12]

---

11 This total was also divided into "Religiously Active Youth" (24 percent) and "Inactive/Non-religious Youth (13 percent). The comparison between these two populations revealed that the religiously active youth had a higher positive response rate than the inactive/nonreligious youth in all but one category: safety (58 percent of nonreligious have safety as an external asset, while only 53 percent of the religious do). On the other side, the differences ranged from only six percentage points (37 percent of religious have cultural competence as an internal asset while only 31 percent of nonreligious) to twenty-five percentage points (51 percent of religious have restraint as an internal asset while only 26 percent of nonreligious claim restraint). Roehlkepartain and Roehlkepartain, *Prescription*, 18–19.

12 *Grounding Asset Building in Lutheran Faith: An Invitation to Reflection and Dialogue* (Minneapolis: Search Institute, 2001), 5.

# Lutherans Noticing Teens

Now we come to the central question of this book as it applies to the first of the characteristics that mark Eutychus: that he is *young*. Is there anything from Lutheran theology as it is applied to youth ministry that is a significant addition to what we already have in the field of youth ministry?

We first of all recognize that the developmental assets, whether internal or external, are all First Article gifts. In fact, as I look at them, I can see a connection between the pyramid from below and the developmental assets. The internal assets are the created gifts, talents, and personality youth receive, while the external assets are the "life experience" environment in which the teens live. As Lutherans, we can readily affirm using helpful guides to notice the young among us.

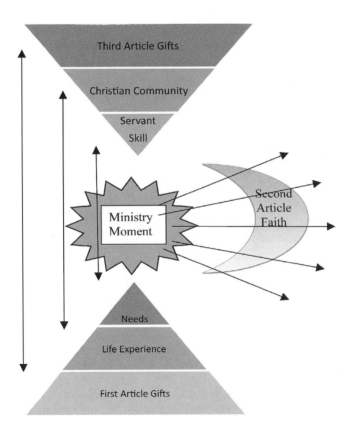

But there is more. As Lutheran Christians, we also want to notice youth among us through the pyramid from above, through the Third Article gifts. The youth in our congregations are baptized children of God. They have been buried with Christ in Baptism and have risen again in newness of life (Colossians 2:10). So as we notice them, we find they are just like us, saints and sinners, battling the devil, the world, and the sinful flesh and doing so with multiple temptations they are meeting for the first time. What does this mean in terms of practical theology? It means we are not surprised by great acts of faith on the part of teens, nor are we surprised by great failures by teens. In our service to teens, we will be ready with the Law when it's necessary to accuse and with the Gospel when we have the chance to declare God's forgiveness through Jesus Christ.

Noticing the young for Lutherans also means confessing that there is a vocation to which youth are called. We have always subscribed to the idea that adults have a vocation toward the young—whether parents or members of a larger community like a congregation. But something we perhaps haven't emphasized strongly enough is the vocation of youth toward adults and the rest of the community. The Harris twins write beautifully about the many hard things that teens have done and are doing. How much more powerful would their argument be if it was grounded in the truth that each teen is a mask, rendering a service on behalf of God, to their families, their peers, and the larger adult community? In *Do Hard Things*, there is frequently mentioned the motivation of honoring God and pleasing God through the acts of service they and other teens are planning and providing.[13] How much more would those same activities be understood and appreciated by the teens themselves if they understood the flip side of the equation—that they weren't working for God's benefit or their own but that God was working His deep will in the world through them!

Noticing the young also means noticing all the teens within our communities, and maybe in our congregations as well, who do not

---

13 One critique I've heard of the Harris book is that it is Law-driven with little recognition of the Gospel as the motivation. I want to be generous in my evaluation and point out that the last chapter is a brief presentation of the Gospel, albeit in the style of Campus Crusade for Christ. There is a need in much of the youth ministry material available today for an approach that regains the central focus on the cross of Jesus Christ as our motivation rather than the Law. "For the love of Christ controls us" (2 Corinthians 5:14), not the demands of the Law.

have faith in Jesus Christ—those who have either never heard or never received what they have heard. The young are a mission field. Who can reach them with the Gospel of Jesus Christ? Do you see where this is going? Those best equipped to reach youth will be youth and those who are leading youth. The idea that youth can reach out to other youth is not a unique contribution of Lutheran theology. The belief that youth have a vocation, a calling in their place and time of life, to be witnesses for Jesus Christ may very well be a unique contribution. And if it is, what a significant addition to make to the field of youth ministry!

## Eutychus the Individual

Is there anything special about Eutychus? I mean, other than the fact that he dies in his fall and comes back to life? If attendees at the upper room preaching marathon had been asked prior to his fall what they knew about Eutychus (what was he like, what were his gifts and talents), would they have been able to give an answer? What had they noticed about this young man?

Peter Benson has a term he uses to describe the unique quality that each teen brings to the world. He calls this quality a spark. "Every teenager has a spark—something inside that is good, beautiful, and useful to the world. Sparks illuminate a young person's life and give it energy and purpose."[14] Benson has found that teens resonate to the concept of sparks. They understand the idea, and it doesn't take them long to identify their own. Sparks give us "energy and joy." When we use our sparks, "we feel alive. We feel useful. Life has purpose." When we are using our sparks, "we lose our sense of time. We are in the moment."[15]

Now, that is an interesting way to describe the First Article gifts that make each young person the unique person he or she is. No two sets of First Article gifts are alike. Even studies done on identical twins have shown differences between them, not based on their genes, but on other influences that affected the timing of their genes. Each one of us is different, and each teen we have the privilege of serving has a

---

14 Peter L. Benson, *Sparks: How Parents Can Help Ignite the Hidden Strengths of Teenagers* (San Francisco: Jossey-Bass, 2008), 17.

15 Benson, 19.

unique combination of traits—both positive and negative—that make the teen the person we seek to love in Jesus Christ. A spark is a helpful way to describe these gifts.

The core Third Article gifts—by way of contrast—are identical: not the community or the servant skill, but the core Third Article gifts of the Word, Baptism, and the Lord's Supper are the same for everyone. The love of God for us through Jesus Christ is not more fervent for you than for me. The amount of forgiveness might vary among individuals, but the quality of the forgiveness is the same for all—pure and holy, complete and sufficient for each of us. The same Jesus meets the needs of each different person.

So we have this interesting situation wherein our core gifts from below have made each of us different while our needs are met by identical core gifts from above for each of us. And, of course, it doesn't even need to be said that the same holds true for teens. Perhaps this gives us the last insight we'll draw from "noticing the young." Our ministry in this regard is ... vocational—assisting youth as they pull together their unique spark with which God has gifted them for the benefit of the world (their vocation) with the one gift we all have received in common: faith in Jesus Christ. Perhaps that's what Mr. Emde is really remembered for. It's certainly what I'd like to be remembered for.

# CHAPTER 11

# Noticing the Bored

**W**hatever I am, I'm not bored—terrified maybe, but not bored. My confirmation on Palm Sunday is only two weeks away, meaning that next Sunday is *Examination Sunday*. In preparation, our pastor is holding our Saturday morning class in church. We are a class of twenty-six, so he's dividing us up evenly: thirteen for first service, thirteen for second. Given my place in the alphabet, I'm slotted for second service. I listen intently to his directions as we rehearse; in fact, the whole class is riveted on every syllable exiting his lips. What kind of questions will we have? The questions will come from the catechism. Which verses should we know? You should know the verses in the catechism. But there are 613 verses! Yes, there are; now listen while I ask you questions, and you practice volunteering your answers.

Like a wedding rehearsal for the bride and groom, the confirmation examination rehearsal does little to lessen my anxiety or the anxiety of my classmates. If only we could catch on that the rehearsal questions are the exact same questions he will ask the following Sunday. Then we would have taken some notes. When the rehearsal is over, Pastor gives the class an interesting offer. Anyone who wants to see what it's like can go one at a time and stand in the pulpit. I, along with several others, take him up on it. I walk into the chancel, over to the west wall, up the two steps, and into the pulpit. I look up to the balcony, glance at the empty pews, and gaze at my assembled classmates. I linger just a tad longer than the others. The pulpit seems a strangely comfortable place to be.

The Day of Judgment arrives, but I'm prepared. To this day I can still rattle off Romans 2:14–15 as I did that morning:

> When the Gentiles, which have not the law, do by nature
> the things contained in the law, these, having not the law,
> are a law unto themselves: Which shew the work of the law
> written in their hearts, their conscience also bearing witness,
> and their thoughts the mean while accusing or else excusing
> one another. (KJV)

On that day, I didn't quite comprehend the verse, but I knew it meant everybody had a problem with their conscience. Nor did I comprehend that morning the anxiety and distress of my classmates. I was too focused on my own circumstance, since it seemed every time the class gets stuck, I got called on.

Forty years later at the Youth Ministry 2006 conference held by the Department of Youth Ministry in Houston, Texas, with the theme of "Abuse," I was struck by comments made by Rev. Terry Dittmer as he spoke on the subject of "Spiritual Abuse." Was Examination Sunday an example of spiritual abuse? Was I abusing children when, as a pastor, I held a Friday evening public examination before parents, elders, and anyone else who wanted to attend? Subsequent discussion assures me that the answer to that question is "it depends." What it depends on is whether my intent was to expose the catechumens' ignorance, thereby publicly shaming them, or to rejoice in what the catechumens had learned and give them an opportunity to tell family and friends about Jesus. I'm relieved because my goal was always the latter and never the former.[1]

---

1 My commitment to this attitude was reinforced by the mother of a catechumen, teacher, and wife of our grade school principal at Zion, Litchfield, Illinois, who, as the class was processing in for examination with me bringing up the rear, whispered in my

My purpose in sharing these moments of adolescent trauma isn't to comment on the relative merits of an examination versus the variety of practices that in many congregations have taken the examination's place.[2] Rather, the point is to illustrate the lengths we will often go in order to motivate youth to learn what we want them to learn. Sometimes those efforts have positive effects, sometimes negative, but what drives us to use them is the realization of how frequently the youth in our youth group or the catechumens in our confirmation classes are unresponsive, indifferent, uninterested, and apathetic about what we are teaching them. In summary, they are bored.

In terms of educational psychology, the issue we are dealing with is motivation. How can we best motivate learning for our youth? What we know from both experience and research is that intrinsic motivation is extremely powerful, with long-lasting effects, while extrinsic motivation is very powerful, but leaves no lasting residue. In other words, if teens want to learn something, they will. If they don't want to learn something, they will learn it if forced, but the learning won't last. In college, we know this procedure as the "cram and flush" process, which results in passable grades but little knowledge.

Intuitively, we know that teaching the faith isn't like teaching an academic subject. Reading, writing, and arithmetic reach the mind, while the goals of catechesis go much deeper: reaching the heart for a lifetime. Religious educators from every religious background have struggled with finding methods and strategies that effectively transmit the faith to the coming generation, and we recognize that the challenge to motivate and engage teens in the faith isn't unique to the Lutheran Church. But is there something in Lutheran theology that uniquely addresses this issue? Is there something that we can add, not only from our long history of catechesis using the Six Chief Parts dating back to Luther, but also in our theology itself?

Remember what we are trying to do here. We are trying to keep Eutychus alert as he sits in the window—in fact, to prompt his curiosity so that he voluntarily slips off the sill and moves closer, with

---

ear, "You know, you're the one who's really on trial here."

2 It is important not to overlook the dual purpose of confirmation instruction—to know the faith well so as to make a public profession of faith (Matthew 10:32–33; 28:19–20) and to be able to examine oneself in preparation for the Lord's Supper (1 Corinthians 11:28–29).

ever-increasing attentiveness, with his eyes fixed on Paul and his body safely out of the clutches of gravity.

# The Catechetical Task

Paul gives us the clearest rendition of the catechetical task in 1 Corinthians 11 as he begins his discourse concerning the Corinthians' practice of the Lord's Supper. He writes, "For I received from the Lord what I also delivered to you" (23a). I actually prefer the translation in the NIV, where the dependent clause reads, "What I also passed on to you." The movement is so crystal clear. Paul received and Paul passed on. Paul doesn't see his function to include any change, alteration, or improvement in what he received. No, the test of his role as an ambassador of Christ (Ephesians 6:20) is the faithfulness with which he passes on the same message that he's received.

This is our task also. We take what we have received and pass it on to the next generation. As simple as this appears, it is really quite difficult. The history of the Christian Church on earth is one long list of problems in passing on what was received. Every major split, every disruptive heresy is an example of somebody deciding an improvement was needed, an innovation was necessary, or a doctrine needed an upgrade.

The conundrum that confronts us is that cultures aren't static; they shift and change. Likewise, language isn't a stationary target, but shifts through the centuries so that something that was quite clear in 1611 ("Suffer the little children to come unto me" [Mark 10:14, KJV], meaning to grant permission) comes under suspicion of child abuse in 2010. Add to this the brief attention spans of modern humans, who easily tire of the same-old-same-old and therefore require some creativity on the part of presenters to ward off boredom, and we see the problem. To pass on what we have received faithfully requires that we be creative without being innovative, imaginative without trying to improve, and able to upgrade our technologies, strategies, and methods without contaminating our message. All our care and attention to passing on what we have received is especially applicable to youth ministry, where the emerging intellectual capacities of youth are engaging old questions with new abilities for the first time in their young lives.

# Two Kinds of Theologies

I don't intend to make this discussion of our battle with boredom more complex than it needs to be, but there is another facet that must be cut into the diamond of our dilemma. I must confess I'm the kind of person who likes to divide things into two categories: not necessarily black and white, but certainly distinguishable shades of gray. In contemporary theology, there are two kinds of theologians: those whose search for answers succeeds and those whose search for answers fails. This is a division without shades of gray.

Confessional theologians are those whose search for answers succeeds. There is a question. The Scriptures, being an authoritative source to be reckoned with, are carefully searched, using every responsible hermeneutical tool, and an answer is found. Now, not every question a confessional theologian might want to ask has an answer found in the Scriptures. But if an answer is contained in the Scriptures, it is the theologian's task to find it, present it clearly, and pass it on. And, given human nature what it is, we aren't surprised to learn that confessional theologians can differ in the answers they find; and as a result there are different confessional groupings—Reformed, Lutheran, Arminian, and so forth. But what crosses the confessional denominational divides is the conviction that the search for answers succeeds. We are able with certainty to speak of things theological on the basis of God's revelation in Scripture.

Romantic theologians,[3] by way of contrast, are theologians whose search for answers fails. However, for the romantic theologian, this failure to secure an answer isn't a letdown. No, the lack of an answer substantiates the rationale behind the theological enterprise, which is really about questions, not about answers. The intellectually respectable theologian is the one following the romantic quest, the journey that begins with profound questions and continues as more data allows the crafting of even more profound questions. To actually come to a conclusion concerning a historical occurrence, the likelihood of

---

3 Some might wonder why I don't use the phrase "liberal theologians" here. My reason is that the distinction being made really isn't between those who look at Scripture as authoritative and those who do not. The distinction really is between those who want to find answers and those who enjoy asking questions. There may be some who give Scripture credit for being authoritative and yet are caught up in the appeal of never-ending questions. Truly scary is the reverse—having definitive answers without an authoritative Scripture, which brings us into the realm of free-floating misbelief.

a miracle, a saying of Jesus, or an ethical decision spoils the whole game, although speculation on the probability of finding an answer is frequently allowed.

Lutheran theology is squarely on the side of theology that succeeds in finding answers. Having found those answers, Lutheran theology is diligent in its desire to transmit those answers to the next generation of believers. For any number of reasons, success in finding answers and then promulgating those answers within the general public is not highly regarded by our contemporary culture. Intellectual credibility is generally awarded to those who work on the questions, not those who claim to have answers. In fact, those who claim certain knowledge in areas of faith or religion will have any number of derogatory adjectives thrown at them, all the way from fundamentalist to bigot.[4]

I fear that now I've bored you with my introductory comments on the problem of adolescent boredom, so I better make my point. Two likely variables in the dynamics of boredom ought to be understood before we devise a theological strategy for motivation.

First, teens are bored in church because they've heard it all before. There's nothing new here, nothing that surprises or entertains. It's booooorrrrriiiinggg. And because the Church is faithfully passing on what it has received without alteration or innovation, this isn't going to get any better, at least from the teens' perspective.[5]

Second, because the Church claims to have answers for many of life's most basic and important questions, the Church lacks intellectual credibility within the culture. As youth encounter teachers and professors, whose mission is to debunk the myths of the spiritual and extol the merits of the material, the reproach they will feel and the disdain they will encounter for their religious convictions may be overwhelming. A faith that might have survived getting shot at could be the faith that is lost when it is laughed at. The boredom I'm describing here is the boredom that results from teens concluding that their faith is irrelevant to the real world, to real academics, and to

---

4 I can't help but share that when I used the synonym function in Microsoft on the word *bigot* one of the words that came up as a synonym was *dogmatist*. Could it be that in current language usage, to hold strong to a belief is the same as being a bigot? This further illustrates the point I'm making.

5 As a teen and on into college, there was nothing I despised more than the Venite in the Matins service of *TLH*. It was the epitome of boring liturgical practice. Oddly enough, I now sing it to myself every morning in my personal devotions.

their own real lives. How shall we respond? With what can Lutheran theology motivate?

# Challenging the Bored without Boring the Challenged

I suggest the place to undermine adolescent ennui is with a return to the ministry moment—that opportunity that inevitably arrives for us as we work with youth when the gifts from above and the gifts from below meet. The moment exists because of some uncertainty, some disequilibration as Piaget might call it, or cognitive dissonance as later psychologists might suggest. Instead of falling back on psychological terms, however, why not just call it a moment of doubt, a time of stress, or a crisis of faith?

The ministry moment forms a creative nexus in which gifts coming from both directions are resources for a faith-enhancing resolution that results in a stronger faith and a growing life of sanctification. You are part of the mix, and your Lutheran theology comes into play as you help teens sort through the effects of Law and Gospel on the situation. You may find yourself reminding teens of the promises they have in their Baptism and the invitation they have to the Supper, which validates God's mercy and forgiveness for them. You may be the one to absolve, explaining what it means to be justified by grace—and grace ALONE. Your own life experience may come into play as you assure teens that they are not schizophrenic—they are just dual-natured saint/sinners like yourself. In the middle of a crisis, you may battle through your own tears in order to lead teens away from dead-end "Why did this happen?" questions and instead guide them to comfort-filled "Who is with me?" questions. Those are the questions you can answer with certainty. You can also be the one to appreciate and affirm for teens how they are God's masks giving care not only to one another but also to you.

All that may be going on—but I would hope not all at once. What I want to point out now is that in the ministry moment, when theology is at its most practical, teens are being challenged. And one thing about being challenged is that it is never, ever boring.

# The Antidote of Vocational Catechesis

There are three key elements, as I shared in chapter 8, that comprise vocational catechesis; knowing oneself well as a saint/sinner, knowing God well as a God who works through the weakness of the cross, and hearing God's call in vocation by acknowledging meaning and purpose in life. Teens who have a grasp of who they are, how God has redeemed them, and the meaningfulness of their lives have an immediate advantage when they find themselves challenged. Teens in the middle of a challenge who have leaders, guides, or mentors ready to affirm these truths also have an immediate advantage. What's common to both the previous sentences is the word *challenge*. A teen faced with a challenge is not a bored teen.

The challenge, however, must be seen as a challenge by the teen or it doesn't work. For a challenge to be effective, teens have to accept the challenge. Something about it needs to appeal to them in a manner they can't refuse, or their life circumstance within the ministry moment must prevent any attempt to escape the challenge. For example a teen's parents getting a divorce, with all the concomitant trials that go along with family breakup, is a challenge that can't be avoided. The invitation to become a core member of the youth ministry leadership team, on the other hand, can readily be declined.

What is asked of us here, using our trinitarian framework, is the hard and sometimes embarrassing job of analyzing the challenges we place before teens. I recall how early on in my parish ministry I tinkered with my confirmation curriculum, trying to find the combination that would be most challenging to my catechumens. Unfortunately, too often what I devised was a curriculum that I as a pastor found challenging, not necessarily what an early adolescent might find challenging.

Don't assume at this point in the discussion that I'm now going to suggest that we dumb down our curriculum for youth ministry even further and fill our time with more games that physically or intellectually challenge teens. If I did that, I would be confusing what is challenging with what is entertaining. My suggestion is that we make the effort to go beyond the interesting and entertaining to what will genuinely stretch teens.

The strange part about what I'm suggesting is that what we do as Lutheran youth leaders challenging teens may not on the surface appear much different from what others do in youth ministry. Everybody goes on retreats, servant events, or training seminars. Everybody has Bible study. What *is* different, and I think unique, is why we do them and what we expect as a result from having done them.

We do not do good works (or meet their challenges) in order to be justified before God, because for believers justification has already happened.[6] Neither do we do good works in order to validate our having been justified, as if we must do a minimum number of good works or our justification by grace will be rescinded due to lack of personal effort.[7] Nor do we do our good works in order to prove to ourselves that we have been justified and are therefore among the elect.[8] As Lutheran Christians we do good works because it is our vocation. Out of love for Jesus Christ, in obedience to God's commands, and guided by the Holy Spirit working through the Means of Grace, we serve others by fulfilling our respective callings.

Our theology, therefore, drives us to be life-directed. The biggest challenge for teens, based on justification by grace through faith, is the identification of their vocation. Who are they to be and what are they to be as baptized believers in Jesus who are moving through adolescence toward adulthood?

What ought we to teach teens to expect as they accept the challenge of vocation? On one hand, we don't teach them to expect too much. Accepting the challenge of finding and fulfilling one's vocation doesn't earn extra stars behind our names, at least that's what Jesus seems to be saying in Luke 17:7–10 when He describes those who labored in the field all day only to return home in time to prepare dinner for the master, and who say, "We are only unworthy

---

6 To connect our good works with our justification confuses the saving work of Jesus Christ on the cross for us with our own works, making us responsible in part for our own salvation—something we are simply incapable of doing!

7 To make our justification dependent on our subsequent good works takes God's unconditional gift of justification by grace through faith alone and makes it conditional on our behavior. Once again, we are made responsible for part of our salvation—something we are incapable of doing!

8 To make our good works the evidence by which we can be assured of our justification means that our certainty for salvation is placed in our own works rather than in the promise of God. If this were true, then it would also be true that our falling to temptation is the evidence by which we can be assured of our condemnation. The most profound influence of Lutheran theology on us is in the recognition that justification is outside of us, in the declaration of forgiveness of sins for Christ's sake.

servants; we have only done what was our duty" (v. 10). True, our vocation is simply doing our duty.

On the other hand, we don't teach them to expect too little. Jesus also teaches that those who follow Him will receive many times more than this world can ever offer (Luke 18:29–30). Can we really expect more than what we have already received—the forgiveness of our sins, peace that passes human understanding, and eternity? Heaven belongs to us. A place has been prepared for us (John 14:2), all before we have done anything. So we don't expect anything because we have already received everything. We do know that our community, our neighbors, and our families benefit because we meet the challenge of our vocation.

## Three Challenges for Teens

With a subtitle like this, you might expect that *Challenge 1* is to bring the wizard the broomstick of the Wicked Witch of the West; *Challenge 2* is dropping the One Ring to bind them all into the fires of Mount Doom from which it was forged; and *Challenge 3* is to kill Lord Voldemort with or without one's own wand. My three challenges are far simpler and more substantial. They involve challenging teens to find vocation through discovery, experience, and debate.

### Discovery

If one aspect of teen boredom with church has to do with the fact that all the great questions have already been answered and there's nothing really to do besides repeat what's written in the Book of Concord,[9] then why not challenge teens to trace the path that got us here and see if they arrive at the same destination? There is curriculum coming from our own sources that will assist. But don't limit the challenge to prepared curriculum. Teens have resources at their fingertips that they use daily for other purposes. Let them use it for this purpose. Challenge them to search the Internet and see what they find.

---

9 This assumes that high school teens have heard of this book. Its very existence may come as a surprise to teens and challenge some of their assumptions about their Church and its history.

- Caution them always to document the URLs of the Web sites they visit and read each source with a critical eye.

- Use their findings as discussion starters that lead back to the Bible and to the catechism.

- Treat all the findings with respect, but be very clear when a Web site is in error; and provide support from Scripture.

- Let youth know that sometimes what is not mentioned is most important.[10]

- Recognize that you won't always have an answer at your fingertips, so be free to tell youth you'll need to check back with them later.

- Use your pastor as a resource when difficult questions come up.

Tracing the doctrines believed by Lutherans is only part of the discovery trip. The greater challenge comes when youth realize that, although many great questions of life and faith were answered by the reformers, many other questions were not. Challenge teens to answer the questions based on what they have learned from their faith. Challenge teens to work through what is Law and what is Gospel in the questions such as "What does it mean to be a sexual being?" or "How can we understand marriage with all that's going on in the culture today?" or "Is there a theological way of looking at health care?" Along with engaging issues that never confronted the reformers, let teens discover that the definitive answers given by the reformers were written for another time and place. Could it be part of their vocation to find ways of connecting those teachings to their own everyday circumstances? How would they go about communicating to peers the Church's answer to questions such as "Why is the Church concerned over who goes to the Lord's Supper and who doesn't?" or "Why is living together anybody's business other than the couple's?"

---

10 Many statements of faith on Web sites read very well until one notices that there is no mention of the Sacraments, or if they are mentioned they are called ordinances. This is a giant red flag for Lutheran Christians.

Perhaps I read too much into Alex and Brett Harris's book *Do Hard Things*, but I suspect when they accuse adults of expecting too little from teens, they are on to something. They encourage teens throughout the book by providing examples of teens organizing missions of mercy or getting involved in the political process in ways normally reserved for adults. Have we set the bar of expectations too low for teens regarding their faith? Have we suppressed their innate gifts for exploration and discovery by challenging them to nothing more than pat "Jesus" answers in our youth Bible studies? Could it be that many are bored because they've been given milk over and over again so often they are gagging on it, while their whole demeanor would change if they got a taste of solid meat?

A retreat dedicated to exploring the faith isn't a new or unique idea. Lutheran Teens Encounter Christ has never been a large organization, but it's been around for thirty years; and it leads youth on a spiritual journey that retraces their steps from the baptismal font to their confirmation promises to being fed at the Lord's Table—all done within the context of training in private Confession and Absolution. A TEC weekend is highly, dramatically experiential as youth recommit on a teen level to the faith they confessed as children. Are there other ways we could spend a weekend with youth, challenging them in their faith? It's just a thought.

## Experience

Youth groups that are vibrant and alive, as defined by willing participation on the part of youth rather than coerced participation, tend to be highly experiential. When ideas are talked about and faith concepts taught, a means to turn the abstract idea into a concrete action are found. We talk about mercy—we volunteer at a food pantry or soup kitchen. We learn about crisis pregnancy centers—we organize a fund-raiser and supply the home with six months' worth of diapers. We study the forgiveness of God for Christ's sake—we learn how to ask one another for forgiveness.

Where is the challenge in this? you might ask. The challenge comes when the teens share in taking the abstract and making it concrete, when they share responsibility for the experience.

Gain the support of the pastor and the church administration in moving toward an experiential youth ministry that draws on teen gifts from below and above.

Ask the teens to make the practical connection for their activities. Let teens brainstorm a concrete response to an abstract belief.

- Support their suggestions and monitor their planning.

- Let teens know there are limits that have to do with safety, liability, and the church treasurer.

- Don't arbitrarily veto a suggestion—let it play out and explore with the teens the process.

- Be comfortable with ideas that fail, and let youth know the experiment with an unexpected result was nevertheless a great learning experience.

- Ask the teens to choose adults from the congregation to join them in the adventure as their guides and mentors. Make experiences cross-generational.

- Support and encourage the adults that respond—they are a special gift.

- Debrief every experience through the filter of vocational catechesis:

  ❏ What have we learned about ourselves by this experience?

  ❏ What have we learned about God by this experience?

  ❏ What does this experience mean for each one of us?

Teens that are challenged aren't bored. Teens that challenge themselves have reached another level of nonboredom. They are on a mission. Perhaps that describes the experience of those teens who I've known through Ongoing Ambassadors For Christ. They are teens who have meaning and purpose. They are on a mission, and they aren't bored. Granted, their experience isn't one that was self-generated. OAFC is very much adult led and adult monitored. But the youth who have gone through OAFC are different. Now, it's possible that they were different before they went through OAFC, but I doubt it. What makes them different is their capacity to turn the abstract into the concrete. They will be leaders in experiential learning in the future. They will want others to experience the satisfaction they have experienced in the mission of Jesus Christ to the world.

## Debate

My third challenge for teens is debate. Actually, what I really mean by debate is apologetics: the intellectually rigorous and demanding defense of the Christian faith through well-reasoned argument. Now, why would I suggest something like this? Didn't I point out in an earlier chapter that Christians are looked at by much of society as argumentative fundamentalists who impose their judgmental conclusions on the rest of society? Am I here suggesting that we develop a training program to develop extremists?

Well, yes, I suppose I am if by extremist you mean someone who is committed to a certain set of beliefs and can articulate rational arguments in defense of those beliefs against those who would be detractors. I am suggesting that we shouldn't let our youth go out into the world, and especially into higher education, without any more armor than the songs they learned in VBS, summer camp, or the district youth gathering. Remember, the Christian faith is ridiculed relentlessly on Comedy Central, and our youth watch Comedy Central. The Christian faith is mocked by best sellers proclaiming that "God Is Not Great," and if they don't read the best sellers, their teachers might. The name of the Savior of the world is constantly used as a curse word all around them, and our youth are not above joining in. Science has long proclaimed God to be unnecessary and prohibits asking questions about design, and most of our youth at best can only answer "And God said, 'Let there be light'" (Genesis 1:3), at which point they find themselves laughed out of the lecture hall.

Adults have not done very well themselves in learning how to defend the faith. Many have remained comfortable with the eighth grade faith with which they were confirmed; they are ill-equipped to defend the faith they received. I believe the next generation of youth can do better. Let's provide them with the armor Paul recommends in Ephesians 6:11–17.

> Put on the whole armor of God, that you may be able to stand against the schemes of the devil. For we do not wrestle against flesh and blood, but against the rulers, against the authorities, against the cosmic powers over this present darkness, against the spiritual forces of evil in the heavenly places. Therefore take up the whole armor of God, that you may be able to withstand in the evil day, and having done all, to stand firm. Stand therefore, having fastened on the belt of truth, and having put on the breastplate of righteousness, and, as shoes for your feet, having put on the readiness given by the gospel of peace. In all circumstances take up the shield of faith, with which you can extinguish all the flaming darts of the evil one; and take the helmet of salvation, and the sword of the Spirit, which is the word of God.

What will help our youth to stand firm? They will need a belt, a breastplate, shoes, a shield, a helmet, and a sword—all with the readiness of the Gospel of peace. This is wonderful language, but what does it mean? It means that we ought to do the following:

- Initiate evening opportunities for youth to gather at church and discuss the challenges to their faith that they encounter, preferably with adults who also want to learn.

- Work into the youth curriculum discussions on ethical issues that present strong arguments for moral behavior, rather than settling for "just say no."

- Introduce youth to the writings of some of the great apologists such as C. S. Lewis. Don't assume that *Mere Christianity* is beyond the reach of a high school student.

- Read up on apologetics yourself, with such authors as Nancy Pearcey, G. K. Chesterton, David Bentley Hart, Francis Schaeffer, and Angus Menuge.[11]

---

11 Nancy R. Pearcey, *Total Truth: Liberating Christianity from Its Cultural Captivity* (Wheaton, IL: Crossway Books, 2004). Gilbert K. Chesterton, *Orthodoxy* (New York: Dodd, Mead and Company, 1936). David Bentley Hart, *Atheist Delusions: The Christian Revolution and Its Fashionable Enemies* (New Haven, CT: Yale University Press, 2009). Angus J. L. Menuge, ed., *Reading God's World: The Scientific Vocation* (St. Louis:

- Follow with your youth the arguments presented by reputable scientists who, though they are by no means creationists, nevertheless provide evidence of design: Guillermo Gonzalez and Francis Collins, to name just a few.[12]

- Invite outside speakers or develop a weekend training seminar on the defense of the faith.[13]

You've probably noticed that most of my bullets above have more to do with you the youth leader than with activities for the youth. In this challenge for youth, your example becomes even more important. As Lutheran Christians, we recognize that no one can be argued into the faith. Faith comes by hearing the Word, we learn in Romans 10, and through that Word the Holy Spirit works to bring people to faith, then to a confession of faith, and then to Baptism. Without the work of the Holy Spirit, no amount of arguing, be it rational or irrational, will bring a person to faith. But a lack of understanding the rationality of our faith may be the crack through which a flaming dart of the evil one reaches the heart of a teen who decides that faith is nothing more than a crutch built on a myth to help humans deal with their own death, which is just what materialism teaches.

## Vocational Catechesis

Discovery, experience, and debate create a formula for moving teens' understanding of their faith forward. Can it have other uses? Couldn't it also be a formula to help teens find the way that God intends, given their gifts from above and gifts from below, to be His mask in the world by serving others? And if discover, experience, and debate can be such a formula, then shouldn't it also be part of our youth ministry?

---

Concordia, 2004).

12 Guillermo Gonzalez and Jay W. Richard, *The Privileged Planet: How Our Place in the Cosmos Is Designed for Discovery* (Washington DC: Regnery, 2004). Francis S. Collins, *The Language of God: A Scientist Presents Evidence for Belief* (New York: Free Press, 2006).

13 *Life's Big Questions, God's Big Answers* by Brad Alles, theology teacher at Milwaukee Lutheran High School, published by Concordia Publishing House, is a good example of a resource around which a program could be designed.

What a list of leading questions! So far, we have looked only at this three-pronged approach in terms of its value for understanding the gifts from above. It also has value for comprehending one's gifts from below. Using many of the same bullet points from above, teens can be challenged to think about the vocations into which they will be called.

Why not spend time in youth group talking about different kinds of employment and doing some discovery work about them? Why not encourage projects among teens, supported by the youth group, to have shadow days—only then debrief the experience within the theological construct of vocation? Since justice and the environment are topics toward which the idealism of youth gravitate, then let's engage in vigorous discussion and debate over what might be the most God-pleasing answers for human relationships and for stewardship of planet Earth. We can do these things, and they won't be boring.

I still remember the Sunday afternoon when the youth leader of our congregation in St. Louis arranged for a youth luncheon followed by a guest speaker. The guest speaker was a friend of hers in the medical profession who frequently gave talks to teens on various aspects of health. On this afternoon, she had the youth sit in a semicircle in front of a table. She stood behind the table with a large plastic bucket beside her. One after another she took diseased body parts out of the bucket to show the teens. Only when she lifted up a human brain, with the spinal cord hanging down, did one youth have to make a dash to bathroom.

"Look at this," she said, holding up a human lung. "Notice how soft and springy it is? Now look at this." She took a second lung from the bucket. "This is a lung taken from a smoker. Come up and touch both. See how discolored and crunchy the diseased lung is? This is what smoking does. Now look at this," as she held up a human liver. "This is the portion of the liver that was destroyed by alcohol." The amazed youth, except the one who left abruptly, gathered around the table, put on plastic gloves, and poked the different body parts. No one was the least bit bored.

I can't be sure what each youth left with that day. It could have been the beginning of a medical vocation for one of them or a behavioral change away from destructive habits by another or a recognition of the marvelous design the Creator put into the human body. There was among all, however, the realization of the gift from below they each had by having a body and what care is necessary to respect that gift.

So this is the three-pronged approach to overcoming boredom; discovery, experience, and debate. As I look at it, I'm a little surprised, as you might be also, that nothing in my list involves an increase in athletic competition, use of computer games, or mass quantities of food mixed with CDs and DVDs. My surprise is tempered, however, by the realization that youth can find sports, games, and entertainment just about anywhere. The only place they will be guided in the discovery of their faith or have the mentoring available to train them into adulthood in their faith or give them the intellectual wherewithal by which to defend the faith and perhaps even lead others by the Holy Spirit working through the Word to faith is right where you are. Those other things soon become boring. The Gospel, properly understood, isn't and never will be.

## Vocational Postscript

Part of the adult Christian vocation is passing on the faith to the next generation. Part of the Christian vocation of youth is to receive the faith, and in the words of the collect, "read, mark, learn and inwardly digest" the faith in preparation for their adult Christian vocation.

The gathering mentioned earlier of over one hundred colleges and universities to discuss the topic of vocation in higher education was designed in such a way that participants were involved in breakout sessions of no more than ten faculty members. In my first breakout session, it didn't take long before someone mentioned the oft-quoted definition of vocation attributed to Frederick Buechner: vocation is "where your deep gladness meets the world's great need." I was astonished as my circle of faculty began to rip Buechner's definition to shreds. Other scholars from places such as Calvin College and Baylor University rejected the statement outright.

Why the negative response? Because, as one of the faculty members pointed out, "Sometimes we are called to sacrifice." What an insight. For the Christian, the deep gladness may have opportunity to meet the world's great need. That is certainly a possibility. I think my life could be an example of that process. Yet, for the Christian, the world's great need may be the Christian's deepest pain. Some are called to sacrifice for the sake of their faith in the Lord Jesus Christ. Others, even in our own day—and perhaps especially in our own day—are called to martyrdom. This, too, is a vocation. And who's to say but that some of our charges in their years to come might not be called to just such an honor? There's nothing boring about that, even for teens.

# Noticing the At Risk

C hris is filled with plans and enthusiasm as I meet him at the inner-city church in Milwaukee on a very bright Wednesday morning in August. I've known Chris since he began taking courses in our Lay Ministry program several years earlier. He's African-American, in his early thirties, and he has a mission. He wants to involve students from the youth ministry program at Concordia in his plans. He believes his mission will give them high-quality urban-ministry experiences, and that's why he called me the week before and invited me to see what's happening at Sherman Park Lutheran Church.

My own congregation, Mount Calvary, is only twelve blocks away. Nevertheless I've never been inside Sherman Park Lutheran, though I've driven past it hundreds of times. We enter the huge, ornate sanctuary and ascend a set of stairs into a side wing containing Chris's temporary office area. We find two comfortable chairs and sit facing each other. Chris begins our discussion with a prayer, and then shares his dream.

"There's so much out there," he begins. There certainly is. The church is across the street from one of the largest public high schools in the city. All Chris has to do in order to encounter the multiple risks that face teens, and not just urban teens, is to look out his office window. "Teens have so many decisions to make. There are so many pressures on them. They don't see any future, only the immediate— what's right in front of them." Chris explains the things that are right in front of them. Nothing in the litany he shares surprises me, nor would it surprise you. Drugs, violence, dropouts, guns, gangs, teen pregnancy, hopelessness, and more are all around.

As I listen, and because I'm in the middle of writing this book, I begin thinking of the environment Chris describes in Eutychian terms. These aren't kids who happen to move out of the crowd and put themselves at risk by sitting in the window. These are kids who are growing up in the window, whose everyday lives are lived in the window. What will it take to get them out of the window?

By "getting them out of the window," I don't mean extracting them from their environment. I mean changing mind-sets that will allow them to be transformative within their environment. The goal is not just nudging them from the window, but also mentoring them in such a way that they find themselves nudging others from the window. So what plan does Chris have up his sleeve?

Sherman Park Lutheran used to be a congregation of over two thousand. The enormous sanctuary testifies to its historical prominence. Now the congregation is a handful by comparison, but it's a committed handful. The church has space, a lot of space: classrooms, gymnasium, meeting rooms. The congregation has begun a grade school, supported by the Milwaukee Parental Choice voucher program. The school has grown to 160 students. But this doesn't address the needs of teens, and teens are the target for Chris's service to Jesus Christ.

He explains. "There are three things we need to do. We need to supply a safe place: a place that's secure where they know they can just be kids. Second, we need to share the Gospel. Nothing is going to change for these kids if they don't have Jesus Christ in their lives. Third, we want them to see how they can live their lives with hope, see that they have a future." The plan is rather simple. There is space below the gymnasium for an after-school youth center. The plans are already drawn up, and the church has a development director working on securing funds for the remodeling that's necessary—lighting, ceiling work, flooring, and furnishings. When finished, the after-school youth program will be safe, Gospel-centered, and a place of hope. "So we want to know if you have any students who might be interested. We should be ready to go in about three months."

## Teens At Risk the View from Above

When we think about teens being at risk, the issues confronting urban teens, many of whom are really not that different from suburban or rural teens, usually come to mind. The life-altering and life-damaging decisions and behaviors that tempt youth aren't that difficult to spot from the vantage point of secure adulthood. If we are at all in the news media loop, we are aware of these dangers and more.

Before going further about teens at risk, we need to define what is meant by "risk." What does risk look like to an adolescent? What does risk look like to a parent? What does it look like to a theologian? What types of risks are there? In a recent conversation with an insurance agent, he asked me to consider what my "risk tolerance" is. I had never really thought about it before, but in his world there's an index of risk tolerance that guides the types of investments that a person might consider: the greater the risk, the higher the potential payout, but the greater the chance of losing everything. The more I think about it, the more I realize that I have a very low risk tolerance, which explains why I have never gone bungee jumping. Risk tends to make me nervous. What risk tolerance do you have for youth ministry?

The perspective I describe here is risk as it might look to professional church workers or volunteer laypersons, all of whom are practical theologians in their own right, working with the youth group at the local congregation. This viewpoint may surprise some because from this angle, the greatest risk isn't in drug addiction, teen pregnancy, STDs, or drag racing at midnight; the greatest risk is losing the faith once received. The greatest risk isn't sin; the greatest risk is despair that denies any hope for redemption. To put it simply, the greatest risk any believing teen faces is the risk of no longer believing. From the standpoint of eternity, this risk trumps all others. A theologian might call this *eschatological* risk.

The biblical foundation for this conviction isn't hard to locate; it nearly jumps out of the Scriptures and slaps us in the face. We have spiritual enemies. Peter identifies the devil to be a roaring lion, hungry and ready to devour whatever is in his path, but being especially fond of the taste of those who are in the faith (1 Peter 5:8). Paul never fails to encourage his readers to hang on tight to the message they have received, because the enemy will try to rip it out of their grasp. "*Hold fast* to the word I preached to you—unless you believed in vain" (1 Corinthians 15:2). "Test everything, *hold fast* to what is good" (1 Thessalonians 5:21). The author of Hebrews exhorts his readers to "*hold fast* our confidence" (Hebrews 3:6); "*hold fast* our confession" (Hebrews 4:14); "*hold fast* to the hope set before us" (Hebrews 6:18); and "*hold fast* the confession of our hope" (Hebrews 10:23). To the Church at Philadelphia, Jesus, by the pen of John, writes, "*Hold fast* what you have, so that no one may seize your crown" (Revelation 3:11). Earlier John gives his own warning when he advises believers: "Test the spirits to see whether they are from God, for many false prophets have gone out into the world" (1 John 4:1, all italics added).

The persistent encouragement not only to appreciate what we have received by faith, but to hang on to it for dear life, is not rhetoric. One doesn't need to hold fast to what can't be lost. The spiritual enemies we have are real, and the result of their victory is of eternal consequence. Paul's words to Timothy are noteworthy in the regret they imply and the pathos they involve when he tells Timothy to "wage the good warfare" (1 Timothy 1:18),[1] because others with whom he worked and about whom he cared a great deal had let the faith slip out of their grasp. "By rejecting this, some have made shipwreck of their faith, among whom are Hymenaeus and Alexander, whom I have handed over to Satan that they may learn not to blaspheme" (1 Timothy 1:19b–20).

The concern over spiritual well-being and its attendant eternal well-being is the dividing line between many helpful and well meaning efforts to assist teens that come from the secular realm and the task of youth ministry. The former can claim success when teens avoid destructive behaviors and follow healthy, life-affirming goals. The latter rejoices in healthy behaviors too, but recognizes a layer of

---

1 This is the well-known phrase "fight the good fight," as translated in the NIV. The ESV more accurately translates the original, and in doing so ratchets up the intensity of the verse a notch. This isn't just a fight. It is war!

concern that goes so much deeper. For this reason, you as a youth leader may have concerns your counterparts in secular organizations will miss.

For example, you may find yourself more genuinely concerned about the super-smart kid with the excellent GPA going off to the elite university than you are about the teen from the dysfunctional family that shows up at every youth group event. Your concern comes from your awareness that when it comes to faith, risk can be just as great for the greatly advantaged as it is for the severely disadvantaged, perhaps more so.

Vocational catechesis sees everyone in need of the whole armor of God (Ephesians 6:10–20), student and leader alike. Each of the armaments provided for spiritual warfare is significant for knowing oneself truly, trusting God completely, and living life meaningfully, aware of the gifts one has received and of one's purpose as a believer in Jesus Christ. There are only six words Paul employs, but they are extremely important: truth, righteousness, peace, faith, salvation, and the Word. These terms describe things all Christians, and especially teenagers, need to know about ourselves if we are to face the risks that life presents.

A youth ministry taking a vocational catechesis approach assists youth in recognizing risk by communicating as clearly as possible the importance of these gifts.

## TRUTH

There is such a thing as truth; truth not only as a proposition but truth as a person (John 14:6). Whereas in previous generations and historical time periods the existence of things that are true was simply taken for granted, we no longer live in a society that does so. Attitudes and perceptions that assume all is a matter of opinion wherein we have the capacity to create our own realities infiltrate the minds of youth and adults alike. To know ourselves as we really are means that we know that both truth and falsehood exist and can be known. What we do with truth and falsehood has serious consequences.

## RIGHTEOUSNESS

No matter how good we might be, our own righteousness is insufficient before the justice and holiness of God. In place of our own righteousness, we have the righteousness of Jesus Christ given [imputed] to us (Romans 5:17). We are free from futile attempts at making excuses for ourselves or justifying ourselves. Why? Because we have already been justified. The reason the righteousness of Jesus Christ is such an effective defense against Satan is that it robs him of the potent weapon of accusation. The sins by which he wants us damned are already punished, and we have the righteousness of Jesus Christ. To know ourselves as we really are means we know what is true about Jesus and what is true about ourselves because of Jesus.

## PEACE

"Therefore, since we have been justified by faith, we have peace with God through our Lord Jesus Christ" (Romans 5:1). Need anything more be said about peace? We live in peace that's given us by Jesus Christ, and as He says, it is "not as the world gives" (John 14:27). As a result, our hearts are not troubled nor are we afraid, even though the world has no peace. To know ourselves as we really are means we know our peace is lasting, eternal, and internal; that is to say, conflicts in our daily life cannot rob us of the peace we have with God through Jesus Christ. Given the volatility of emotions for many teens, having feet shod with the shoes of peace can't be overemphasized. This peace passes understanding because it exists so often in spite of conditions that under ordinary circumstances would seem to make peace impossible. Can teens demonstrate the peace of God consistently? Teens can do this no better than adult Christians who also find themselves beset by many "fears within, without."[2] But peace is ours, and in our vocation we remind one another over and over again of the gifts we have received.

## FAITH

Faith is a shield that's proven its effectiveness over and over again for God's people and will continue to do so for teens as they understand their lives to be lived under the canopy of a calling from

---

2 "Just as I Am, without One Plea" (*LSB* 570:3).

God—a vocation to be God's servant in meaningful ways for the neighbor. Faith "is the assurance of things hoped for, the conviction of things not seen" (Hebrews 11:1). Faith opens adolescent and adult eyes to realities about which materialist worldviews are ignorant. Faith trusts in God's promises even when the evidence before our eyes denies its possibility. This is why Abraham laughed (Genesis 17:17), and so did Sarah (Genesis 18:12), when they were told they would be parents in their extreme old age. This is why adolescents struggling to leave a dangerous window have hope in spite of addictions, obsessions, and family conflicts. Faith is a shield through which no fiery darts of the devil pass.

## SALVATION

Salvation is the result of the Gospel having its way with the human heart. Paul is not ashamed of the Gospel of Jesus Christ because it has the power to save (Romans 1:16). But the word *save* creates questions for adolescents. "Saved from what? Saved for what?" Paul calls salvation a helmet for a reason. The helmet protects the head from blows that would otherwise render the individual unconscious. The helmet of salvation protects from the devastating blows that come from guilt and sin, the consequences of our transgressions and iniquities. The Gospel of Jesus Christ's life, death, and resurrection is our salvation, saving us from God's wrath and saving us for service as His people. Vocational catechesis emphasizes not only the "from" of salvation, but also the "for."

## THE WORD OF GOD

The Gospel is what saves us, but the Gospel that saves comes to us through the Word of God. The Word is the sword of the Holy Spirit, because the Spirit uses the Word of God to pierce the heart. This is how the Spirit "convict(s) the world concerning sin and righteousness and judgment" (John 16:8). God's Word is the authoritative source for our knowledge of the Gospel. The Word is where we meet truth. The constant attacks on the authority of Scripture that come from diverse directions over time can dull the blade of the Word. Youth leaders need to be sensitive to the manner in which the Word is treated, or mistreated, because it can lead to doubt in the accuracy, effectiveness, and truth of God's Word. How can the Word be mistreated in youth ministry?

- When the Word is used in such a way that in the mind of an adolescent it moves from being *the* authority to being *an* authority, the first line has been crossed.

- When Scripture is used in such a way that in the mind of an adolescent it moves from *being* God's Word to *containing* God's Word, the second line has been crossed.

- When Scripture is used in such a way that in the mind of an adolescent God's Word is no longer the measuring line for life, but other measuring instruments take precedence, such as our fluctuating emotions, our frail and faulty human reason, or our convenience, that last line has been crossed.

Vocational catechesis in youth ministry assumes the task of maintaining the sword of the Spirit, the Word of God, firmly in the grasp of our young people as the authority they can trust because it is God's Word, telling us who we are, what God has done for us, and what we now do in our various vocations.

This overview of Ephesians 6:10–20 summarizes how a student of theology might look at adolescent risk-taking behaviors, and respond with a scripturally informed perspective grounded in God's Word. In our trinitarian framework, this is the view of adolescent risk from above—according to our Third Article gifts—the gifts given to the believing teen; God's Word, a worshiping community, and a mentor (you) who use all the God-given skills available to connect youth to the Means of Grace, which build faith.

Now let's take a look at adolescent risk behaviors from the perspective of First Article gifts—the gifts from below. This is the viewpoint that we find in psychology and sociology as they also examine adolescent risk-taking behavior.

# The View from Below

When thinking about what risk looks like to adolescents or their parents, let's be honest; it's really the view from below that we are talking about. What gifts has God given to each of us as His creation? How do we encounter the environments within which we mature in the adolescent years? These are questions that focus on healthy development rather than on spiritual truths, and though from the theological perspective healthy development really cannot be separated from spiritual truth, they are separated in the rich literature on adolescent risk-taking behaviors found in secular research.

How should we define risky behavior among adolescents? In a study designed to find correlations between variables that would help teens avoid harmful behaviors, two adolescent researchers offered this rather wide definition.

> A risk behavior is any behavior that impedes successful adolescent development and that may compromise a sense of competency, skill development, or the acquisition of socially approved roles.[3]

There is much to be said in favor of having a broad definition of risk behavior, since just about any activity taken to extremes can impede successful development. There are ways in which we can narrow the definition by looking at various theories that have been proposed to explain adolescent risk-taking behaviors.

Some approach adolescent risk taking from a very individualistic perspective, meaning that the phenomenon is best understood as a personal disposition issue resulting from personality traits. Others approach the origin of risk-taking behavior by inspecting genetic factors or the effects of physiological changes due to puberty or developmental tasks attached to exploring the world and declaring independence (i.e., having a sense of autonomy). Still others are intrigued by the possibility that "sensation-seeking" (thrill seeking) drives much adolescent risk taking, or that it is a "locus of control" issue, referring to the assumption that some adolescents have an internal locus of control in which good or bad things happen to them as a result of their own actions (internal control), while others have an external locus of control in that good or bad things happen and there is nothing they can do about it (external control). A review of studies

---

3 Jay A. Mancini and Angela J. Huebner, "Adolescent Risk Behavior Patterns: Effects of Structured Time-Use, Interpersonal Connections, Self-System Characteristics, and Socio-Demographic Influences," *Child and Adolescent Social Work Journal* 21, no. 6 (December 2004): 648.

on risk taking among adolescents concluded "it appears that none offer conclusive insight into the risk-taking behavior of adolescents."[4]

Interpreting research on adolescent risk-taking behavior is difficult and sometimes frustrating. As an example, take the distinction between internal and external locus of control that I just mentioned. Using that comparison, consider what you might hypothesize about teens. Would the teen who feels that he has control over the good and bad that happens to him be less likely to engage in risky business because he recognizes that his actions have specific effects? Or, feeling himself in control, would he engage in more risky behavior because he believes himself in control and trusts his own competencies? Likewise, if a teen feels she has no control over what happens, would that increase risky behaviors since "whatever will be, will be" anyway, thus ignoring or minimizing risk? Or does it inhibit risk because she feels the need to be more protective of herself in such a totally random world? What would you guess?

Making the investigations even more complex are two more constructs that are well documented in the literature: the imaginary audience and the personal fable. The imaginary audience accounts for the painful self-consciousness that so many early adolescents display. The imaginary audience is a way of describing the onset of interpersonal perspective taking—meaning that the child realizes for the first time that others are watching him or her. Previously unaware, the child becomes self-conscious. But the imaginary audience effect results in interpersonal perspective taking being blown all out of proportion. "The imaginary audience is the adolescent's assumption that his or her preoccupation with personal appearance and behavior is shared by everyone else."[5] During this period of time, hair, clothes, and complexion must all be right or nothing is right.

The personal fable builds on the imaginary audience. "Thinking of himself or herself as the center of attention, the adolescent comes to believe that it is because he or she is special and unique."[6] The personal fable is the belief that bad things happen to other people, but they can't happen to me. Frankly, I like the personal fable, and

4 Mary R. Rolison and Avraham Scherman. "Factors Influencing Adolescents' Decisions to Engage in Risk-Taking Behavior," *Adolescence* 37 (2002): 586.

5 Amy Alberts, David Elkind, and Stephen Ginsberg, "The Personal Fable and Risk-Taking in Early Adolescence," *Journal of Youth and Adolescence* 36 (2007): 72.

6 Alberts, 72.

there is still a trace of the personal fable in the construction of my own world and universe. Its existence might correlate with having a male ego; nevertheless, I don't mind occasionally thinking of myself as "different."[7]

When applied to adolescent risk-taking behavior, however, the implications of the personal fable become apparent. Others will lose control of themselves if they drink too much, but I won't. Others will contract an STD from promiscuous sexual activity, but I won't. In a very real sense, the personal fable allows adolescents to feel themselves invulnerable; adolescent psychologists theorize that this invulnerability enhances the likelihood of bad choices and risky behavior because adolescents are certain that, while accidents may happen to you, nothing bad can happen to them.

This makes sense to me and offers a reasonable explanation why those boys on the fifth floor of the hotel in suburban Chicago felt little hesitation when they grasped the sheets extended from the girls on the sixth floor and climbed out and up into the annals of youth ministry lore forever, proving once and for all the existence of guardian angels ready to lift us up lest we dash our feet against the glass ceiling atrium below.[8] Researchers have found that the effect of the "personal fable" increases from the sixth to the ninth grade, and these measures of invulnerability are higher for boys than for girls.[9]

Just when we think we have a handle on a complex issue, however, new information reframes our questions in unexpected ways. Just when I think I have enough evidence to convict invulnerability as the culprit in adolescent risk-taking behavior, more research arrives to contradict. According to Laurence Steinberg,

> Systematic research does not support the stereotype of
> adolescents as irrational individuals who believe they
> are invulnerable and who are unaware, inattentive to, or
> unconcerned about the potential harms of risky behavior.
> In fact, the logical-reasoning abilities of 15-year-olds are
> comparable to those of adults, adolescents are no worse than

---

7 In a good way, not a dorky way.

8 See chapter 1 for the context of this reference.

9 Alberts, 74.

adults at perceiving risk or estimating their vulnerability to it.[10]

What's the answer this time around? If it is true that the reasoning capacities of the adolescent are comparable to those of adults, then why aren't the decisions regarding risk comparable? The answer has something to do with adolescent cognitive control network and its relationship to adolescent socioemotional network, both of which are neural networks in the brain.

> This new view begins from the premise that risk taking in the real world is the product of both logical reasoning and psychosocial factors. However, unlike logical-reasoning abilities, which appear to be more or less fully developed by age 15, psychosocial capacities that improve decision making and moderate risk taking—such as impulse control, emotion regulation, delay of gratification, and resistance to peer influence—continue to mature well into adulthood.[11]

What does this mean? It means that there are two drivers at the controls of the adolescent: one rational and logical and the other more attuned to social and emotional influences. According to brain research, both drivers are in operation, but under some circumstances the rational and logical gets hijacked by the social and emotional, which hasn't yet fully matured and won't be fully matured until well into the twenties.

Here we have clues why the fifteen-year-old is just about ready for calculus but is not ready for the car keys. In fact, the use of car keys is the scenario one study tapped in order to demonstrate the theory. Adolescents, young adults, and adults were all measured for risk-taking maneuvers while playing a video driving game. When playing the video game alone, there was no difference in the driving patterns of all three groups. They all scored about the same number of crashes per minute. *But when playing the game in the presence of friends*, the results were dramatically different. In the presence of friends, adolescents had three times as many crashes per minute, young adults had twice as many crashes per minute, and adults crashed at the same rate as if they

10 Laurence Steinberg, "Risk Taking in Adolescence: New Perspectives from Brain and Behavioral Science," *Current Directions in Psychological Science* 16, no. 2 (2007): 55.

11 Steinberg, 56.

were playing alone. "In adolescence, then, not only is more merrier—it is also riskier."[12]

Psychologists call the power of a variable to affect an outcome "salience." The presence of friends in the study was the salient variable that dramatically changed the risk-taking behavior of the adolescent, and to a lesser extent the young adult participants in the study. This information seems to say that the youth clutching the sheets out the hotel window knew very well the risks they were taking, but felt the social benefits of their action a more immediate and powerful concern, in other words, more "salient." Thus in spite of full knowledge of the risks involved in their action, they did it.

Laurence Steinberg, the author of this study, provides a much more detailed description of the intricate brain development that occurs during adolescence and young adulthood—like myelination of neurons and synaptic pruning that increase brain efficiency. These, he points out, are developmental issues that for the present are beyond our ability to alter or change. They explain why programs of intervention "designed to alter knowledge, attitudes, or beliefs have proven remarkably disappointing."[13] The suggestion Steinberg offers for limiting adolescent risk-taking behaviors is that adults pay more attention to the situations and circumstances in which adolescents find themselves, with the goal of "limiting opportunities for immature judgment to have harmful consequences. . . . Some things just take time to develop, and, like it or not, mature judgment is probably one of them."[14]

# Youth Leaders Roles and Responsibilities

The first conclusion that I draw from this information is that our culture once again has things backwards. Rather than giving adolescents so much freedom as early as possible, we would be better off functioning as do many other cultures that closely monitor the behavior of the young through family structures that only gradually

---

12 Steinberg, 57.

13 Steinberg, 55.

14 Steinberg, 58.

allow freedom.[15] But since our culture is not going to change dramatically in the direction of fewer freedoms for adolescents anytime soon, I might as well quit complaining and suggest something helpful in our current situation.

## Adolescent risk-taking behaviors will continue to happen

We live in a fallen world where the devil, the world, and our own sinful flesh continue to seek our destruction; teenagers are not immune from these effects, nor can we immunize them. The psychological and physiological explanations cited above do not invalidate the previous sentence. These explanations merely add to the vocabulary at our disposal to describe the phenomenon. "Salience" might just be a euphemism for how temptation works, and immaturity will continue to be our fall-back commentary when temptation has won over common sense regarding risk-taking behaviors. Recognizing this to be the case, youth workers have a responsibility to minimize the impact of immaturity, or to use Steinberg's words, to limit "opportunities for immature judgment to have harmful consequences."

What is Steinberg suggesting? He is suggesting that we become experts at predicting what could go wrong and who would be the most likely source for the wrong-going. It means that we must take every precaution, not for the purpose of inhibiting growth and maturity nor to repress spontaneity, but to preclude opportunities for poor decision making. Some of this is simply common sense. On trips, housing arrangements aren't made at random. Medical forms must be available in case of an accident. Sufficient adult supervision is required at all times and if unavailable, the event should be postponed.

Finally, as Lutheran youth leaders, we will not only be fully prepared with rules (the Law), but we will also be ready with words of forgiveness (the Gospel) when our youth mess up. I don't believe this can be overemphasized—that when Lutherans talk about youth *ministry*, ministry isn't the task of making people perfect through effective programming; ministry is applying the life, death, and

---

15 A colleague of mine describes the presence of a chaperone throughout the years he was dating his wife. By the time of the wedding, everyone knew the new family member very well.

resurrection of Jesus to sinful people who need God's grace. Our challenge as leaders is learning how best to be conduits of the message of God's love.

## Adolescent risk-taking behaviors do not occur in a vacuum

There is always a context. The context can be the Church, the school, the home, or someplace in between those three. To be effective in noticing the at-risk adolescents, youth leaders need to be in a solid team-working relationship with the church staff, with teachers and administrators in the school system, and with parents in the home.

Granted, any one of those three sources could conceivably be part of the problem for the teenager, but from the start these three sources are the three-legged stool support mechanism for anyone in youth work. Some aphorisms are in order here, such as "Youth Ministry Is Family Ministry." If you are doing youth ministry, then you will inevitably be engaged in family ministry, either through the enlistment of families as core support team members of the youth program or families as the targets of ministry efforts in support of troubled teens. One way or the other, getting to know your teens will mean learning about their families, or as systems theory would describe it, their "families of origin."

## Youth leaders recognize their limits in working with troubled teens

When youth leaders notice an adolescent at risk, they are often tempted to believe their ministry goal is to cure, heal, or fix the problem. If the problem is a flat tire, then of course getting it fixed is the proper course of action. But here I'm referring to encountering a teen who is exhibiting problems that transcend an easy fix. Youth leaders have limits in their expertise. You may be the first one on the scene, you may be the one to share words of comfort, and you may be the one who provides the background support, but you are not a therapist, a counselor, or a social worker.[16]

---

16 Unless, of course, you are a licensed therapist, counselor, or social worker, who
   happens also to be volunteering as a youth leader at your congregation. If you are,
   however, you are also then aware of the issues of dual-relationships that may make

Realizing the limits of your role is no small part of being an effective youth leader. You really are on the front line for those youth whom you've come to know well and even for a few that are on the fringes of the youth group. Before parents suspect there is a problem, you already may know what the problem is. If it was within your power to fix the difficulty, no doubt you would, but that magic wand wasn't included in the deal when you volunteered, were hired, or received your call into youth ministry. Your role in a crisis may simply be that of being the "nonanxious presence" that reminds people that God is not absent from the room. Your role in an emergency may be basically that of maintaining calm and notifying authorities. Your role in listening to a teen suffering from a chronically debilitating situation or condition may be to recognize the kind of help the teen needs and arrange for the teen to get it.

The truth is that more expertise is required in serving teens than you are capable of mastering. Accurately recognizing your own weaknesses can be one of your greatest strengths in ministry, however. And of course, these really aren't so much weaknesses as they are simply areas of expertise for which you have never been trained. Resources are available, and it is your responsibility to familiarize yourself with Christian caregiving professionals—counselors, physicians, therapists, social workers—who can be your source for referrals when you need them. These phone numbers will be in your cell phone address book.

## Types of Risk

Noticing someone sitting in a window and losing consciousness isn't really hard to do; the evidence of impending disaster is readily discerned. But most of the risks that match the definition provided above by Mancini and Huebner[17] are more subtle. In order to get a grasp on all that we want to be aware of, I find it helpful to arrange risks into five categories: personality, behavioral issues, self-destructive

---

your ability to serve as the counselor difficult. Referral may very well still be the most appropriate course of action.

17 "A risk behavior is any behavior that impedes successful adolescent development and that may compromise a sense of competency, skill development, or the acquisition of socially approved roles" (648).

activities, families at risk, and sexuality.[18] Each category covers situations that range from the obvious, meaning they are impossible to ignore, to the extremely well hidden, which will only be shared with the most trusted of friends or mentors.

## Personality

Teens can sometimes begin to display symptoms of a personality disorder. You might notice differences in how a teen interacts with others. It's one thing to be shy, but it's another thing to lack the social confidence to look at others or talk with them. Without specialized training, youth leaders find it difficult to determine what might be a passing phase that's really no big deal and what is a serious condition that might grow worse with time. Some years ago, when a teen approached me to share that the voices the teen was hearing were telling the teen to come and talk to pastor, it didn't take me long to realize this was not a case for pastoral counseling but a situation for medical attention.[19] In this category we notice behaviors that coalesce around issues such as anxiety, depression, inferiority, panic attacks, phobias, anger management, shyness, obsessive/compulsive behaviors, and more severe forms of mental illness.

Many of these difficulties have hopeful resolutions through therapy and medication. Your role as the youth leader may be that of the catalyst, working with the family, who assists the teen in securing the medical attention needed. On the other hand, your challenge may be in raising the Christian maturity level of other teens in the group by teaching them how to respond in love rather than rejection. How do we do that? We begin by guiding teens through appropriate Scripture that describes their vocation within the scenario. We share information with teens, within the limits of privacy and confidentiality, so that they have a sufficient understanding of the illness that can inform and guide

---

18 For anyone wishing to dig deeper, I suggest looking at three books in particular: Les Parrott III, *Helping the Struggling Adolescent: A Guide to Thirty-Six Common Problems for Counselors, Pastors, and Youth Workers* (Grand Rapids: Zondervan, 2000); Rich Van Pelt and Jim Hancock, *The Youth Worker's Guide to Helping Teenagers in Crisis* (Grand Rapids: Zondervan, 2005); and the companion volume, *The Parent's Guide to Helping Teenagers in Crisis* (Grand Rapids: Zondervan, 2008).

19 Hearing voices and similar phenomena are usually understood to be the early onset of schizophrenia that often begins to manifest itself in mid-adolescence. The earlier the diagnosis and treatment is initiated, the better the prognosis for mental health.

their emotional responses. Without that knowledge, their reaction could be harmful if not unchristian.

This pattern of response is not all that different from how we respond for the benefit of teens experiencing any other kind of illness or teens living with a permanent disability of one kind or another. These teens need the affirmation that will come from their youth leader teaching them about their own special vocation—which under the circumstances consists of providing their peers with the chance to serve, and by serving grow. I think of the girl in confirmation class with cerebral palsy so severe she required an aide to be with her at all times; not only do I recall how brilliant she was in class (she was the brightest confirmation student I have ever taught), but I also remember how her presence in the classroom raised the level of maturity and helpfulness among her classmates. Her vocation was training them in meaningful Christian care by being the object of their love and care.

## Behavioral Issues

Behavioral issues tend to be the things that get youth in trouble with parents, teachers, and peers, yet they aren't the kind of behaviors that might cause harm or injury to self or others. You might become aware of the problems when others bring it to your attention through complaints or criticisms. These are often acting out behaviors that have very deep-rooted sources, making it difficult to understand why these behaviors are happening. On the other hand, these may also be the behaviors resulting from an inability to withstand social pressures. The teen is challenged and can't refuse to act on the dare.

In this category, we might include bullying or being bullied, cheating, getting in trouble with the law through shoplifting or driving violations, dropping out of school, and a variety of problems resulting from peer pressure. Whereas our previous category involved many situations that are involuntary, the behavioral issues center on teens making a series of bad choices. Is this the immaturity, the lack of brain development that was discussed earlier in this chapter, or is it a manifestation of the old Adam, the fallen human nature, rendering itself visible by sinful acts? This, I believe, is a false dichotomy: not an either/or but precisely a both/and. That many of these problems begin to fade as the teen moves into the twenties indicates the developmental side. That many of these problems remain throughout the lifespan bears witness to the fallen human nature side. How does the youth leader respond? Behavior that hurts self and others can't be tolerated or excused. The youth group has a set of rules—a code of behavior—that is articulated and enforced. No one who presents a danger to others can participate. It is the responsibility of the youth leader to make clear behavior that's unacceptable. At the same time, these are the kind of issues for which Lutheran theology stresses repentance. Where there is sorrow over transgressions because the Law has been felt or spoken, then there is the ministry opportunity to apply the forgiveness of the Gospel to the stricken conscience. In working with the youth group, the leader doesn't put the group at risk by ignoring what's unacceptable; but the leader also doesn't put the offender at risk by withholding the forgiveness that comes through the cross of Christ. Behavioral issues provide us with opportunities to put the distinction between Law and Gospel into living practice with our youth.

## Self-Destructive Activities

Self-destructive activities can be frightening to youth leaders. What would motivate students to do things that are so obviously harmful? Yet it happens with high levels of frequency. Again we might ask if the behavior is rooted in poor decisions, misperceptions, or developmental issues. The causes are so varied, and the exploration of them so far beyond the training of volunteers and full-time church workers alike, that we realize intuitively that we will need help if we are to help teens caught in self-destructive activities. After we have found the best source of help we can, our next role will be to assure teens that we aren't going to abandon them, and neither will God.

Self-destructive activities include but are not limited to substance abuse (drugs and alcohol), eating disorders (bulimia and anorexia), cutting and embedding, non-drug-related addictions (video games, Internet, etc.), and suicide ideation culminating in successful or unsuccessful attempts. Of these destructive behaviors, the one I was least familiar with until a few years ago was cutting and its more recent offshoot, embedding. Cutting is the ritualized cutting of one's body so that it bleeds. Embedding is the practice of inserting foreign material, like a paper clip, underneath the skin and in the flesh and leaving it there.

One distinction needs to be immediately drawn: cutting is not considered a prelude to suicide. Rather cutting, and perhaps embedding, is a ritualized practice that releases a buildup of stress and tension for the teen. Some speculate this practice brings the distressed teen a sense of peace and control, and if this is true, then we can see a link between cutting and eating disorders in that both give teens who feel no control over what's happening to them in life at least control over what enters her or his body.

Eating disorders tend to affect girls more often than boys and for different reasons. Issues of control and body image are of prime importance for girls, while athletics in which weight class drives competition can initiate eating disorders for boys. Further reading on this subject will reveal how often self-perception becomes skewed for girls suffering from anorexia, as dangerously slender girls still think themselves fat. Certain circumstances highly correlate with anorexia, such as high family expectations and personal perfectionism. Bulimia, the practice of binging (overeating) and purging (induced vomiting), is often felt to originate because overeating compensates for social stresses—with food assuming the role of comforter. Eating disorders are serious medical conditions that can result in permanent physical disabilities or death.

Suicide probably should be in a category by itself. How often is a successful suicide attempt a cry for help that's gone wrong? Van Pelt and Hancock suggest that if one suspects a person may be suicidal, a series of questions asked in private using the outline SLAP helps to evaluate the risk.

- **S**—Specific Details: Is there a plan, a method?

- **L**—Lethality of Method: Guns are more successful than pills; is it a cry for help?

- **A**—Availability of Method: Are the means accessible?

- **P**—Proximity to Helping Resources: Is the plan in an isolated area or where interruption could take place?[20]

---

20 Van Pelt and Hancock, 43–44. Particularly significant is the following observation: "Can he name someone who'd want to stop him if he tried to kill himself? A person who has difficulty naming such a person is at high risk. He may be wrong in his assessment—but if he believes it's true, he may act as if it were true" [italics in original] (44).

From a theological perspective, self-destructive behaviors, like all the difficulties we encountered so far, have a connection to sin and to the fallen world in which we live. Satan seeks the destruction of God's creation and God's creatures, especially us. Whether through depression, a desire to make whatever pain there is in life go away, or because of weak impulse control after hearing about another teen's suicide, we would do well to think of teen suicide as a victory for Satan, whose deceptions have in this case led to their ultimate conclusion rather than focus on the eternal state of the deceased, about which we have no final word.

Still, we find self-destructive behaviors difficult to understand. What can bring healing? Our approach should not cut off or disparage the help that comes from psychology and psychiatry. The counselor and the psychiatrist have a valid vocation to fulfill on behalf of teens struggling with self-destructive behaviors, and as youth leaders we will rely on them to fulfill their vocation. Our vocation, which is to be present with God's Word and the strength that comes with the Sacraments, dare never be underestimated. A stronger faith and a firmer relationship with Jesus Christ are outcomes for which we work and pray. This is no simplistic response but is relying on the Holy Spirit to be present in the lives of troubled teens. The Spirit's presence may find itself felt by troubled teens as you, along with others, intervene in order to get the help that's needed to combat an addiction or other self-destructive behavior.[21]

## Families At Risk

The fourth category describes teens who are at risk not because of their own beliefs or behaviors, but because of the actions of the adults around them. Because a family is at risk of imploding, the teens in the household are at risk for unhealthy attitudes and behaviors when they see their homes disintegrating before their eyes. Within this category we find divorce, abuse, alcohol and drug addictions by parents, and problems between siblings that go far beyond simple rivalry. Because

---

21 Interventions are procedures used in order to use family, community, and church resources to confront an individual for the purposes of bringing him or her to a realization of the real condition and to get the person into some form of treatment. Interventions are led by trained individuals who carefully prepare members of the team before the intervention is made. For more information, see the works by Parrott and Van Pelt and Hancock mentioned earlier.

divorce is so frequent, the experience of divorce by children has nearly achieved the status of a new norm for childhood development. As much as our cultural practice might want to make divorce free from unfortunate side effects for children, divorce still hurts, even years later.[22]

The teen you work with whose family is dissolving feels anger, embarrassment, remorse, and guilt. There is anger that the adults in his or her world have betrayed their vocation to care and nurture their child.[23] There is embarrassment that the family has now become a topic of discussion within the community, and there is remorse over a lost home. Of greater seriousness, however, is the emergence of feelings of guilt—to what degree does the child feel responsible for the breakup? Surprisingly, even older children can feel traces of guilt, even though as adults they know better.

You probably will encounter in your youth ministry a situation in which adult betrayal has exploded into full-blown danger for members of the family—spousal abuse and child abuse, often alcohol related, isn't uncommon and carries with it a whole set of counterintuitive dynamics. For example, the abused spouse defends the abuser, and children want to remain in the home even though the conditions are intolerable. Is it likely to find such a circumstance within the homes of the church's youth group? Perhaps, and we dare not be naïve to what's possible in a fallen world and fail to see an at-risk youth living in an at-risk household.

The ministry response at the dissolution of a family will bear a striking resemblance to what might happen when a death occurs, because in reality there is a death—the death of the marriage. Teens experiencing this loss will need to grieve, and as you would respond at a death, in this situation your care is one of bringing the comfort of your presence, God's Word, and hope for the future. Because you are guided by a theology of the cross, you can assure teens that God has not left them, but is right beside them through each step. No less

---

22 See Judith S. Wallerstein and Joan Berlin Kelly, *Surviving the Breakup: How Children and Parents Cope with Divorce* (New York, Basic Books, 1980) and the follow-up study: Judith S. Wallerstein, Julia Lewis, and Sandra Blakeslee, *The Unexpected Legacy of Divorce: A 25 Year Landmark Study* (New York: Hyperion, 2000).

23 Yes, you are correct in seeing that teens wouldn't describe their family's situation as a failure of vocation. I'm only suggesting that we look at it through a theological lens, and when we do so, this is one of the pictures that emerges.

practical will be the realization that for most, the divorce means a decrease in family resources. What teens could do before, they might no longer be able to afford. You can be sensitive and supportive as all these changes take place.

## Sexuality

The heading I'm using for the final category is representative of the difficulty. Why should sexuality be the heading for a fifth category of risk behaviors for adolescents? Of course, we know why it is a category for risk—incest, sexual abuse, sexual intercourse outside of marriage, sexually transmitted diseases, pornography, pregnancy,[24] sexual identity confusion, homosexual behavior, and multiple variations of the preceding list.

University of Texas at Austin professor Mark Regnerus in his research of adolescent sexuality presents a thorough, academic, dispassionate description of the attitudes and behaviors he discovers.[25]

Regnerus describes the emotional pain and scars caused by the poor choices that teens make regarding sexuality. Most teens are ill-equipped to deal with the complex issues surrounding human sexuality.[26] This moral complexity is the brick wall of confusion into which adolescents collide when the hormonal transformations of puberty kick into gear. The questions, articulated and hidden, in the minds of teenagers cannot be excluded from the ministry moments inherent in youth ministry. So your challenge is simply this—will you communicate in meaningful ways to teens in your youth program that there is more to human sexuality than what is healthy or wise—behaviors that the culture readily endorses? Will you go beyond the bar of cultural mores in order to communicate what is God-pleasing and right?

Is this risky and uncomfortable? Of course it is, because as Regnerus mentions, "Sex is far from a *simple* pleasure." We have our own attitudes, feelings, and embarrassments with which to deal. Let's

---

24 I was about to write "unwed mothers," but that term is so outdated I couldn't bring myself to use it.

25 Mark D. Regnerus, *Forbidden Fruit: Sex and Religion in the Lives of American Teenagers* (New York: Oxford, 2007).

26 Regnerus, 211.

not let those obstacles get in our way. The subject is too important, the ministry moment too intense, to ignore. Adolescents need adults who are willing to confirm that what God's Word has to say about the most intimate of relationships is not only workable, it is ultimately the most satisfying.

Here is what I suggest. The information about what is God-pleasing and right is easily obtained. It's right there in our catechisms.[27] Our clear communication begins with a solid theological foundation. We recall that sex is a gift from God, a First Article gift for which our Creator has intended purposes that bless us not only with the opportunity to be co-creators with God in bringing the next generation into the world, but to do so in a way that brings two people so closely together that they become one. Without recognition of the core goodness of God's gift of sex, we run the risk of mistaking the gift for the problem, rather than the misuse of the gift.

From this starting point, our next step is to learn as much as we can about human sexuality.[28] We can't afford to be misinformed about our First Article gifts. If we aren't familiar with the vocabulary used by teens, then let's ask them—the slang changes year by year and what meant one thing last year may mean something quite different today. There's no reason to miscommunicate because we don't know the language.

Next, we need to understand our role, which is not to replace parents, who have the primary responsibility. So whatever we might choose to do in terms of curriculum, we will do it with the knowledge, approval, and participation of parents. We also recognize our responsibility as mandatory reporters, a responsibility that varies in degree from state to state. In most states, if we learn of situations

---

27 *Luther's Small Catechism* (St. Louis: Concordia, 1943), Question 61: "What is marriage? Marriage is the lifelong union of one man and one woman unto one flesh. Marriage was instituted by God and is entered into by rightful betrothal, or engagement." *Luther's Small Catechism with Explanation* (St. Louis: Concordia, 1991), Question 64: "How do we lead a sexually pure and decent life? We lead a sexually pure and decent life when we
A. Consider sexuality to be a good gift of God;
B. Honor marriage as God's institution, the lifelong union of one man and one woman;
C. Reserve sexual intercourse for the marriage partner alone; and
D. Control sexual urges in a God-pleasing way."

28 See Roger Sonnenberg, *Human Sexuality: A Christian Perspective* (St. Louis: Concordia, 1998).

of abuse, it becomes our responsibility to inform authorities. In an abusive situation, it isn't just our legal responsibility, it is our moral responsibility. Resources are available to guide us in these difficult situations.[29]

Our focus thus far has been on the gifts from below. Let's remember that the heart of our service to teens rests on the gifts from above. Each sexual category of risk, and I don't think I provided an exhaustive list, is rooted in temptations to sin and acts of sin, whether they be in thought, word, or deed. And of course we all would recognize, as did Jesus in the Sermon on the Mount, that a high percentage of sexual sin and guilt is the result of thought.[30] Where there is sin, there needs to be repentance, Confession, and Absolution. From a ministry perspective, one of the reasons for accurate information about sex for adolescents is to counter the murky and confused conscience that is ready to accuse a teen of terrible things, when in fact all that is happening is normal physical development. Wet dreams are a case in point. Real guilt needs forgiveness. Misinformed guilt needs explanation.

Vocational catechesis has a place in this discussion too. Why not explain in clearest of terms that God does work in the world for the benefit of our neighbor through our sexuality? That benefit is found in our respect for the boundaries of sex within marriage. How might this be expressed for a teen? My sexual purity as a male teen is not simply for my own benefit in my relationship to God, but is also for the benefit of my girlfriend, whose purity is maintained as I fulfill my vocation toward her as a Christian brother in Christ. My sexual purity as a female teen is not simply for my own benefit in my relationship to God, but is also for the benefit of my boyfriend, whose purity is maintained as I fulfill my vocation toward him as a Christian sister in Christ. And should the relationship mature into public vows of lifelong fidelity in marriage, the vocation changes from that of respecter of the gift of sex to participant in the gift of sex, as the vocation of husband and wife is fulfilled with the possibility of an even more profound vocation as mom and dad.

---

29 Van Pelt and Hancock provide a listing of Child Protective Services by state (230–36).

30 Matthew 5:28: "But I tell you that anyone who looks at a woman lustfully has already committed adultery with her in his heart" (NIV).

Granted, this may not be a view toward sex that's easily understood or put into practice. Others will no doubt say this is impractical, unrealistic, and pie in the sky. So? The important question is this: is it true?

## Eutychus At Risk

Life not only *can* be confusing to teens, but it usually *is* confusing. Trying to figure out the world and one's place in it is the norm for adolescents. What then is your role regarding the five categories of risk that I've outlined? Remember that you are not the expert, but you are the observer. You need enough familiarity with the difficulties of adolescent existence to notice when something is going really wrong and have the awareness to act upon your observations, not as an individual but as a member of a ministry team that may include pastors, parents, and other professionals. But as you share these responsibilities, don't overlook the theological importance of the ministry moment that brings together the gifts from below and the gifts from above—you and a hurting teen—for the benefit of faith in Jesus Christ. The guilty conscience needs to hear that forgiveness is given. The hurting heart needs to hear that God is love.

CHAPTER 13

# Looking for Eutychus

L et's assume for a moment that Eutychus is in the upper
room listening to Paul, and he realizes he's getting tired.
He looks around to see what he might do to relieve
his fatigue, and he notices the window. "If I can just
maneuver myself over to that window," he thinks, "I'll get
some fresh air. That should revive me." Gradually, he moves through
the crowd toward the window and carefully positions himself on the
ledge. He's pleased with himself for having solved the problem and
turns his attention once more to the words that continue to flow
unabated from Paul's mouth. The fresh air fails to revive him, however,
and it is only a short time before his condition is more precarious than
ever before.

In a world in which the number of windows offering fresh air
to bored youth seems beyond count, many of those windows are no
less risky than the third-story casement of the room in Ephesus.[1] The

---

1 I can't help but point out that many temptations for youth today come through the
computer, and, of course, much of that comes through Windows.

statistics are startling when we finally bring ourselves to look at them. Ken Ham and Britt Beemer summarize the research in their book *Already Gone*. Sixty-one percent of teens who are involved in a church walk away from church in their twenties.[2] The authors report the situation in England to be much worse, but warn that it's happening in America as well. In their analysis, they find two sources that systematically engender unbelief.

- The Bible is no longer relevant to the skeptic because he/she has not been taught convincing apologetics for its historical accuracy beginning at Genesis 1:1.

- The believer has found the Church to be irrelevant because of hypocrisy, a watering down of God's Word, and an unwillingness to be flexible with cultural forms in order to stay true to the principles of God's inerrant Word.[3]

While this may be true of Christendom at large, could it also be true among us? What I find most disconcerting in this research is the implication that youth are being lost not because of the attractive draw of the world reaching out to them, but because the Church is failing to pass on to the next generation what is truly valuable.

## Prioritizing Youth Ministry

Let me see if I can better explain what I mean. In the last several chapters, we have explored a wide range of risky behaviors. If we are to do youth ministry competently and faithfully, we must be aware of the difficulties of being young, bored, and at risk and be willing to notice and respond appropriately. But risky behavior is not the greatest risk youth face. The greater danger is risky theology, and by that I mean attitudes and beliefs—worldviews—that are easily accepted and approved by culture, while simultaneously undermining faith in Jesus Christ. Remember Moralistic Therapeutic Deism?[4] Do we have

---

2 Ken Ham and Britt Beemer, *Already Gone: Why Your Kids Will Quit Church and What You Can Do to Stop It* (Green Forest: Master Books, 2009), 25.

3 Ham and Beemer, 84.

4 (1) A God exists who created and orders the world and watches over human life on earth.
(2) God wants people to be good, nice, and fair to each other, as taught in the Bible

any reason to believe that our youth are immune from this pervasive worldview? Are they even aware of the difference between "MTD" and genuine, historic Christianity?

Here's my suspicion—the drop-off from participation and the loss of souls to faith in Jesus Christ is due more to risky theology than it is due to risky behavior, more to unfulfilled catechesis than to the lure of the world. From multiple directions, youth are led to believe that personal opinion is more and the authority of God's Word is less, that faith is merely a matter of feelings and not the stuff of facts. Tragically, in the middle of great spiritual hunger that leads even major secular universities to study the spirituality of both students and faculty, youth today don't trust the Church to feed them. Could that mistrust have roots in misguided priorities? Is that the realization that so many youth ministry organizations are coming to when they lament the failures of contemporary youth ministry initiatives?

Let's put it this way. If our main concern is that youth grow up healthy in mind and body, then we are really engaged in youth social services, not youth ministry. Youth ministry is not unconcerned about the healthy mind and body, but its primary concern is a healthy soul, a healthy spirit, connected to a loving God through faith in Jesus Christ by the power of the Holy Spirit, from which a healthy mind and body may follow. Don't misunderstand. I'm not saying mind and body are unimportant, nor am I saying they are of no concern for youth ministry. I am arguing that the center of youth *ministry* is theology. And if the center is theology, what theology brings youth closest to a living, loving, sustainable relationship with Jesus Christ?

## What Lutheran Theology Brings

Lutheran theology applied to youth ministry[5] adds much to the practice of youth ministry. Ultimately, this is what this book is about—not an attack on other theologies or denominations as they go about

and by most world religions.
(3) The central goal of life is to be happy and to feel good about oneself.
(4) God does not need to be particularly involved in one's life except when God is needed to resolve a problem.
(5) Good people go to heaven when they die (Smith and Denton, 162–63).

5 Notice I did not say "a Lutheran theology of youth ministry." Such a thing doesn't exist. As I have said before, what we do have is Lutheran theology applied to youth ministry.

reaching their youth nor a gleeful attempt to elevate Lutheranism by pointing out the shortcomings of others, but to provide an answer to the question whether or not Lutheran theology has something to offer, something to add that is of value not only for Lutherans but for other Christians as well who want to serve their young people in the name of Jesus Christ.

I'm going to summarize what I have proposed by working our way back to the beginning. In doing so, we will discover that our theology is not difficult or complicated. It is rooted in Scripture and in the chief doctrine of the Christian religion: justification by grace through faith in Jesus Christ. Our theology recognizes mystery, miracle, and paradox as precious components of God's message to humankind and also appreciates how these three elements appeal to youth and draw them, as well as ourselves, toward God. We also discern that nothing is changing in our theology—it is the same we have received for generations. What makes it different is only that we are applying this theology to the wonderful and amazing time of life we call adolescence.

## Vocational Catechesis

Luther's doctrine of vocation teaches that God serves our neighbors through the talents, abilities, and possessions He has given us. Teens who grasp they are the "masks of God" for their neighbor have a ready answer for the deep, challenging questions of adolescence: who am I, and why am I here? Lifelong instruction in the faith that emphasizes vocation emphasizes living under the theology of the cross. Mature Christian faith grows as difficulty and suffering in life is understood not as God's absence but as God's purpose, perhaps hidden from human eyes but nevertheless precious in His sight and filled with intention and meaning.

The fact that teens as well as adults struggle in their vocation of service reminds us of our dual nature, our schizoid existence as saint/ sinner: perfect in Christ yet battling toe-to-toe against the devil, the world, and our own sinful flesh. Vocational catechesis stresses that we are children of God who are leery of our capacity for sin but confident of our ability to do good for Jesus' sake by the Holy Spirit's power. Such a worldview transforms our ordinary and mundane lives into components of God's mission in the world. Don't think vocation won't do for teens what it already does for so many adults. But this begs the question that, as we work our way back, asks: How did we get this way?

## Means of Grace Theology

We got this way by God's grace wholly without our own merit or works. This sounds so Lutheran, so Reformation driven, and indeed it is. We got this way because God works through an authoritative Word attached to certain elements whereby God's promises are given. The promises tell us three incredibly important things about ourselves. We are called, we are washed, and we are fed, all things needed by children who are being cared for by a loving parent—a heavenly Father. These are also things needed by adolescents looking to find where they fit in and feeling terribly awkward, self-conscious, and needy in the process.

The very first thing a Means of Grace theology provides teens is truth. One cannot trust if one doubts the existence of truth, and many teens today doubt whether or not truth really exists. How can it be known with certainty? What does it look like? Truth, Lutheran theology tells us, begins with words—with promises. We know because God Himself gives us words, His words. We read them, speak them, memorize them, and believe them because they are God's words and they are true. They are true because God cannot lie.

Yet today simply telling young people that God's Word is true and trustworthy isn't enough. Yes, of course the Holy Spirit will work through the Word to bring faith to the heart. But while that is going on, skeptics fill classrooms and bookstores with alternatives. Go to Borders or Barnes & Noble, and peruse the offerings of the current crop of militant atheist authors. Check out the latest interpretation of Gnostic writings, reviews of the Gospel of Thomas or the Gospel of Judas. Realize how much the curiosity of adolescents is pricked when they see things that undermine, cast doubt, or deny what they learn in confirmation and Bible class. There is a natural suspicion about the adult world—that adults are hiding something from us, and we must crack the code in order to uncover the truth.[6]

---

6 A moment's consideration reveals that this was certainly true in prior generations, but the secrets being withheld were all about sex. Today there are *no* secrets about sex or anything else for that matter. The suspicion remains, however.

Therefore, our vocational catechesis, supported by our Means of Grace theology, requires an apologetic bent. Teens need to be informed about the opponents of the Christian faith—even the opponents from the first centuries. Rather than trying to hide teens from the detractors of the faith, we need to school teens in arguments for the faith. It won't take a great deal of effort to show teens the difference between a Gnostic text and Holy Scripture. Explaining the difference between suppressing an alternative expression of Christianity (the supposed reason Gnosticism didn't survive) and rejection of a false religion (the real reason Gnosticism didn't survive) isn't all that difficult. Likewise, teens should not discover in a high school class or college course that there are textual variants in Scripture—a time and place where the information will be used to discredit the faith. Wouldn't it be better for teens to learn about the thousands of New Testament texts and fragments in church, at a time and place where they can learn how "textual criticism" provides us with Scriptures that are better attested to than any other ancient writings, and that—wonder of wonders— instead of discrediting the Christian faith, such knowledge supports the Christian faith by the amazing transmission of the Word to us today. But to include such information in a youth ministry curriculum does assume some knowledge in this area that, if the youth leaders lack, can be filled in by the pastor.

What I'm suggesting is that we do a preemptive educational strike so that our young people have answers to the attacks that will come against God's Word. And why should we do this? We do this not to worship the Bible, but to remove doubt about the promises God has made. If God promises through the writing of Peter that we are born again through the living Word of God (1 Peter 1:23), then we are. If God promises the forgiveness of sin and the gift of the Holy Spirit through Baptism even for children through the preaching of Peter (Acts 2:38–39), then we have forgiveness and the Holy Spirit when we are washed with water and the Word. If Jesus promises His body and His blood, shed for the forgiveness of sins when we eat the bread and drink the cup of His Supper (Matthew 26:26–27), then we receive into our own bodies the gift He promises.

God cares enough about us to call us, wash us, and feed us. Trusting God's promises brings us ever closer to one another as part of His family, the community of the Church. This is not lost on growing adolescent faith as it remembers the scrubbing of Baptism and walks up to kneel at the altar to receive the meal that feeds the soul. These promises are precious to us, and they raise another question. What is it that leads us to these promises?

## Law and Gospel

Certainly it is the Holy Spirit that opens hearts and minds to the truth of God's Word and brings us to faith. But the Word that is heard first is the word of the Law. Either our conscience hammers us by our own failings or our consciousness burns us by the evil that so often surrounds us. At the very deepest levels, under all our pretense and bravado, we know the truth about our sinful selves. The truth leaves us helpless, hopeless, and hurt. The Law does its work, and we need little help in understanding it. It is, after all, written in our hearts (Romans 2:13–14).

To be sure, our hopelessness is not without purpose. The Holy Spirit has brought us to this point of despair precisely to bless us with the message of the Gospel. Jesus Christ is our substitute who has taken our place—the hammer will not strike us because it has already struck Him. Jesus Christ has defeated sin, death, and the devil, and they can burn us no longer because in turning back death into life by the resurrection, Jesus Christ has turned the enemies back on themselves. We believe these promises because the Holy Spirit has brought us the Word that cannot lie, and we realize that here is truth—and not only truth, but in Jesus Christ we have the way and the life too (John 14:6). These gifts are far above us, and we are not worthy of them. Knowing this, we confront one last question as we work our way back in our theological foundations: Why does God do all this for us?

## Trinitarian Framework

God does this because He is rich in mercy (Ephesians 2:4; Titus 3:5). God is a gift-giving God who is merciful. He gives us gifts from below through His creative power and gifts from above through the Means of Grace. Third Article gifts (the work of the Holy Spirit, the community of the Church, and the servant's skill) are received in the context of First Article gifts (created skills and abilities, life experiences, and human needs) for the benefit of Second Article faith in Jesus Christ. Within the trinitarian framework, we receive all that we need from the hand of our loving God. There are ministry moments in the lives of teens, just as there are ministry moments in our own lives, when all this comes together—when who we are meets what we do. Within a trinitarian framework, the moments all point to Jesus Christ and faith in Him.

# Final Disclaimer

Will others from different traditions find these theological distinctives helpful? I can't say, but I do know they are helpful for me as I work with those who want to work with youth in the Church. Lutheran theology has a lot to offer ministry to youth because Lutheran theology responds to the paradoxes of life with the grace and mercy won for us through Jesus Christ. Lutheran theology teaches us to notice Eutychus in our midst and to explore ways to nudge him from the window.

I must apologize, however, to all who read this book waiting for the chapter on "how to do youth ministry and be an astounding success so you can write books about it." I have given you no icebreakers, no list of best games, no organizational charts, and only referenced two movies—far too few to be of real help in programming youth nights. I warned you about this at the beginning. This isn't a book telling you how to do it. It is a book telling you why to do it, with which beliefs about God and youth to do it, and why doing it as a Lutheran Christian is something for which to be eternally grateful. Above all, this book encourages all adults, not just youth workers, to notice teens, to appreciate their gifts, and to guide them along the path to Christian adulthood.

Eutychus came to hear Paul teach about Jesus Christ that warm evening so long ago in Troas on the coast of Asia Minor. He didn't come to play games; he came to listen. There must have been some question on his mind, some desire in his heart, for which he had no answer. Young and bored, it is his story that prompts me, and I hope prompts you as well, to notice when the Eutychuses among us put themselves at risk. But when you notice, take care to approach carefully. Remember not to shout—that will only be misunderstood. Instead, gently nudge, and while nudging away from the danger, listen ever so carefully so that you might speak ever so lovingly. In so doing, you will guide our Eutychuses safely into the arms of Jesus.